DISCARDED

DATE DUE	
GAYLORD	PRINTED IN U.S.A.

Manual of Ready Reference to The Authors' Digest

CONTAINING BRIEF ANALYSES OF

THE WORLD'S GREAT STORIES

AND ANALYTICAL INDEXES OF THE
CHIEF ELEMENTS FOUND THEREIN

Johnson, Rossiter, ed.
11

MARION MILLS MILLER, LITT. D.
(*Princeton*)

ISSUED BY
AUTHORS PRESS
NEW YORK

COPYRIGHT, 1909
By AUTHORS PRESS

FOREWORD

WHILE this volume will be found in itself a valuable guide to the reader and student of fiction, nevertheless it is primarily intended for use as a manual of ready reference to THE AUTHORS' DIGEST. The abridgments of novels in this larger work are analyzed in the Manual, and the elements found therein, historical and biographical facts, scientific and philosophical theories, etc., are noted and classified. Accordingly all the indexes of the Manual refer *to* these abridgments of stories, but always *through* their analyses, which compose the text proper of the Manual (pages 3 to 105). Thus the table of contents on page iii, which serves as an index of the authors and titles of the novels whose abridgments are found in THE AUTHORS' DIGEST, refers to the analyses of the abridgments as these are numbered in the Manual. The reader, turning to the analyses, finds references in turn to the volumes and pages in THE AUTHORS' DIGEST where biographies of the authors will be found, and abridgments of their works.

The Index of Proper Names (page 107) is divided into two sections, one relating to persons, and so serving as an index of Biography, and the other relating to places, and therefore forming an index of the subjects of Geography and Travel.

The most valuable index of all is that of Subjects, on page 116, with a number of entries, such as Character (or Psychology) and

FOREWORD

History, that with their many subdivisions form indexes within the index, as it were.

The items under each entry are classified, so far as possible, according to similarity, and are arranged in the order in which the stories to which they refer appear in the Manual. This enables an investigator of a particular subject, Ethics for example, to run through the analyses in their page order, departing from it only when two stories in different parts of the book are entered side by side in the index as treating of the same phase of the subject. In short, the index is designed to be both practical and logical.

M. M. M.

CONTENTS

I. AUTHORS

NOTE: Numbers refer to analyses on pages 3 to 105

About, Edmond François Valentin, 91, 92.
Achard, Louis Amédée, 80
Aguilar, Grace, 377, 378
Aide, Charles Hamilton, 426, 427
Ainsworth, William Harrison, 321, 322
Alarcon, Pedro Antonio de, 146
Alcott, Louisa M., 598, 599
Aldrich, Thomas Bailey, 603, 604
Aleman, Mateo, 145
Alexander, Mrs. (Mrs. Alexander Hector, née Annie French), 409, 410
Allen, James Lane, 638, 639
Amicis, De, Edmondo, 161
Andersen, Hans Christian, 687, 688
Annunzio, Gabrielle D', 163, 164
Anstey, F. (Thomas Anstey Guthrie), 484-487
Arthur, Timothy Shay, 565
Astor, John Jacob, 664
Astor, William Waldorf, 632
Auerbach, Berthold, 179
Austen, Jane, 256-261
Austin, Jane Goodwin, 595
Azeglio, Massimo Taparelli D', 153

Bacheller, Irving, 657
Balestier, Wolcott, 659
Balzac, Honoré de, 21-42
Banim, John, 279
Baring-Gould, Sabine, 431
Barr, Amelia Edith, 597
Barrie, James Matthew, 498, 499
Barrili, Anton Giulio, 158
Bates, Arlo, 641
Baylor, Frances Courtenay, 631
Bazin, René, 140
Beaconsfield: see Disraeli
Beckford, William, 223
Bede, Cuthbert (Edward Bradley), 414
Beecher, Henry Ward, 575
Behn, Aphra, 198
Bellamy, Edward, 642, 643
Bentzon, Thérèse (Madame Blanc) 126

Bernard, De, Charles, 71
Besant, Walter, 437-439
Bird, Robert Montgomery, 553
Björnson, Björnstjerne, 692, 693
Black, William, 454-457
Blackmore, Richard Doddridge, 411
Boccaccio, Giovanni, 149-150
Boisgobey, Du, Fortuné Castille, 90
Borrow, George Henry, 309
Bourget, Paul, 139
Boyesen, Hjalmar Hjorth, 695
Braddon, Mary Elizabeth (Mrs. John Maxwell), 440, 441
Bremer, Fredrika, 686
Brontë, Anne (Acton Bell), 396, 397
Brontë, Charlotte (Currer Bell), 373-376
Brontë, Emily (Ellis Bell), 380
Brooks, Charles William Shirley, 379
Broughton, Rhoda, 446, 447
Brush, Christine Chaplin, 617
Buchanan, Robert, 458
Bulwer-Lytton, Edward George Earle 283-308
Burnett, Frances Hodgson, 634-636
Burney, Frances, 221
Butti, Enrico Annibale, 165
Bynner, Edwin Lassetter, 618

Cable, George Washington, 621
Caine, Thomas Henry Hall, 477
Cambridge, Ada, 460
Camoëns, Luis de, 197
Cantu, Cesare, 155
Carcano, Giulio, 157
Carleton, William, 276
Catherwood, Mary Hartwell, 628
Cervantes, Miguel Saavedra de, 144
Chambers, Robert William, 667
Chamisso, Adelbert von, 173
Charles, Elizabeth Rundle, 418
Chateaubriand, François René de, 13, 14
Chatrian, Alexander: see Erckmann
Cherbuliez, Victor, 94
Cholmondeley, Mary, 495

CONTENTS—AUTHORS

Churchill, Winston, 672
Claretie, Arsène Arnaud Jules, 125
Cobb, Sylvanus, Jr., 584
Cockton, Henry, 325
Collins, William Wilkie, 402–407
Connor, Ralph (Charles William Gordon), 699
Conway, Hugh (Frederick John Fargus), 462
Cooper, James Fenimore, 520–550
Coppée, François, 128
Corelli, Marie (Minnie Mackay), 509
Crawford, Francis Marion, 648, 649
Crockett, Samuel Rutherford, 500
Croly, George, 266
Cummins, Maria Susanna, 588
Curtis, George William, 586

Daudet, Alphonse, 113–124
Davis, Rebecca Harding, 594
Davis, Richard Harding, 665
[For De Amicis, etc., see Amicis, De,]
DeFoe, Daniel, 199
Dekker, Eduard Douwes, 689
Deland, Margaretta Wade, 654
Dickens, Charles John Huffham, 338–352. (See also 320.)
Dinarte, Sylvio, 701
Disraeli, Benjamin, Earl of Beaconsfield, 310–320
Dodge, Mary Mapes, 608
Dole, Nathan Haskell, 646
Doyle, Arthur Conan, 493, 494
[For Du Boisgobey, etc., see Boisgobey, Du,]
Dumas, Alexandre (Fils), 88, 89
Dumas, Alexandre (Père), 43–60

Ebers, Georg Moritz, 193, 194
Edgeworth, Maria, 227, 228
Edwards, Amelia Blandford, 428
Eggleston, Edward, 605
Eggleston, George Cary, 613
Eichendorff, Joseph von, 174
Eliot, George (Mary Ann Evans Cross), 387–393
Erckmann, Emile; and Alexander Chatrian, 186

Farjeon, Benjamin Leopold, 430
Fenn, George Manville, 429
Fern, Fanny (Sarah Payson Parton), 569
Ferrier, Susan Edmonstone, 269
Feuillet, Octave, 84, 85
Fielding, Henry, 204–207
Flaubert, Gustave, 81–83
Fogazzaro, Antonio, 160

Ford, Paul Leicester, 666
Fothergill, Jessie, 475
Fouqué, Friedrich de la Motte, 171, 172
Fowler, Ellen Thorneycroft (Mrs. Alfred Felkin), 516.
France, Anatole (Jacques Anatole Thibaut), 129
Frederick, Harold, 652
Freeman, Mrs.: see Wilkins
Freytag, Gustav, 185

Gaboriau, Emile, 97, 98
Galdos, Benito Perez, 147, 148
Galt, John, 265
Gaskell, Elizabeth, Cleghorn Stevenson, 327
Gautier, Théophile, 76, 77
Genlis, De, Stephanie, 11
Glasgow, Ellen Anderson Gholson, 673
Godwin, William, 222
Goethe, Johann Wolfgang von, 167–169
Gogol, Nikolai Vasilievitch, 677
Goldsmith, Oliver, 217
Goncourt, De, Edmond and Jules, 87
Grand, Sarah, 481
Grant, James, 398
Grant, Robert, 647
Gras, Felix, 130
Gray, Maxwell (Mary Gray Tuttiett), 497
Green, Anna Katherine (Mrs. Charles Rohlfs), 625
Greene, Mrs. Franklin Lynde (Sarah Pratt McLean), 651
Gréville, Henri (Alice Durand-Fleury) 127
Griffin, Gerald, 308
Grossi, Tommaso, 152
Guerrazzi, Francesco Domenico, 154

Habberton, John, 616
Hackländer, Friedrich Wilhelm von, 183
Haggard, Henry Rider, 488, 489
Halévy, Ludovic, 100, 101
Hamerton, Philip Gilbert, 432
Harben, William Nathaniel, 656
Harder, Ludwig, 192
Hardy, Arthur Sherburne, 629, 630
Hardy, Thomas, 448–451
Harland, Henry, 660
Harland, Marion (Mrs. Edward P. Terhune), 593
Harris, Joel Chandler, 633
Harrison, Constance Cary (Mrs. Bur-

CONTENTS—AUTHORS

ton Harrison), 626
Harte, Francis Bret, 612
Hartner, Eva (Emma von Twardowska), 196
Hauff, Wilhelm, 175
Hawthorne, Julian, 624
Hawthorne, Nathaniel, 554–559
Hay, John, 610
Hay, Mary Cecil, 452
Hearn, Lafcadio, 644
Hewlett, Maurice, 502, 503
Heyse, Paul, 191
Hichens, Robert Smythe, 511, 512
Hoffman, Charles Fenno, 561
Holland, Josiah Gilbert, 581
Holmes, Oliver Wendell, 566–568
Homer, 1
Hope, Anthony (Anthony Hope Hawkins), 506
Howard, Blanche Willis (Mrs. Von Teuffel), 627
Howells, William Dean, 606, 607
Hughes, Thomas, 399
Hugo, Victor-Marie, 62–67

Ingelow, Jean, 395
Irving, Washington, 518, 519

Jackson, Helen Hunt, 596
Jacobs, William Wymark, 508
James, George Payne Rainsford, 281
James, Henry, 619, 620
Jerome, Jerome Klapka, 496
Jewett, Sarah Orne, 637
Johnson, Samuel, 208
Johnston, Mary, 670
Johnston, Richard Malcolm, 583
Jokai, Maurus, 691
Juncker, Elisabetta, 195

Keenan, Henry Francis, 623
Kennedy, John Pendleton, 551
Kimball, Richard Burleigh, 576
Kingsley, Charles, 381–386
Kingsley, Henry, 423, 424
Kipling, Rudyard, 513–516
Kirk, Ellen Olney, 615
Kjelland, Alexander Lange, 696
Kock, De, Charles Paul 18,

Laboulaye, Edouard René de Lefebvre, 79
Lamartine, Alphonse Marie Louis de, 17
Lang, Andrew, 461
Lepelletier, Edmond, 131
Lesage, Alain-René, 6
Lever, Charles James, 323, 324

Lewald, Fanny, 178
Lewis, Matthew Gregory, 255
Lie, Jonas Lauritz Edemil, 694
London, Jack, 674
Longfellow, Henry Wadsworth, 562
Loti, Pierre (Louis Marie Julien Viaud), 138
Lover, Samuel, 278
Ludlow, James Meeker, 614
Lyall, Edna (Ada Ellen Bayly), 492

Maartens, Maarten (Joost Marius Willem van der Poorten-Schwartz), 690
McCutcheon, George Barr, 668
MacDonald, George, 408
Mackenzie, Henry, 219
Macleod, Fiona (William Sharp), 491
Macquoid, Katherine Sarah, 453
Major, Charles, 653
Malot, Hector, 95
Manzoni, Alessandro, 151
Marlitt, E. (Eugénie John), 188, 189
Marryat, Frederick, 273–275
Martineau, Harriet, 282
Massa, De, Philippe, 96
Maturin, Charles Robert, 268
Maupassant, De, Henri René Albert Guy, 134–137
Maurier, Du, George Louis Palmella Busson, 434, 435
Melville, Herman, 578, 579
Mendoza, Diego Hurtado de, 143
Meredith, George, 415–417
Mérimée, Prosper, 61
Mille, De, James, 697
Mitchell, Donald Grant, 582
Moore, George, 478, 479
Moore, John, 218
Moore, Thomas, 264
More, Hannah, 220
Morier, James, 267
Morris, William, 436
Mühlbach, Luise (Clara Mundt), 180–182
Mulock, Dinah Maria (Mrs. George Lillie Craik), 412, 413
Murger, Henri, 86
Murray, David Christie, 463
Musset, De, Alfred, 75

Norris, Frank, 671
Norris, William Edward, 464

Ohnet, Georges, 132, 133
Oliphant, Laurence, 421
Oliphant, Margaret Oliphant Wilson, 419, 420

vi CONTENTS—AUTHORS

Osborne, Duffield (Samuel Duffield Osborne), 655
Ouida (Louise de la Ramée), 444, 445

Parker, Gilbert, 700
Pater, Walter Horatio, 443
Payn, James, 425
Peacock, Thomas Love, 270
Pemberton, Max, 507
Phelps, Elizabeth Stuart (Mrs. Herbert Dickinson Ward), 622
Phillpotts, Eden, 504
Poe, Edgar Allan, 563, 564
Porter, Jane, 262, 263
Prentiss, Elizabeth Payson, 577
Prévost D'Exiles, Antoine François, 8
Pushkin, Alexander Sergyevitch, 676

Quiller-Couch, Arthur Thomas, 505
Quincey, De, Thomas, 271

Radcliffe, Anne Ward, 224, 225
Raimund, Golo, 187
Reade, Charles, 353-365
Reid, Christian (Mrs. Frances Fisher Tiernan), 640
Reuter, Fritz, 177
Rice, James, 437
Richardson, Samuel, 201-203
Richter, Jean Paul Friedrich, 170
Ritchie, Leitch, 280
Rives, Amélie (Princess Troubetzkoy), 663
Roberts, Charles George Douglas, 698
Roche, Regina Maria, 226
Rousseau, Jean Jacques, 9
Rowson, Susanna Haswell, 517
Ruffini, Giovanni Domenico, 156
Russell, William Clark, 459

Sadlier, Mrs. James, 394
Saintine, Joseph Xavier Boniface, 20
Sand, George (Amantine Lucile Aurore Dupin Dudevant), 68-70. (See also 32, 75.)
Sandeau, Jules, 78
Savage, Marmion W., 400
Schreiner, Olive, 703
Schücking, Christoph Bernhard Levin, 184
Schultz, Amélie, 141
Scott, Michael, 272
Scott, Walter, 229-254
Seawell, Molly Elliot, 658
Serao, Matilde (Signora Edoardo Scarfoglio), 162
Shaw, George Bernard, 482, 483

Shelley, Mary Wollstonecraft Godwin, 277
Sheppard, Elizabeth Sara, 422
Shorthouse, Joseph Henry, 433
Sienkiewicz, Henryk, 702
Simms, William Gilmore, 560
Sinclair, May, 501
Smith, Francis Hopkinson, 611
Smollett, Tobias George, 212-216
Souvestre, Emile, 74
Spielhagen, Friedrich von, 190
Spofford, Harriet Prescott, 601, 602
Staël-Holstein, De, Anne Louise Germaine Necker, 12. (See also 58, 60.)
Steel, Flora Annie, 465
Stendhal (Marie-Henri Beyle), 15, 16
Stephens, Ann Sophia, 594
Stepniak, Sergius (Sergius Michaelovitch Kravtchinski), 685
Sterne, Laurence, 209, 210
Stevenson, Robert Louis Balfour, 466-474
Stimson, Frederic Jesup (J. S. of Dale), 650
Stockton, Francis Richard, 600
Stoddard, Elizabeth Drew Barstow, 585
Stowe, Harriet Beecher, 570-573
St. Pierre, De, Henri Jacques Bernardin, 10
Sturleson, Snorre, 4
Stuart, Ruth McEnery, 645
Sue, Marie Joseph Eugène, 72, 73
Swift, Jonathan, 200

Tarkington, Newton Booth, 669
Tautphœus, Jemima Montgomery, Baroness, 176
Taylor, Bayard, 587
Thackeray, Anne Isabella (Mrs. Richmond Ritchie) (daughter of William Makepeace Thackeray), 442
Thackeray, William Makepeace, 328-337. (See also 320.)
Theuriet, Claude André, 99
Thompson, Daniel Pierce, 552
Tolstoi, Lyof Nicolaievitch, 680-684
Tourgee, Albion Winegar, 609
Trollope, Anthony, 367-372
Trowbridge, John Townsend, 589, 590
Turgeniev, Ivan, 678, 679

Verga, Giovanni, 159
Verne, Jules, 93
Vigny, De, Alfred Victor, 19
Virgil (Publius Virgilius Maro), 2
Voltaire, François-Marie Arouet, 7

CONTENTS—AUTHORS

Wallace, Lewis, 591
Walpole, Horace, 211. (See also 672.)
Ward, Mary Augusta (Mrs. Humphry Ward), 476
Warner, Charles Dudley, 592
Warner, Susan, 580
Warren, Samuel, 326
Weyman, Stanley John, 480
Wharton, Edith, 662
Wilde, Oscar Fingall O'Flahertie, 490

Wilkins, Mary Eleanor (Mrs. Charles M. Freeman), 661
Wood, Ellen Price (Mrs. Henry Wood), 366
Wyss, Johann Rudolf, 675

Yonge, Charlotte Mary, 401

Zangwill, Israel, 510
Zola, Émile, 102-112

II. TITLES OF STORIES

NOTE: Numbers refer to analyses on pages 3 to 105

Abbé Constantin, The, 100
Abbé Mouret's Transgression, The, 104
Abbot, The, 241
Abdullah, 79
Abner, Daniel, 656
Absentee, The, 228
Adam Bede, 387
Æneid, The, 2
Afloat and Ashore, 542
African Farm, An, Story of, 703
Agnes Grey, 396
Agnes of Sorrento, 573
Agnes Surriage, 618
Alice, or The Mysteries, 293
All Sorts and Conditions of Men, 438
Alone, 593
Alroy, 313
Altiora Peto, 421
Alton Locke, 381
Amelia, 207
Andrée de Taverney, 60
Anglomaniacs, The, 626
Anna Karénina, 681
Anne of Geierstein: or, The Maiden of the Mist, 252
Antar, The Romance of, 3
Antiquary, The, 231
Antonina, 402
Archibald Malmaison, 624
Armadale, 405
Arne, 692
Arthur Gordon Pym, The Narrative of, 563
Ashes of Empire, 667
Atala, 13
At Sunwich Port, 508
At the Red Glove, 453
Aucassin and Nicolette, 5
Auf der Höhe (On the Heights), 179
Aus dem Leben eines Taugenichts (The Happy-Go-Lucky), 174
Avenger, The, 271
Awakening of Helena Richie, The, 654
Azarian, 601

Bachelor's Establishment, A (*Un ménage de garçon*), 36
Bachelor of the Albany, The, 400
Bad Boy, The Story of a, 603

Barchester Towers, 368
Barnaby Rudge, 342
Barry Lyndon, 329
Beatrice Cenci, 154
Beatrix, 32
Bel Ami, 136
Belle-Rose, 80
Ben Hur, 591
Benefits Forgot, 659
Berlin and Sans-Souci, 181
Bessy Conway, 394
Betrothed, The (Manzoni), 151
Betrothed, The (Scott), 248
Black Arrow, The, 471
Black Dwarf, The, 232
Black Tulip, The (*La tulipe noire*), 57
Bleak House, 346
Blithedale Romance, The, 557
Bohemian Life, 86
Bothwell, 398
Bow of Orange Ribbon, A, 597
Boyne Water, 279
Brave Lady, A, 413
Bravo, The 530
Breadwinners, The, 610
Bride of Lammermoor, The, 236
Brunhilde, 146

Caleb Williams, 222
Called Back, 462
Camille, 88
Can You Forgive Her? 370
Cape Cod Folks, 651
Captain Fracasse, 77
Captain of the Janizaries, The, 614
Captains Courageous, 514
Captain's Daughter, 676
Cardinal's Snuff-Box, The, 660
Career of a Nihilist, The, 685
Carlotta's Intended, 645
Carmen, 61
Cashel Byron's Profession, 483
Casting Away of Mrs. Lecks and Mrs. Aleshine, The: The Dusantes, 600
Castle Dangerous, 254
Castle of Otranto, The, 211
Castle Rackrent, 227
Catherine: A Story, 328

viii

CONTENTS—TITLES OF STORIES

Catherine de' Medici, 35
Caxtons, The, 300
César Birotteau, 31
Chainbearer, The, 544
Charles Auchester, 422
Charles O'Malley, 323
Charlotte Temple, 517
Chartreuse of Parma, The, 16
Chevalier de Maison-Rouge, The, 53
Chicot the Jester, 49
Childe Christopher and Goldilind the Fair, 436
Children of the Abbey, The, 226
Children of the Ghetto, 510
Choir Invisible, The, 639
Chouans, The, 21
Christie Johnstone, 354
Cid, The, 142
Cinq-Mars, 19
Circuit Rider, The, 605
Clarissa Harlowe, 202
Claude's Confession, 102
Clemenceau Case, The, 89
Cloister and the Hearth, The, 358
Cœlebs in Search of a Wife, 220
Colette, The Story of, 141
Collegians, The, 308
Colonel Carter of Cartersville, 611
Colonel's Opera Cloak, The, 617
Coming Race, The, 304
Confession d'un enfant de siècle (Confession of a Child of the Century), 75
Confessions d'un ouvrier (Confessions of a Workingman), 74
Confessions of a Child of the Century (Confession d'un enfant de siècle), 75
Confessions of a Workingman (Confessions d'un ouvrier), 74
Coningsby, 316
Conquest of Rome, The, 162
Conscience, 95
Conscript, The, 186
Consuelo, 69
Contarini Fleming, 312
Cord and Creese, 697
Corinne, 12
Corsican Brothers, The (Les frères corses), 46
Cosmopolis, 139
Count of Monte Cristo, The, 44
Count Robert of Paris, 253
Countess de Charny, The, 59
Country Doctor, A, 637
Country Doctor, The, 25
Cousin Bette, 39
Cousin Pons, 40

Cranford, 327
Crater, The, 546
Crime of the Opéra, The, 90
Cudjo's Cave, 590

Daisy Miller, 619
Dame aux camellias, La (Camille), 88
Damiano, 157
Damnation of Theron Ware, The, 652
Daniel Deronda, 393
Das Geheimniss der alten Mamsell (The Old Mam'selle's Secret), 188
David Balfour, 472
David Copperfield, 345
David Elginbrod, 408
Dead Souls, 677
Débâcle, Le (The Downfall), 110
Debit and Credit (Soll und Haben), 185
Decameron, The, 149
Deemster, The, 477
Deerslayer, The, 537
Deliverance, The, 673
Devereux, 286
Diana of the Crossways, 417
Die Wahlverwandtschaften (Elective Affinities), 169
Disowned, The, 285
Distinguished Provincial at Paris, A, 33
Divine Fire, The, 501
Doctor Antonio, 156
Doctor Johns, 582
Dombey and Son, 344
Donovan, 492
Don Quixote, 144
Dorothy South, 613
Dorothy Vernon of Haddon Hall, 653
Dosia, 127
Dossier No. 113, Le (File No. 113), 97
Double Marriage, A: or, White Lies, 356
Double Thread, A, 516
Downfall The (Le Débâcle), 110
Drink (L'Assommoir), 105
Duke of Stockbridge, The, 643
Dusantes, The, and The Casting Away of Mrs. Lecks and Mrs. Aleshine, 600

East Lynne, 366
Eben Holden, 657
Eddas, The, 4
Egoist, The, 416
Elective Affinities (Die Wahlverwandtschaften), 169
Eleventh Commandment, The (L'undecimo comandamento), 158

CONTENTS—TITLES OF STORIES

Elsa, 696
Elsie Venner, 566
Emma, 259
Enchantment (*L'incantesimo*), 165
Endymion, 320
Epicurean, The, 264
Ernest Maltravers, 292
Esther Waters, 478
Ettore Fieramosca, 153
Eugene Aram, 288
Eugénie Grandet, 26
Evangelist, The, 120
Evelina, 221
Evelyn Innes, 479

Fair Maid of Perth, The: or St. Valentine's Day, 251
Falkland, 283
Fall of the House of Usher, The, 564
Fallen Idol, A, 487
Family Feud, A, 192
Fanshawe, 554
Far from the Madding Crowd, 448
Fashion and Famine, 574
Fathers and Sons, 678
Fécondité, La (Fruitfulness), 111
Felix Holt, the Radical, 391
Ferdinand, Count Fathom, The Adventures of, 214
File No. 113 (*Le Dossier No. 113*), 97
First Violin, The, 475
Fisher-Maiden, The, 693
Fiskerjenten (The Fisher-Maiden), 693
Fool's Errand, A, 909
Footsteps of a Throne, The, 507
Forbidden Fruit (*Namenlose Gesichten*), 183
Forest Lovers, The, 502
Fortunes of Nigel, The, 243
Forty-Five Guardsmen, The, 50
Foul Play, 361
Frankenstein: or, The Modern Prometheus, 277
Frères Corses, Les (The Corsican Brothers), 46
Friends: a Duet, 622
Friendship, 445
Fromont and Risler, 114
Fruitfulness (*La Fécondité*), 111

Gabriel Conroy, 612
Gabriel Tolliver, 633
Garden of Allah, The, 512
Gentleman from Indiana, The, 669
Gentleman of France, A, 480
Gerfaut, 71
Germinal, 108
Giant's Robe, The, 485

Gil Blas, 6
God and the Man, 458
Godolphin, 289
God's Fool, 690
Golden House, The, 592
Good-Bye, Sweetheart, 446
Gordian Knot, The, 379
Grandison, Sir Charles, History of, 203
Grandissimes, The, 621
Grannarna (The Neighbors), 686
Graustark, 668
Graziella, 17
Great Expectations, 350
Green Carnation, The, 511
Green Mountain Boys, The, 552
Grettir The Outlaw, 431
Greyslaer, 561
Griffith Gaunt, 360
Guardian Angel, The, 567
Guenn, 627
Gulliver's Travels, 200
Gunmaker of Moscow, The, 584
Gunnar, 695
Guy Mannering, 230
Guzman d'Alfarache, Life and Adventures of, 145

Hajji Baba of Ispahan, The Adventures of, 267
Hammer und Amboss (Hammer and Anvil), 190
Hammer and Anvil (*Hammer und Amboss*), 190
Han d'Islande (Hans of Iceland), 62
Handy Andy, 278
Hans Brinker: or, the Silver Skates, 608
Hans of Iceland (*Han d'Islande*), 62
Happy-Go-Lucky, The (*Aus dem Leben eines Taugenichts*), 174
Hard Cash, 359
Hard Times, 347
Harold, 299
Headlong Hall, 270
Headsman, The, 532
Heart of Midlothian, The, 235
Heavenly Twins, The, 481
Heidenmauer, The, 531
Heideprinzesschen (A Little Moorland Princess), 189
Heir of Redclyffe, The, 401
He Knew He was Right, 372
Helen's Babies, 616
Henrietta Temple, 314
Henry Esmond, The History of, 332
Henry Masterton, 281
Henry the Eighth and His Court, 180
Hereward the Wake, 386

CONTENTS—TITLES OF STORIES

Herr Paulus, 439
Historie d'un conscrit de 1813 (The Conscript), 186
Home as Found and Homeward Bound, 534
Home Influence, 377
Homo Sum, 194
Honorable Peter Stirling, The, 666
Horseshoe Robinson, 551
Hour and the Man, The, 282
House in Bloomsbury, A, 420
House of Mirth, The, 662
House of the Seven Gables, The, 556
Hulda, 178
Humphrey Clinker, 216
Hypatia, 382
Hyperion, 562

Iliad, The, 1
Il Santo (The Saint), 160
Immortal, The, 121
Indiana, 68
Inheritance, The, 269
Initials, The, 176
Ink-Stain, The (Un tache d'encre), 140
Innocencia, 701
In Paradise, 191
In the Days of My Youth, 428
In the Year '13, 177
Intruder, The, (L'Innocente), 163
Iron Heart, The, 175
Ironmaster, The (Le maître des forges), 133
Irrational Knot, The, 482
It's Never Too Late to Mend, 355
Ivanhoe, 238

Jack, 115
Jack Sheppard, 322
Jack Tier, 547
Jacqueline, 126
Jane Eyre, 373
Jane Field, 661
Japhet in Search of a Father, 273
John Godfrey's Fortunes, 587
John Halifax, Gentleman, 412
John Inglesant, 433
John Marchmont's Legacy, 441
Jonathan Wild, 205
Joseph Andrews, The Adventures of, 204
Joseph Balsamo, 54
Joshua Marvel, 430
Journey in Other Worlds, A, 664
Juif errant, Le (The Wandering Jew), 73
Jungle Book, The, 515

Kenelm Chillingly, 305
Kenilworth, 242
Kidnapped, 470
King Noanett, 650
King of the Mountains, The (Le roi des montagnes), 92
King Solomon's Mines, 488
Kings in Exile (Rois en exil), 117
Kreutzer Sonata, The, 682

Labor (Le Travail), 112
La Conquista di Roma (The Conquest of Rome), 162
Lady Audley's Secret, 440
Lady of Quality, A, 636
Lady Rose's Daughter, 476
La femme de trente ans (A Woman of Thirty), 23
La Fiammetta, 150
Lamplighter, The, 588
Land, The (La Terre), 109
La peau de chagrin (The Magic Skin), 22
L'Assommoir (Drink), 105
Last Days of Pompeii, The, 290
Last of the Barons, The, 297
Last of the Mohicans, The, 525
Lavengro, 309
Lawrie Todd, 265
Lazarillo de Tormes, 143
Lazarre, 628
Leavenworth Case, The, 625
Legend of Montrose, A, 237
Legend of Sleepy Hollow, The, 519
Leiden des jungen Werther, Die (The Sorrows of Young Werther), 167
Leila, or the Siege of Grenada, 294
Le lys dans la vallée (The Lily of the Valley), 29
Le Maître des forges (The Ironmaster), 133
Le roi des montagnes (The King of the Mountains), 92
Les illusions perdues (Lost Illusions), 30
Les Misérables, 64
L'homme à l'oreille cassée (The Man with the Broken Ear), 91
L'homme qui rit (The Man Who Laughs), 66
Life, A (Une vie), 135
Light that Failed, The, 513
Lilac Sunbonnet, The, 500
Lily of the Valley, The (Le lys dans la vallée) 29
L'incantesimo (Enchantment), 165
L'innocente (The Intruder), 163
Lionel Lincoln, 524

xii   CONTENTS—TITLES OF STORIES

Lion's Brood, The, 655
Little Dorrit, 348
Little Lord Fauntleroy, 635
Little Minister, The, 499
Little Moorland Princess, A (*Heideprinzesschen*), 189
Little Parish Church, The (*La petite paroisse*), 123
Little Savage, The, 275
Little Women, 599
Lodsen og hans Hustru (The Pilot and His Wife), 694
Looking Backward, 642
Lorna Doone, 411
Lost Illusions (*Les illusions perdues*), 30
Lost Sir Massingberd, 425
Lothair, 319
Louis Lambert, 24
Louisa de Clermont, 11
Love Me Little, Love Me Long, 357
Lovel the Widower, 336
Lover's Heart, The (*Decameron*), 149
Lucretia, 298
L'undecimo comandamento (The Eleventh Commandment), 158
Lusiad, The, 197
Lys rouge, Le (The Red Lily), 129

Macleod of Dare, 457
Madame Bovary, 82
Madame Chrysanthème, 138
Madame Sans-Gêne, 131
Madeleine, 78
Mademoiselle de Maupin, 76
Mademoiselle Duval, 101
Magic Skin, The (*La peau de chagrin*), 22
Maid of Belleville, The (*La pucelle de Belleville*), 18
Malavoglia, The, 159
Man and Wife, 407
Man of Feeling, The, 219
Manon Lescaut, 8
Mansfield Park, 258
Man Who Laughs, The (*L'homme qui rit*), 66
Man with the Broken Ear, The (*L'homme à l'oreille cassée*), 91
Marble Faun, The, 558
Marco Visconti, 152
Margarethe, 195
Margherita Pusterla, 155
Marguerite de Valois, 48
Marianela, 148
Marie Antoinette and Her Son, 182
Marius the Epicurean, 443
Martin Chuzzlewit, 343
Master and Man, 683

Master of Ballantrae, The: A Winter's Tale, 469
Master of the Ceremonies, The, 429
Mauprat, 70
Max Havelaar, 689
Mayor of Casterbridge, The, 450
Melmoth the Wanderer, 268
Member for Arcis, The, 41
Memoire d'un medicin (Memoirs of a Physician), 55
Memoirs of a Physician, The, 55
Memoirs of Barry Lyndon, The, 329,
Mercedes of Castile, 536
Middle Classes, The, 42
Middlemarch, 392
Midshipman Easy, Mr., 274
Miles Wallingford, 543
Mill on the Floss, The, 388
Minister's Wooing, The, 572
Mistress Regained, The (Decameron), 149
Moby Dick, 579
Modern Instance, A, 606
Modeste Mignon, 38
Monarch of Mincing Lane, The, 454
Monastery, The, 240
Money-Makers, The, 623
Monikins, The, 533
Monk of Fife, A, 461
Monk, The, 255
Monsieur de Camors, 85
Monsieur Lecoq, 98
Mont Oriol, 134
Moods, 598
Moonstone, The, 406
Morgesons, The, 585
Mortal Antipathy, A, 568
Morton House, 640
Mother's Recompense, The, 378
Mr. Isaacs, 648
My Novel, 301
Mystères de Paris, Les (The Mysteries of Paris), 72
Mysteries of Paris, The, 72
Mysteries of Udolpho, The, 225
Mystery of Edwin Drood, The, 352

Nabob, The, 116
Nameless Nobleman, A, 595
Namenlose Gesichten (Forbidden Fruit), 183
Nana, 107
Nancy, 447
Narrative of Arthur Gordon Pym, The, 563
Neighbor Jackwood, 589
Neighbors, The (*Grannarna*), 686
Newcomes, The, 333

CONTENTS—TITLES OF STORIES xiii

New Héloïse, The (*La Nouvelle Héloïse*), 9
New Race, A, 187
Nicholas Nickleby, 340
Nick of the Woods, 553
Night and Morning, 295
'Ninety-Three, 67
No Name, 404
Northanger Abbey, 261
Norwood, 575
Not Angels Quite, 646
Notre Dame de Paris, 63
Nouvelle Heloïse, La (The New Héloïse,) 9
Numa Roumestan, 118

Oak Openings, The, 548
Off the Skelligs, 395
Old Curiosity Shop, The, 341
Old Mam'selle's Secret, The (*Das Geheimniss der alten Mamsell*), 188
Old Mortality, 233
Old Myddleton's Money, 452
Oldtown Folks, 571
Oliver Twist, 339
On Both Sides, 631
On the Face of the Waters, 465
On the Heights (*Auf der Höhe*), 179
Ordeal of Richard Feverel, The, 415
Orley Farm, 369
Oroonoko: or, The Royal Slave, 198
O. T., 687
Our Mutual Friend, 351

Page d'amour, un (A Page of Love), 106
Page of Love, A, 106
Page of the Duke of Savoy, The, 52
Pamela, 201
Papa Bouchard, 658
Parisians, The, 306
Passé Rose, 630
Pathfinder, The, 535
Paul and Virginia, 10
Paul Bronckhorst, 184
Paul Clifford, 287
Paul Kelver, 496
Pausanias the Spartan, 307
Pearce Amerson's Will, 583
Peg Woffington, 353
Pelham, 284
Pendennis, 330
Père Goriot, 27
Peregrine Pickle, 213
Persuasion, 260
Peter Ibbetson, 434
Peter Schlemihl, 173
Petite paroisse, La (The Little Parish Church), 123
Peveril of the Peak, 244

Pharais, 491
Philip, The Adventures of, 337
Picciola, 20
Pickwick Papers, 338
Picture of Dorian Gray, The, 490
Pierre and Jean, 137
Pilot, The, 523
Pilot and His Wife, The (*Lodsen og Hans Hustru*), 694
Pioneers, The, 522
Pirate, The, 239
Pit, The: A Story of Chicago, 671
Portrait of a Lady, The, 620
Prairie, The, 527
Precaution, 520
Pride and Prejudice, 257
Prince Otto, 467
Princess of Thule, A, 456
Prince Zilah, 125
Prisoner of Zenda, The, 506
Professor, The, 376
Promessi Sposi, I (The Betrothed), 151
Pucelle de Belleville, La (The Maid of Belleville), 18
Put Yourself in His Place, 362

Quarante-cinq, Les (The Forty-Five Guardsmen), 50
Quatre-vingt treize ('Ninety-Three), 67
Queen's Necklace, The, 56
Quentin Durward, 245
Quick or the Dead, The, 663
Quo Vadis? 702

Ramona, 596
Rasselas, History of, The, 208
Ravenshoe, 424
Ready-Money Mortiboy, 437
Recollections of Geoffry Hamlyn, 423
Red and Black (*Rouge et noir*), 15
Redgauntlet: A Tale of the Eighteenth Century, 247
Red Lily, The (*Le lys rouge*), 129
Red Pottage, 495
Red Rover, The, 526
Redskins, The, 545
Reds of the Midi, The, 130
Reine des bois, La (A Woodland Queen), 99
René, 14
Renée Mauperin, 87
Resurrection, 684
Return of the Native, The, 449
Reynard the Fox, 166
Richard Carvel, 672
Richard Yea-and-Nay, 503
Rienzi: Last of the Tribunes, 291
Right of Way, The, 700
Rip Van Winkle, 518

CONTENTS—TITLES OF STORIES

Rise of Silas Lapham, The, 607
Rita: An Autobiography, 426
Robber of the Rhine, The, 280
Robinson Crusoe, 199
Rob Roy, 234
Roderick Random, 212
Rogue, The, 464
Rois en exil (Kings in Exile), 117
Roman Singer, A, 649
Romance of a Poor Young Man, The (*Le roman d'un pauvre jeune homme*), 84
Romance of a Schoolmaster, The (*Il romanzo d'un maestro*), 161
Romance of the Forest, The, 224
Romance of Two Worlds, A, 509
Romance of Youth, A (*Toute ma jeunesse*), 128
Roman d'un jeune homme pauvre, Le (The Romance of a Poor Young Man), 84
Romanzo d'un maestro, Il (The Romance of a Schoolmaster), 161
Romola, 390
Rose and Ninette, 122
Rouge et Noir (Red and Black), 15
Ruth Hall, 569

St. Ives, 474
St. Leger, 576
St. Ronan's Well, 246
Saint, The (*Il Santo*), 160
Salammbô, 82
Salathiel, 266
Salem Chapel, 419
Samuel Brohl and Company, 94
Sappho, 119
Saragossa, 147
Satanstoe, 541
Scarlet Letter, The, 555
Scènes de la vie de Bohème (Bohemian Life), 86
Schönberg-Cotta Family, The, 418
Scottish Chiefs, The, 263
Sea Lions, The, 549
Sea-Wolf, The, 674
Sense and Sensibility, 256
Sentimental Education, 83
Sentimental Journey, A, 210
Septimus Felton, 559
Serge Panine, 132
Seraphita, 28
Sevenoaks, 581
Severa, 196
Sforza, 632
Shabby-Genteel Story, A, 334
She, 489
Shirley, 375

Silas Marner, 389
Silence of Dean Maitland, The 497
Simpleton, A, 364
Sintram and His Companions, 172
Sir Charles Grandison, 203
Sir Launcelot Greaves, The Adventures of, 215
Sister to Evangeline, A, 698
Sky Pilot, The, 699
Small House at Arlington, The, 371
Smoke, 679
Soldiers of Fortune, 665
Soll und Haben (Debit and Credit), 185
Sons of the Morning, 504
Sorrows of Werther, The (*Die Lieden des jungen Werther*), 167
Soutien de Famille, Le (The Support of the Family), 124
Splendid Spur, The, 505
Spy, The, 521
Start in Life, A (*Un début dans la vie*), 37
Stepping Heavenward, 577
Stillwater Tragedy, The, 604
Story of Margaret Kent, The, 603
Strange Adventures of a Phaeton, The, 455
Strange Case of Dr. Jekyll and Mr. Hyde, The, 468
Strange Story, A, 303
Study in Scarlet, A, 493
Summer in Arcady, 638
Support of the Family, The (*Le Soutien de Famille*), 124
Swiss Family Robinson, The, 675
Sybil: or, The Two Nations, 317

Taking the Bastile, 58
Tale of Two Cities, A, 349
Talisman, The, 249
Tancred, 318
Tartarin of Tarascon, 113
Tenant of Wildfell Hall, The, 397
Ten Nights in a Bar-room, 565
Ten Thousand a Year, 326
Terre, La (The Land), 109
Terrible Temptation, A, 363
Tess of the D'Urbervilles, 451
Thaddeus of Warsaw, 262
That Lass o' Lowrie's, 634
Thérèse Raquin, 103
Thief in the Night, The, 602
Three Miss Kings, The, 460
Three Musketeers, The (*Les trois mousquetaires*), 43
Three Rings, The (Decameron), 149
Timar's Two Worlds, 691

CONTENTS—TITLES OF STORIES

Tinted Venus, The, 486
Titan, 170
To Have and to Hold, 670
Toilers of the Sea, 65
Tom Brown's School Days, 399
Tom Burke of Ours, 324
Tom Cringle's Log, 272
Tom Jones, The History of, 206
Toute ma jeunesse (A Romance of Youth), 128
Tower of London, The, 321
Travail, Le (Labor), 112
Travailleurs de la mer (Toilers of the Sea), 65
Treasure Island, 466
Trilby, 435
Trionfo della morte, Il (The Triumph of Death), 164
Tristram Shandy, 209
Triumph of Death, The (*Il trionfo della morte*), 164
Trois mousquetaires, Les (The Three Musketeers), 43
Trumps, 586
Tulipe Noire, La (The Black Tulip), 57
Twenty Thousand Leagues Under the Sea (*Vingt mille lieues sous les mers*), 93
Twenty Years After (*Vingt ans après*), 45
Two Admirals, The, 538
Two Baronesses, The, 688
Two Dianas, The, 51
Two Years Ago, 384
Typee, 578

Uarda, 193
Uncle Tom's Cabin, 570
Un début dans la vie (A Start in Life), 37
Under Two Flags, 444
Undine, 171
Une Vie (A Life), 135
Unleavened Bread, 647
Un ménage de garçon (A Bachelor's Establishment), 36
Un tache d'encre (The Ink-Stain), 140
Ursule Mirouët, 34

Valentine Vox, 325
Vanity Fair, 331
Vathek: An Arabian Tale, 223
Venetia, 315
Verdant Green, Mr., Adventures of, 414
Vicar of Wakefield, The, 217
Vice Versa, 484
Vicomte de Bragelonne, The, 47

Village on the Cliff, The, 442
Villette, 375
Vingt ans après (Twenty Years After), 45
Vingt mille lieues sous les mers (Twenty Thousand Leagues Under the Sea), 93
Virginians, The, 335
Vivian Grey, 310
Voyage of Discovery, A, 427

Waiting for the Verdict, 594
Wandering Jew, The (*Le juif errant*), 73
War and Peace, 680
Warden, The, 367
Water Babies, The, 385
Water Witch, The, 529
Waverley, 229
Way of the World, The, 463
Ways of the Hour, 550
Weir of Hermiston, 473
Wenderholme, 432
Wept of Wish-ton-wish, The, 528
Westward Ho! 383
What Will He Do With It? 302
Wheel of Fire, A, 641
Which Shall It Be? 409
White Company, The, 494
White Lies, 356
Wide, Wide World, The, 580
Wife's Revenge, The (Decameron), 149
Wilhelm Meister's Apprenticeship, 168
Willy Reilly, 276
Wind of Destiny, The, 629
Window in Thrums, A, 498
Wing and Wing, 539
Woman-Hater, A, 365
Woman in White, 403
Woman of Thirty, A (*La femme de trente ans*), 23
Wondrous Tale of Alroy, The, 313
Woodland Queen, A (*La reine des bois*), 99
Woodstock: or, The Cavalier, 250
Wooing o't, The, 210
Wreck of the Grosvenor, The, 459
Wuthering Heights, 380
Wyandotte, 540

Yemassee, The, 560
Young Duke, The, 311
Youma, 644

Zanoni, 296
Zadig, 7
Zeluco, 218
Zibeline, 96

ANALYSIS OF THE WORLD'S
GREAT STORIES

Analysis of the World's Great Stories.

GIVING the chief elements of each in the order of their importance; the central idea; and any distinctive features there may be in plot, historical reference, delineation of character, etc. The authors are arranged by countries, in the chronological order of their births, the date of the earliest author of each country fixing the order of countries. By reading the stories in this order, a complete course of study in the world's greatest fiction, from the earliest times to the present, classified both by countries and authors, may be obtained. All these elements, special features, etc., are covered in a general index following this list of stories.

GREECE.

HOMER (NINTH CENTURY B. C.), XIX, 261.

1. THE ILIAD, X. 326. 1. Mythology. 2. War. The tale of the siege of Troy, in which legendary heroes, such as Achilles, Agamemnon, Menelaus, Diomed, etc., of the Greeks, contend with Hector, Paris, Æneas, etc., of the Trojans, the heroes being assisted by the partisan gods, Athene, Hera, Aphrodite, Ares, etc. The tale ends with the death of Hector at the hands of Achilles, and the victor's dragging him behind his chariot.

ROME.

VIRGIL (70 B. C.–19 B. C.), XIX, 413.

2. THE ÆNEID, XVII. 129. 1. Poetry. 2. Legend. 3. Mythology. An epic of the legendary founding of the Latin kingdom, recounting the martial exploits of gods and heroes.

ARABIA.

3. THE ROMANCE OF ANTAR (sixth century), I. 312. 1. Heroism. 2. War. 3. Love. An Arabian epic narrating the adventures in war and love of an heroic mulatto chief.

ICELAND.

SAEMOND SIGFUSSON (TWELFTH CENTURY, A. D.).
SNORRE STURLESON (1179–1241), XIX. 395.

4. THE EDDAS (12th and 13th centuries A. D.), VIII. 128. 1. Mythology. 2. Poetry. Collections of sagas, giving the Norse cosmogony and mythology.

FRANCE.

5. AUCASSIN AND NICOLETTE (12th century), I. 362. 1. Love. 2. Adventure. The story of the troubled course of love between a brave youth and fair maiden, which ended happily. Written in archaic poetic diction.

ALAIN-RÉNÉ LE SAGE (1668–1747), XIX. 291.

6. GIL BLAS (1735), XI. 391. 1. Adventure. 2. Character. 3. History. 4. Spanish Life. A tale of rambling adventure among all classes in Spain, in the first half of the 17th century. The narrator writes himself down as a rascal, among other shady transactions procuring a mistress for the Crown Prince, afterward Philip IV.

VOLTAIRE (1694–1778), XIX. 414.

7. ZADIG (1760), XVII. 135. 1. Detection. 2. Wisdom. 3. Adventure. A Babylonian philosopher uses his reason in unfolding mysteries, detecting crimes, solving puzzles, etc., and by his wisdom wins a princess and a kingdom.

ABBÉ PREVOST (1697–1763), XIX. 345.

8. MANON LESCAUT (1731), XIII. 279. 1. Love. 2. Pathos. A young student of theology becomes infatuated with a young woman, a courtesan by nature, and gives up his career to live with her. He is separated from her by his father. Later, he sees her about to be transported to Louisiana with other loose women, and forsakes all to accompany her thither, where he wins her in fight from the man to whom she has been assigned, and flees with her into the wilderness. She dies, and he hollows her a grave in the sand with his hands, and lies upon it to await death, from which welcome end he is saved to pass his life in sadness.

JEAN JACQUES ROUSSEAU (1712–1778), XIX. 354.

9. THE NEW HELOISE (1760), XIV. 119. 1. Love. 2. Ethics. A girl has an amour with her tutor whom it is impossible for her to marry. Later, she marries, and reveals her past to her husband, who forgives her, and permits her to continue a close friendship with the lover, and, when she dies, wills that he tutor her children.

BERNARDIN DE SAINT-PIERRE (1737–1814), XIX. 129.

10. PAUL AND VIRGINIA (1788), VI. 374. 1. Youth. 2. Love. 3. Tragedy. A low-born lad and high-born maid, playmates on the Isle of

Mauritius, love each other in idyllic fashion, but are separated by the summons of the girl to France by a rich aunt. She remains true to her lover, and refuses to marry the choice of her aunt, who disinherits her and sends her home. She is wrecked in sight of her lover, and he grieves himself to death.

STEPHANIE FELICITIE DE GENLIS (1746–1830), XIX. 118.

11. Louisa de Clermont (1802), VI. 255. 1. Ethics. 2. Love. 3. Tragedy. A princess loves a nobleman of inferior rank, being attracted by his high moral qualities. He nobly resigns her to the claims of the State which point to a higher alliance for her. But she refuses to let him go and secretly marries him. They are separated by her brother and the lover is mortally wounded in hunting, leaving her determined to remain his widow for life.

MADAME DE STAËL (1766–1817), XIX. 132.

12. Corinne (1807), VI. 385. 1. Travel. 2. Love. 3. Pathos. A young Scotch nobleman traveling through Italy, meets and is attracted by an authoress. She becomes his mistress, but learning of a former amour of hers, he returns to a sweetheart at home. The mistress follows him, but, discovering the purity and devotion of the Scotch sweetheart, returns to Italy without revealing herself.

FRANÇOIS RÉNÉ AUGUSTE DE CHATEAUBRIAND (1768–1848), XIX. 90.

13. Atala (1801), IV. 372. 1. American Indian Life and Character. 2. Love. 3. Religion. The romance of two Indian lovers, one of whom dying, enjoins the other that he become a Christian. This he does and suffers martyrdom.

14. Réné (1802), IV. 378. 1. American Indian Life and Character. 2. Incestuous Love. 3. Religion. A sequel to Atala. The hero, a Frenchman, finding that his sister has immured herself in a convent because of her incestuous love for him, which he had not suspected, flees to America and marries an Indian maiden, but is not able to escape his melancholy, despite the appeals of a missionary to turn to religion.

(HERE MAY FOLLOW 173.)

STENDHAL [HENRI BEYLE] (1783–1842), XIX. 384.

15. Red and Black (1830), XV. 419. 1. Ambition. 2. Religion. 3. Tragedy. An ambitious young man enters the priesthood for purposes of selfish advancement. To prove to himself his attractions, he seduces a married woman, and makes the daughter of a noble his mistress. The jealous wife betrays him, and he shoots her. She is only wounded, but he admits his murderous intention, and is guillotined, both of the women who loved him attending him to the last.

16. THE CHARTREUSE OF PARMA (1840), XV. 431. 1. History. 2. The Church. 3. Adventure. An ambitious young Italian, after a number of exciting adventures, contrives to join Napoleon's army in time to fight at Waterloo. Returning to Italy, he is helped in his career by a duchess who loves him. He enters the priesthood. He kills a man in self-defence, is arrested for the murder, makes love to the jailer's daughter, and escapes by help of her and the duchess. On the death of the jailer's daughter, he distributes his property and enters a monastery, where he shortly dies.

ALPHONSE M. L. DE LAMARTINE (1790–1869), XIX. 288.

17. GRAZIELLA (1849), XI. 365. 1. Autobiography. 2. Italian Life. 3. Love. A love story, recalling the author's own experiences on the Isle of Ischia.

CHARLES PAUL DE KOCK (1794–1871), XIX. 121.

18. THE MAID OF BELLEVILLE (1830), VI. 279. 1. Character. 2. Intrigue. 3. Humor. A demure French girl has various escapades with lovers, for which she contrives that another girl be blamed. The sly puss suffers no penalties for her trickeries; her friend forgives her, and both are happily married.

ALFRED DE VIGNY (1797–1863), XIX, 133.

19. CINQ-MARS (1826), VI. 392. 1. History. 2. Conspiracy. 3. Adventure. A romance of derring-do, founded on the historic conspiracy of the Marquis de Cinq-Mars, during the reign of Louis XIII. The king, his queen, Anne of Austria, Marie de Gonzaga, Cardinal Richelieu, and Father Joseph, appear as characters in the story.

XAVIER SAINTINE [JOSEPH FRANCOIS BONIFACE] (1798–1865), XIX. 359.

20. PICCIOLA (1832), XIV. 167. 1. Imprisonment. 2. Religion. 3 Love. 4. Botany. 5. History. A political prisoner, a conspirator against Napoleon I., takes a deep interest in the growth of a flower between the flagstones of his prison yard. The daughter of a fellow prisoner loves him for his tenderness to the flower, and, when it withers for lack of soil, journeys to the Empress Josephine to plead for its relief, and secures this and also his pardon. An agnostic, he is converted to belief in God by the study of the plant.

HONORÉ DE BALZAC (1799–1850), XIX. 26.

21. THE CHOUANS (1829), II. 47. 1. History. 2. Revenge. 3. Love. A story of the insurrection in La Vendée. A woman spy loves the man she is sent to capture, and by so doing causes the death of the soldiers of her side by his command. She plans revenge, and, repenting too late, dies with her lover.

ANALYSIS OF THE WORLD'S STORIES 7

22. THE MAGIC SKIN (1831), II. 58. 1. Magic. 2. Symbolism. 3. Self-Indulgence. 4. Nemesis. A young man becomes possessed of a magic piece of leather, which enables him to gratify any wish, but at the expense of its size, which measures his life span. He dies of self-indulgence. His sweethearts, an evil and a good genius, typify, one, Illusion, the other, Society.

23. A WOMAN OF THIRTY (1832), II. 66. 1. Character. 2. Marriage. 3. Motherhood. 4. Nemesis. 5. History. Six stories grouped around the character of an ambitious woman, who is an unfaithful wife and loveless mother, punished at last for her sins. Napoleon I. appears in the first story.

24. LOUIS LAMBERT (1832), II. 97. 1. Philosophy (Swedenborgianism). 2. Medicine. 3. Love. The romance of a mystical genius, a follower of Emanuel Swedenborg, who fell into a catalepsy on the day set for his wedding, and was faithfully attended thereafter by her who was to have been his wife.

25. THE COUNTRY DOCTOR (1833), II. 88. 1. Character. 2. Philanthropy. 3. Medicine. A Paris physician is jilted by his betrothed on her discovery that he has a natural son. The death of this son following, the physician retires to a country district and devotes himself to good works, adopting orphans, etc. He dies in harness greatly beloved. Incidentally the story contains an idealization of Napoleon I. by an old peasant, one of his soldiers.

26. EUGENIE GRANDET (1834), II. 95. 1. Love. 2. Pathos. 3. Avarice. 4. Character. The story of a self-sacrificing daughter of a miser, who devotedly loved a fortune-seeker and place-hunter, and secretly aided him although he had jilted her.

27. PÈRE GORIOT (1835), II. 106. 1. Pathos. 2. Family Love. 3. Parisian Life. The story of a father who gave all of his substance and soul, and finally his life, to two heartless, ambitious daughters. It contains, incidentally, a graphic picture of life in a Parisian lodging-house.

28. SERAPHITA (1835), II. 117. 1. Mysticism. 2. Swedenborgianism. 3. Symbolism. The story of a mystical being, appearing as a man to a feminine admirer, a woman to a masculine lover, who is represented as the spiritual manifestation of Swedenborg, and who symbolizes celestial perfection.

29. THE LILY OF THE VALLEY (1836), II. 129. 1. Character. 2. Love. 3. Pathos. 4. Symbolism. The story of a man who expected to find all feminine perfections in one woman, and whose various loves discard him because of his praises of qualities in other women lacking in themselves. One love is a married woman, whose renunciation of him for her daughter strikes a note of pathos in the book. This woman, and her complement in character, another object of the man's affection, sum up the ideal of earthly feminine perfection.

30. Lost Illusions (1837), II. 140. 1. Business (Printing and Paper-making). 2. Rascality. 3. Heroism. 4. Parisian Society. A story of business rivalry and intrigue, in which the hero (an inventor) and heroine (his wife) are ruined, but retire with honor to a happy life in the country. The sub-plot is one of social intrigue, in which the central character is a selfish, ambitious poet.

31. Cèsar Birotteau (1838), II. 151. 1. Business (Perfumery). 2. Rascality. 3. Loyalty. A story of the rise, decline, and rehabilitation in fortune and honor of a Parisian manufacturer. The loyalty of his chief clerk is the dominant note of the romance.

32. Beatrix (1839), II. 162. 1. Love. 2. History. 3. Character. 4. Social Rivalry. The story of a young man's pure first love, and how two older women, rivals in literary and artistic society, make it a pawn in their game of intrigue. The originals of the rivals were "George Sand" and "Daniel Stern," and of other characters, Liszt and Gustave Planche.

33. A Distinguished Provincial at Paris (1839), 173. 1. Parisian Society. 2. Rascality. 3. Journalism. 4. Pathos. The hero is the chief figure in the sub-plot of "Lost Illusions" (30). His rise and fall in Parisian society and journalism are depicted, ending with the pathetic death in poverty of his mistress.

34. Ursule Mirouët (1841), II. 184. 1. Love. 2. Rascality. 3. Mesmerism. 4. Religion. A materialistic physician is converted to Catholicism by the faith of his granddaughter, and the performance of a mesmerist. The girl loves a young nobleman and persuades her grandfather to rescue him from prison where he is held for debt. Relatives try to separate not only the lovers, but grandchild and grandparent, overwhelming the girl with sorrows, from which she finally emerges triumphant.

35. Catherine De' Medici (1841), II. 193. 1. History. 2. Religion. 3. Astrology. A romance of the career of a queen who sacrificed everything to preserve and strengthen her dominion. Francis II., Mary, Queen of Scots, Charles IX., Henry IV., Calvin, and other of her contemporaries appear in the story. She is represented as a devotee of astrology.

36. A Bachelor's Establishment (1843), II. 212. 1. Character. 2. Gambling. 3. Art. 4. History. A story of the interplay of various types of character, the most notable being two brothers, one a dissipated gambler, the other, a hard-working artist. The introduction relates to events of the French Revolution and the empire of Napoleon I.

37. A Start in Life (1844), II. 223. 1. Character. 2. Business. 3. Parisian Life. The story of a raw, blundering youth, who by his errors gets repeated set-backs in his career, but, profiting by his experience, finally attains success.

ANALYSIS OF THE WORLD'S STORIES

38. MODESTE MIGNON (1844), II. 233. 1. Love. 2. Comedy. A young girl, debarred from the acquaintance of men, imagines herself in love with a poet, whose works she admires, and writes him a virtual declaration of love. His secretary corresponds with the girl in the poet's name, and finally impersonates him. The girl being an heiress, the poet himself becomes a suitor, leading to a comedy situation resulting happily in the marriage of the girl and the secretary.

39. COUSIN BETTE (1846), II. 244. 1. Character. 2. Rascality. 3. Honor. 4. Pathos. The story of a family, and of the conflict of noble and ignoble designs of its members, with tragic effects. The titular character is an old maid who has been slighted, especially in a love matter, by her rich relatives, and who achieves her revenge.

40. COUSIN PONS (1847), II. 255. 1. Character. 2. Antiquarianism. 3. Friendship. 4. Rascality. 5. Pathos. The story of a friendship between an antiquary and a musician, and of the shabby treatment of the antiquary by his relatives.

41. THE MEMBER FOR ARCIS (1854), II. 266. 1. Politics. 2. Intrigue. A story of political intrigue connected with a contest for a seat in the French Parliament.

42. THE MIDDLE CLASSES (1854), II. 277. 1. Psychology. 2. Rascality. 3. Detection. The story of an adventurer and his dupe, and the frustration of the rascal's designs by a detective.

ALEXANDRE DUMAS [PÈRE] (1802–1870), XIX. 160.

43. THE THREE MUSKETEERS (1844), VII. 307. 1. History. 2. Adventure. 3. Melodrama. The story of four comrades-in-arms, who serve the Queen of France, and outwit her enemy Cardinal Richelieu and his clever agent, a female criminal. The agent is discovered to be the evil wife of one of the Musketeers. His private execution of her is the tragic climax of the story. Historic characters are Louis XIII., his queen, Richelieu, and the Duke of Buckingham.

44. THE COUNT OF MONTE CRISTO (1844), VII. 319. 1. Revenge. 2. Crime. 3. Adventure. 4. Wealth. An innocent man is imprisoned by two men covetous, one of his place, one of his wife. He cleverly escapes from prison, gains possession of a great store of treasure, and incognito wreaks a terrible vengeance on his enemies.

45. TWENTY YEARS AFTER (1845), VII. 331. 1. History. 2. Adventure. A continuation of "The Three Musketeers." The four Musketeers take service under Cardinal Mazarin, the power behind the throne of Louis XIV. They aid him in the insurrection of the Fronde, and he sends them to England to aid Cromwell. Instead they attempt to rescue Charles I. of England from the block. In this they are foiled by the son of the criminal woman of "The Three Musketeers" (43). Returning

to France they are imprisoned by the Cardinal, but soon reverse the situation by imprisoning him; he ransoms himself by giving the four Musketeers rewards and dignities.

46. THE CORSICAN BROTHERS (1845), VII. 342. 1. Psychic Phenomena. 2. Revenge. Twins, one in Paris, one in Corsica, are in telepathic accord with each other. The Parisian brother is killed in a duel, and the Corsican at once is mysteriously made cognizant of the fact, and, setting out for Paris, he challenges and kills the duellist.

47. THE VICOMTE DE BRAGELONNE (1845), VII. 350. 1. History. 2. Adventure. A continuation of "Twenty Years After" (**45**). The four Musketeers aid in restoring Charles II. of England to his throne. With the son of one of them (the titular hero), they are implicated on opposing sides in the troubles between Fouquet and Louis XIV. Mazarin, Condé, Colbert, Queen Anne of Austria, Queen Henrietta Maria, and General Monk also appear in the story.

48. MARGUERITE DE VALOIS (1845), VII. 361. 1. History. 2. Intrigue. 3. Tragedy. The first of the "Queen Margery" series. Queen Marguerite of Valois, sister of Charles IX. and wife of Henry of Navarre, later Henry IV., is the central figure of a mesh of political and amorous intrigue. The Massacre of St. Bartholemew is the dominating situation. Historical characters are: Charles IX., his brother Henry, Henry of Navarre, Marguerite, Coligny, Guise, Alençon, and Catherine de' Medicis.

49. CHICOT THE JESTER (1845), VII. 372. 1. History. 2. Adventure. The second of the "Queen Margery" series. Adventures of minions of the court of Henry III., chief of whom is Bussy d'Amboise. He is in love with a lady of the court, whose husband leads a band of assassins against him, whom he annihilates before he is slain. The plot centers around the conspiracy of the Holy League to make the Duke of Anjou king. Catherine de' Medicis, Henry of Navarre, and Alençon also appear in the novel.

50. THE FORTY-FIVE GUARDSMEN (1846), VII. 382. 1. History. The third of the "Queen Margery" series. It relates the exploits of a band of guards of Henry III., and the revenge of Bussy d'Amboise's mistress on his murderers, one of whom was the Duke of Anjou. The book ends with the alliance of Henry III. with Henry of Navarre against the Holy League, under the Duke of Guise, and the assassination of Henry III.

51. THE TWO DIANAS (1846), VII. 392. 1. History. The young Count Montgomery finds that his sweetheart Diana, daughter of Diana of Poitiers, has been married to another by the order of Henry II., who admits he is her father. She becomes a widow, and the Count is informed that another bar remains between them—Diana of Poitiers was his father's mistress, and the count may be her daughter's half-brother. The daughter is immured in a convent. It is captured by the English, with whom the French are at war. The Count Montgomery storms the place and rescues her, only to see her immured again in a convent. By accident he kills the king in a tourney. He enters the religious wars as a Huguenot; is captured, and beheaded. The Duke of Guise, Coligny, Catherine de' Medicis, Francis II., and Mary Stuart also appear as characters in the story.

52. THE PAGE OF THE DUKE OF SAVOY (1846), VII. 400. 1. History. 2. Magic. The same historical events are treated as in "The Two Dianas" (51). A page of a royal duke is a girl in disguise. A tender but pure relation subsists between the two; she is a prophetess, and warns him of dangers ahead.

53. THE CHEVALIER DE MAISON-ROUGE (1846), VII. 411. 1. History. The hero is a royalist conspirator during the Revolution; he plots with a woman to rescue Queen Marie Antoinette from prison. Two revolutionists, one in love with her, are involved by a series of circumstances. The conspiracy fails, and the conspirators are executed.

54. JOSEPH BALSAMO (1848), VII. 422. 1. History. 2. Charlatanism. 3. Hypnotism. A romance founded on the career of Cagliostro, the charlatan. The names of Swedenborg, Fairfax, Paul Jones, Lavater, Ximenes, Rousseau, and Voltaire are introduced. Louis XV. and his mistress Du Barry enter into the story, and Balsamo predicts the fate of Marie Antoinette.

55. MEMOIRS OF A PHYSICIAN (1848), VIII. 1. 1. History. 2. Charlatanism. 3. Hypnotism. 4. Tragedy. A continuation of "Joseph Balsamo" (54). It ends with the death of Louis XV. Louis XVI., Marie Antoinette, Madame Du Barry, Rousseau, and Marat are introduced in the story. Balsamo's medium, who is also his wife, is murdered by an old magician.

56. THE QUEEN'S NECKLACE (1848), VIII. 12. 1. History. 2. Crime and its Detection. 3. Charlatanism. 4. Hypnotism. A continuation of "Memoirs of a Physician" (55), containing the same elements of hypnotism and magic. Balsamo, now known as Cagliostro, prophesies the fates of various nobles. Mesmer is a character in the story. The plot narrates the theft of Marie Antoinette's diamond necklace by a clever adventuress who impersonates and compromises the Queen. Exposure of the woman exonerates the Queen, but the necklace is lost. Madame Du Barry, Cardinal de Rohan, and Louis XVI. also appear in the story.

57. THE BLACK TULIP (1850), VIII. 23. 1. History. 2. Flowers. 3. Tragedy. A tale of the "tulip mania" of Holland, in which the rivalry of two tulip-growers is implicated with the political events of the time. The execution of the De Witt brothers, and the administration of William of Nassau are described.

58. TAKING THE BASTILE (1853), VIII. 31. 1. History. A tale of the beginning of the French Revolution. A farmer and his workman are represented as leaders of the assault on the Bastile. Louis XVI., Marie Antoinette, M. Necker, and Madame de Staël, Lafayette, and De Launay, Governor of the Bastile, appear in the story.

59. THE COUNTESS OF CHARNAY (1853), VIII. 42. 1. History. 2. Charlatanism. 3. Invention. Cagliostro reappears as the central figure of a group of revolutionary conspirators, including St. Just and the Duke of Orleans. Other new characters are Mirabeau, Guillotine (inventor of the beheading-machine), and Robespierre. Former characters are Louis XVI. and Marie Antoinette (whose arrested flight from Versailles is described), Marat, and Lafayette.

60. ANDRÉE DE TAVERNEY (1855), VIII. 53. 1. History. 2. Tragedy. The execution of Louis XVI. and of Marie Antoinette is the central scene. The chief actors in the French Revolution appear: Bailly, Lafayette, Brissot, Condorcet, Robespierre, Marat, Danton, Narbonne, Dumouriez, Madame de Staël, Madame Roland, Napoleon Bonaparte, Rouget de l'Isle (composer of the Marseillaise), Vergniaud, and Cagliostro, who bears the name of Zanoni.

PROSPER MÉRIMÉE (1803–1870), XIX. 318.

61. CARMEN (1847), XII. 317. 1. Spanish Life and Character. 2. Tragedy. A Spanish gipsy girl, a smugglers' spy and their decoy, tires of her jealous lover, and submits herself to be killed by him rather than live with him.

VICTOR HUGO (1802–1885), XIX. 265.

62. HANS OF ICELAND (1823), XI. 1. 1. Melodrama. 2. Imagination. A fantastic tale of ferocious passions and bloody deeds. The scene is laid in Norway.

63. NOTRE DAME DE PARIS (1831), X. 388. 1. Melodrama. 2. Archæology. A wild tale of a gipsy girl, reputed a sorceress, who is secretly beloved by a humble hunchback, who protects her from villains, and, when she is hanged as a witch, who avenges her. The scenes are laid in and about the old cathedral of Paris, which is described. Mediæval customs are depicted.

64. LES MISÉRABLES (1862), X. 400. 1. Ethics. 2. Character. 3. Adventure. 4. History. 5. Crime and its Detection. A discharged convict robs a priest who had succored him; the priest shields him. The convict is converted, and becomes a good and useful and benevolent man. He, however, is hounded by a detective, faithful to his office. But the reformed convict saves this man from death in the Revolution of 1832. Then the detective solves the conflict of duty and gratitude by suicide. The ex-convict is exonerated of the crime for which the detective pursued him. There are many other characters, all types expressive of special human relations.

ANALYSIS OF THE WORLD'S STORIES

65. TOILERS OF THE SEA (1866), X. 424. 1. Sea Life. 2. Labor. 3. Renunciation. 4. Adventure. A sailor salves a wrecked vessel with endless patience and marvellous skill, and then renounces the prize of his deed, the hand of the shipowner's daughter, because he has discovered she loves another. While working on the wreck he has a desperate fight with a giant octopus.

66. THE MAN WHO LAUGHS (1869), XI. 13. 1. Melodrama. 2. Love. 3. English Aristocracy. The hero has been stolen and made a monstrosity as a child for use by a mountebank. The heroine is a blind companion. They love each other. It is discovered that he is a lord, and he takes his place among the aristocracy of England, the vices of whom are described. Disgusted, he returns to the heroine, whom he finds dying. He drowns himself to regain her in the other world.

67. NINETY-THREE (1874), XI. 24. 1. History. 2. Tragedy. 3. Ethics. A tale of the French Revolution, the scene of which is laid in Brittany. A battalion of Republicans besiege a tower defended by Royalists, who hold three children, adopted by the battalion, in the upper story. The Royalists, leaving by a secret way, fire the town. Their leader returns and rescues the children, at the cost of his capture. The Republican leader aids him to escape, and is sentenced to death for the treason by his best friend, who, upon the execution of the sentence, kills himself. Robespierre, Danton, and Marat are characters in the story.

GEORGE SAND [MADAME DUDEVANT] (1804–1876). XIX. 360.

68. INDIANA (1832), XIV. 181. 1. Love. 2. Fidelity. 3. French Colonial Life. The heroine is a Creole lady in the Isle of Bourbon. Unhappily married, she is tempted by a villain, but saved by a devoted friend, whom she finally marries.

69. CONSUELA (1842), XIV. 193. 1. Music. The career of an Italian prima donna. Haydn and Porpora appear as characters in the story.

70. MAUPRAT (1846), XIV. 206. 1. Love. 2. Character. The hero, a man of strong passions, is reared among outlaws. He meets a refined woman, who loves him, but who refuses to yield to his turbulent wooing, until her confession of love will save him from punishment, when she succumbs.

CHARLES DE BERNARD (1804–1850). XIX. 115.

71. GERFAUT (1838), VI. 234. 1. Seduction. 2. Tragedy. A former lover seduces a wife; this is discovered, and her husband challenges him to a duel. The husband is killed and the wife commits suicide.

EUGÈNE SUE (1804–1857), XIX. 396.

72. THE MYSTERIES OF PARIS (1842), XVI. 197. 1. Social Reform. 2. Melodrama. A story of the life of the poor of Paris, depicting abuses of the penal system, of the hospitals, etc. The plot is one of wild melodrama.

73. The Wandering Jew (1845), XVI. 211. 1. Legend. 2. Imagination. 3. Melodrama. Based on the legend of the Jew Ahasuerus condemned for his inhumanity to Christ at the crucifixion to roam the earth till Christ's second coming. He introduces the cholera wherever he goes. This motive enters but slightly into the plot, which is one of romantic melodrama.

EMILE SOUVESTRE (1806–1854), XIX. 381.

74. Confessions of a Workingman (1851), XV. 367. 1. Labor. 2. Education. 3. Ethics. The career of a mason, showing the advantages of industry, honesty, and application to books.

ALFRED DE MUSSET (1810–1857), XIX. 127.

75. Confessions of a Child of the Century (1836), VI. 354. 1. Autobiography. 2. Character. A neurotic youth finds his mistress is deceiving him, and, despite her protestations, leaves her. He falls in love with a widow, and yet cannot forget his false mistress. The widow returns his love, but, older than himself, realizes his mental condition, and offers to resign him. He, however, gives her up to a better man. The story is based on the author's relations with George Sand.

THÉOPHILE GAUTIER (1811–1872), XIX. 201.

76. Mademoiselle de Maupin (1835), IX. 106. 1. Adventure. 2. Disguise. 3. Love. 4. Marriage. A woman desires to see men as they are, and so goes among them disguised as a cavalier, meeting many adventures. Learning the weakness of her own sex (she is beloved by a woman), as well as of the other, she disavows matrimony.

77. Captain Fracasse (1863), IX. 115. 1. Adventure. 2. The Theatre. A poor young baron joins a troupe of strolling players, and meets with more romantic adventures in real life than they performed on the mimic stage.

JULES SANDEAU (1811–1883), XIX. 361.

78. Madeleine (1848), XIV. 217. 1. Labor. 2. Love. 3. Ethics. An heiress becomes a working-girl to save her lover from a career of dissipation.

ÉDOUARD LABOULAYE (1811–1883), XIX. 287.

79. Abdullah (1859), XI. 354. 1. Oriental Life. 2. Youth. 3. Imagination. 4. Ethics. A parable concerning selfishness and altruism, in the form of an Oriental tale.

LOUIS AMÉDÉE ACHARD (1814–1875), XIX. 4.

80. Belle-Rose (1850), I. 27. 1. Adventure. 2. Love. 3. Melodrama. A low-born hero aspires to the hand of a high-born lady, and enters the army to win renown. He serves the king, Louis XIV., in the Low

ANALYSIS OF THE WORLD'S STORIES

Countries, and in the wars of 1667 and 1672, and, after a melodramatic career, achieves his purpose.

GUSTAVE FLAUBERT (1821-1880), XIX. 186.

81. MADAME BOVARY (1857), VIII. 367. 1. Character. 2. Marital Infidelity. 3. Medicine. The wife of a country doctor is unfaithful to him, and, to escape exposure, commits suicide. The husband idealizes her, until her past is exposed by old letters.

82. SALAMMBÔ (1862), VIII. 378. 1. History. 2. Archæology. 3. Paganism. 4. War. 5. Torture. 6. Description. A romance of ancient Carthage in the days of Hamilcar. The unpaid mercenaries besiege the city. Their leader steals the sacred veil of the patron goddess of Carthage, and falls in love with her priestess, Salammbô. She is sent to recover it at the price of her virtue. But the rebel general grants her the veil freely and sues for her love as a favor. She returns with the veil to the city; its recovery attracts half the mercenaries to the city's side. Salammbô is married to their leader. The rebel general is captured, and is done to death by the finger-nails of the populace. Description is the leading feature of the story.

83. SENTIMENTAL EDUCATION (1869), VIII. 389. 1. Character. 2. Marriage. A self-indulgent young law student in Paris devotes himself to women, who waste his time and money. His attempts to make a rich marriage are provokingly frustrated at the moment of seeming success, and he returns to the love of his youth to find her married to a better man.

OCTAVE FEUILLET (1821-1890), XIX. 176.

84. THE ROMANCE OF A POOR YOUNG MAN (1858), VIII. 301. 1. Love. 2. Character. A steward of an heiress, distrustful of men, loves her, and is loved in return, though she will not confess it, even to herself. She is betrothed to a fortune-hunter. The steward and the heiress are locked up by mischance in a desolate tower. She charges him that it is by design. He tells her that he would never marry her while he is poor; he leaps down to save her honor and is injured. Then he learns that he is the true heir of her wealth, but conceals the fact. She breaks with her fiancé, and considers giving away her wealth. Then he agrees to share the inheritance with her.

85. MONSIEUR DE CAMORS (1867), VIII. 310. 1. Character. 2. Selfishness. 3. Ethics. A man follows a code of heartless self-gratification, left him by his father, with the result that he becomes an outcast, feared and shunned by his associates, his wife, and even the child he loves.

HENRI MURGER (1822-1861), XIX. 327.

86. BOHEMIAN LIFE (1848), XIII. 23. 1. Humor. 2. Parisian Student Life. The fantastic deeds of the Bohemian denizens of the Latin Quarter, in their hand-to-mouth existence.

EDMOND DE GONCOURT (1822-1896); JULES DE GONCOURT (1830-1870), XIX. 119.

87. RÉNÉE MAUPERIN (1864), VI. 264. 1. Character. 2. Tragedy. A young girl of strong will and moral nature, secretly attempts to unmask the pretentions of her immoral, ambitious brother, and thereby causes his death in a duel. She dies of grief.

ALEXANDRE DUMAS [FILS] (1824-1895), XIX. 162.

88. CAMILLE (1848), VIII. 64. 1. Prostitution. 2. Love. 3. Pathos. A dramatic story of the love of a courtesan, a consumptive, who renounces her lover at the plea of his father, and dies, her end being hastened by grief.

89. THE CLEMENCEAU CASE (1867), VIII. 76. 1. Prostitution. 2. Tragedy. 3. Character. A dramatic character study of a born harlot, whom her husband kills to save her from prostitution.

FORTUNÉ H. A. DU BOISGOBEY (1824-1891), XIX. 159.

90. THE CRIME OF THE OPÉRA (1879), VII. 297. 1. Crime and its Detection. 2. Intrigue. A mysterious murder is committed which is never publicly cleared up, but the reader is let into its secret, which is a maze of intrigue, leading to the suicide of the murderer.

EDMOND FRANÇOIS VALENTINE ABOUT (1828-1855), XIX. 3.

91. THE MAN WITH THE BROKEN EAR (1862), I. 1. 1. Medicine. 2. Comedy. 3. Love. A soldier of Napoleon I., condemned to death as a spy, is desiccated by a German physiologist, and so held in suspended animation for three generations, when he is restored to life in the full vigor of youth. Grotesque results follow, such as his falling in love with a girl who proves to be his own grandchild, and making her lover furiously jealous. Napoleon III. appears in the story.

92. THE KING OF THE MOUNTAINS (1856), I. 13. 1. Satire. 2. Adventure. A German botanist and two English women, mother and daughter, are captured by a Greek bandit. The bandit banks his gains with the London firm in which the ladies have an interest. Discovering this, the botanist contrives that the ransoms are paid, unknown to the bandit, from the bandit's own funds. But the botanist himself is buncoed by the bank, and left a prisoner. After clever and daring attempts to escape (whereat the bandit is grieved because of his perfidy), the botanist is rescued by two resourceful Americans. While prisoners together he had made love to the English girl encouraged by both ladies. On rejoining them when free, however, he is "cut dead."

JULES VERNE (1828-1905), XIX. 412.

93. TWENTY THOUSAND LEAGUES UNDER THE SEA (1873), XVII. 118. 1. Invention. 2. Adventure. 3. Piracy. A deeply injured man becomes a pirate upon the commerce of the world, inventing and operating a submarine boat for the purpose.

CHARLES VICTOR CHERBULIEZ (1829-1899), XIX. 92.

94. SAMUEL BROHL AND COMPANY (1877), IV. 381. 1. Imposture. 2. Character. A low-born Jew assumes the character of a Hungarian noble in order to win an heiress. He is exposed. Portrayal of his character is the distinctive feature of the novel.

HECTOR MALOT (1830-1907), XIX. 305.

95. CONSCIENCE (1878), XII. 159. 1. Medicine. 2. Crime and its Punishment. 3. Character. 4. Ethics. 5. Love. 6. Hypnotism. A struggling physician loves a poor school-teacher, and, unable to marry, makes her his mistress. He murders a usurer—who will lend him money only on condition he will marry a rich, dissolute woman and make way with her—and robs his safe. He marries his mistress. Her brother is accused of her husband's crime, and is transported. The doctor suspects that his wife knows of his crime, and hypnotizes her to make certain. She is ignorant of his guilt, but learns it from his talking in his sleep, and leaves him. The story closes with the return of the convict, and the doctor going to face him, his mother, and his sister.

PHILIPPE DE MASSA (1831-   ), XIX. 122.

96. ZIBELINE (1892), VI. 302. 1. Love. 2. Gambling. A young soldier gambles away his estate to an adventurer. Twenty years later, advanced in position but not wealth, he meets a rich young woman, who invites his attentions, and chooses him from younger and wealthier suitors as her husband. She takes him to his lost estates, which he finds are now his own property, and he learns that she is the daughter of the man who had won them from him in play.

EMILE GABORIAU (1833-1873), XIX. 196.

97. FILE No. 113 (1867), IX. 57. 1. Detection of Crime. 2. Impersonation. The cashier is accused of a bank robbery. A man is introduced to him as a friend of his father's. It is really Lecoq, the great detective. Lecoq unearths the real criminal, who is blackmailing the banker's wife, pretending to be her illegitimate son, and wooing the banker's daughter, who is beloved by the cashier.

98. MONSIEUR LECOQ (1869), IX. 64. 1. Detection of Crime. The hero is the detective of "File No. 113" (97). He draws shrewd deductions from the circumstances attendant on a murder, and penetrates various ruses of the prisoner to hide his identity. He proves to his own satisfaction after the prisoner escapes, that he is a nobleman.

ANDRÉ THEURIET (1833-1907), XIX. 404.

99. A WOODLAND QUEEN (1890), XVI. 411. 1. Love. 2. Nature. A young girl, loving the woods and fields, is beloved by two young men. It is revealed to her in confidence that one is her natural brother. She forces herself to be cold to him, and he enlists as a soldier and is killed.

She mourns for him so sincerely that the other lover believes the dead man had her heart. Then she reveals the secret, and all is well.

LUDOVIC HALÉVY (1834-1908), XIX. 241.

100. THE ABBÉ CONSTANTINE (1882), IX. 345. 1. Love. A poor young man loves an American heiress, who, seeing that he is too proud to propose, asks him to marry her.

101. MADEMOISELLE DUVAL (1880), IX. 356. 1. Youth. 2. Character. 3. Love. A wealthy young school-girl's diary, in which she naively sets down her maiden triumphs of dress, etc., and her final conquest of a man of title.

(HERE MAY FOLLOW 434 AND 435.)

EMILE ZOLA (1840-1902), XIX. 429.

102. CLAUDE'S CONFESSION (1865), XVII. 301. 1. Poverty. 2. Love. 3. Pathos. A poor student in Paris writes his brothers in the country of two women, one a harlot, in name and soul, and one only in name, who loved him. The death of the innocent one is pathetically described.

103. THÉRÈSE RAQUIN (1867), XVII. 312. 1. Vice and Crime. 2. Love. 3. Tragedy. The lawless loves of a low Parisian household, ending with suicide.

104. THE ABBÉ MOURET'S TRANSGRESSION (1875), XVII. 321. 1. Religion. 2. Pathos. The love of a priest for a young girl ends in his repentance and return to the church, and in her suicide.

105. DRINK (1877), XVII. 331. 1. Temperance. 2. Labor. 3. Parisian Life. 4. Pathos. The tragedy wrought by liquor in the family of a workingman.

106. A PAGE OF LOVE (1878), XVII. 340. 1. Medicine. 2. Psychology. 3. Love. 4. Pathos. A little girl, inheriting a tendency to insanity, has a fit and the mother, a widow, calls in a doctor. Though married, he falls in love with the widow. Though she is engaged to a good man she cannot resist the doctor's passion, and enters into a *liaison* with him. She neglects her child, who dies in consequence, leaving her mother a victim of remorse.

107. NANA (1881), XVII. 352. 1. Vice and Crime. 2. Tragedy. 3. History. The ruin wrought by a harlot of the Parisian stage. The story ends with the opening of the Franco-Prussian War.

108. GERMINAL (1885), XVII. 364. 1. Labor. 2. Tragedy. A sequel to "Nana." *Nana's* brother becomes a miner. A labor strike is depicted, and the tragedies of mining are thrillingly presented.

109. THE LAND (1887), XVII. 376. 1. Labor. 2. French Peasant Life. 3. Avarice. 4. Crime. A tragedy resulting from the greed for land among some peasants.

110. THE DOWNFALL (1892), XVII. 387. 1. History. 2. Pathos. The pathetic story of a French private in the Franco-Prussian War.

111. Fruitfulness (1899), XVII. 398. 1. Labor. 2. Sociology. A contrast between the happiness resulting from child-bearing and industry, and the miseries of race-suicide and idleness.

112. Labor (1901), XVII. 409. 1. Labor. 2. Imagination. A picture of an ideal industrial condition brought about by constructive labor reforms, in opposition to anarchistic methods.

(HERE MAY FOLLOW 444 AND 445.)

ALPHONSE DAUDET (1840–1897), XIX. 111.

113. Tartarin of Tarascon (1872), VI. 80. 1. Humor. 2. Satire. 3. Character. 4. Hunting. A satire upon the exuberant temperament of the Southern Frenchman. Two characters are shown contending in the hero, one of the romantic Don Quixote, the other of the sensual Sancho Panza. This leads to many amusing situations. The hero fights pirates in the Mediterranean who prove to be hotel porters, lions in Africa, which daylight reveals to be donkeys, etc.

114. Fromont and Risler (1874), VI. 92. 1. Character. 2. Business. 3. Family Relations. The wife of the elder member of a firm plays fast and loose with his partner and younger brother, resulting in her husband's financial ruin and suicide, and other tragedies.

115. Jack (1876), VI. 102. 1. Family Relations. 2. Youth. 3. Pathos. 4. Character. The pathetic story of a son to whom, boy and man, his mother, vain and unfaithful, was an evil genius.

116. The Nabob (1878), VI. 124. 1. Parisian Society. 2. Character. 3. Politics. 4. The Theater. 5. Tragedy. A rich man dazzles Paris with his munificence, patronizing artists, actresses, etc. His loyal secretary tries to guard him from the intrigues which beset him, but in vain. The Nabob enters politics, but is defeated and disgraced, because he will not humiliate his old mother by revealing that her other son is a scoundrel. His crucifixion takes place in a theater, where he dies of a broken heart.

117. Kings in Exile (1879), VI. 113. 1. Politics. 2. Character. 3. Loyalty. A royal family are exiled in Paris. The king forgets honor and duty in the pleasures of the city, and sells his claim to the throne. The Queen has one devoted subject, who, by accident, blinds the young prince, leading to the revelation of the subject's love for her.

118. Numa Roumestan (1881), VI. 149. 1. Character. 2. Politics. 3. History. The hero is a character study of Gambetta. He is the political idol of the South of France. He cannot refuse the plea of a friend, or the advances of a woman, and through this weakness loses the respect and love of his wife.

119. Sappho (1884), VI. 135. 1. Character. 2. Prostitution. A Parisian courtesan ruins a young man from the provinces, and when he sacrifices his career for her, she leaves him for a former lover, a forger.

120. The Evangelist (1885), VI. 158. 1. Religion. 2. Character. A religious fanatic drives her husband to suicide, and ruins the life of her schoolmate.

121. The Immortal (1888), VI. 168. 1. Literary Forgery. 2. The French Academy. 3. Character. 4. Tragedy. A forger of MSS. deceives and ruins a French Academician. The Academician's son is a "struggle-for-lifeur" who schemes successfully to advance in life by fascinating rich and titled women, and his wife is a cruel woman who insults him in his downfall. He kills himself because of his disgrace and their actions.

122. Rose and Ninette (1892), VI. 182. 1. Divorce. 2. Character. 3. Pathos. A man with a bad wife agrees to a divorce, on condition that the two daughters be allowed to visit him. He loves a good woman, similarly separated from a bad man, whom she can not forget. His daughters are jealous of her and he repudiates them, whereupon he finds himself alone in the world.

123. The Little Parish Church (1895), VI. 187. 1. Character. 2. Infidelity. 3. Forgiveness. A roué elopes with a married woman, whose masterful mother-in-law has made home intolerable to her. The husband blames his mother, who repents, seeks the girl, whose lover has abandoned her, and brings her home a penitent. The husband is away; returning, he finds the seducer murdered at his doors. Charged with the crime, he refuses to exculpate himself, believing his wife has done the deed. The murder is fixed on another injured husband, and the prisoner and his wife meet in loving reconciliation.

124. The Support of the Family (1899), VI. 195. 1. Character. 2. Family Life. 3. Journalism. 4. Selfishness. The elder son of an orphaned family regards himself and is regarded as its mainstay, but this is really the younger son. The elder is congenitally selfish. As a journalist he makes copy out of his family, to their shame. One spark of manhood remains: when the younger son is conscripted the elder takes his place. Physiological reasons are advanced to explain the difference in character.

JULES ARSÈNE ARNAUD CLARETIE (1840–   ), XIX. 95.

125. Prince Zilah (1884), IV. 424. 1. Love. 2. Patriotism. A Hungarian noble and gipsy-girl are drawn to each other by the common passion of patriotism. A former lover of the girl separates them, and she pines away. However, they are reunited before her death.

THÉRÈSE BENTZON [MADAME BLANC] (1840–1907), XIX. 47.

126. Jacqueline (1893), III. 23. 1. Character. 2. Family Life. 3. Self-Sacrifice. 4. Love. The story of a young girl and her suitors. Her step-mother would force upon her her own paramour. However, she marries a fine young man, through the self-sacrifice of a friend who is in love with him herself, but hopelessly.

HENRI GRÉVILLE [MADAME DURAND] (1842-1902), XIX. 325.

127. Dosia (1876), IX. 269. 1. Love. A madcap girl and an intellectual woman are loved respectively by a serious officer and his dashing but rather brainless comrade. The men marry their loves after suffering pangs of doubt and jealousy.

FRANÇOIS COPPÉE (1842-1908), XIX. 103.

128. A Romance of Youth (1897), VI. 1. 1. Autobiography. 2. Youth. 3. Pathos. 4. Family Life. A semi-autobiographical romance of youth, thwarted ambition, and unsatisfied love. The mother of a family dies, the father kills himself through loneliness, the son's beloved is seduced by a friend, whom he compels to marry her; the friend dies and the hero marries the widow, whose heart is in the grave.

ANATOLE FRANCE [JACQUES ANATOLE THIBAULT] (1844-), XIX. 193.

129. The Red Lily (1894), IX. 30. 1. Love. 2. Character. A married woman has a lover, to whom she yields, not through love, but pity for his utter devotion. She meets another man whom she loves passionately. She discards the first lover for him, but the second, on learning of the first amour, forsakes her, leaving her desolate.

FELIX GRAS (1844-1901), XIX. 232.

130. The Reds of the Midi (1896), IX. 221. 1. History. 2. Tragedy. A graphic description of the Marseilles battalion that at a critical period in the French Revolution entered Paris singing Rouget de l'Isle's hymn, and helped storm the Tuileries. Louis XVI., Marie Antoinette, and Danton appear in the story, and it closes with a description of an execution by the guillotine.

EDMOND ADOLPHE LEPELLETIER (1846-), XIX. 289.

131. Madame Sans-Gêne (1895), XI. 380. 1. History. 2. Character. 3. Comedy. The story of Napoleon Bonaparte's laundress, whose fortunes rose with the "Little Corporal's," until she became the wife of a Marshal and the Duchess of Dantzic, although remaining coarse and "slangy" in her manners and conversation.

GEORGES OHNET (1848-), XIX. 329.

132. Serge Panine (1881), XIII. 67. 1. Family Life. 2. Business. 3. Rascality. 4. Tragedy. A childless man and wife, who have amassed a fortune in the flour business, adopt a girl. Shortly after a daughter is born to them. In time the girls are betrothed, the elder to a banker, the younger to a civil engineer. To disturb this arrangement enters a Polish adventurer. The lover of the elder girl, he marries the younger, who is the heiress. The mother averts disgrace to the family by killing him.

133. THE IRONMASTER (1882), XIII. 81. 1. Love. 2. Pathos. 3. Business. A rich ironmaster, a self-made man of plebeian origin, is accepted as a husband in a moment of pique, by a high-born maiden, whose aristocratic lover has jilted her for a rich plebeian. When the husband discovers why his wife married him, he is cut to the heart, and lives with her as a husband only in name. She learns to love him, but fears he hates her and so hides her love. Her former lover tries to establish his old hold upon her, and her husband has gone to the field of honor with him, to protect her, when she rushes in, stops with her hand the bullet intended for her husband, and thus reveals her repentance and love.

GUY DE MAUPASSANT (1850–1893), XIX. 123.

134. MONT ORIOL (1883), VI. 307. 1. Character. 2. Intrigue. 3. Business. The opening of a watering-place brings together a rich Jew (the investor) and his Christian wife, and a countryman (the owner) and his two daughters. The Jew's wife is pregnant by a lover, who is repelled by her condition, and woos one of the farmer's daughters. The birth of the child gives the Jew's wife the object of love which her heart craved, and she is content.

135. A LIFE (1883), VI. 316. 1. Domestic Infelicity. 2. Vice. 3. Motherhood. A woman has an unfaithful, vicious husband, whom she forgives for the sake of bearing children, whom she may love. He is killed by a husband he has wronged. His boy grows up like him, but the son of a servant girl the father had seduced becomes a stay to the widow, and the daughter of her wayward son a convict.

136. BEL AMI (1885), VI. 326. 1. Character. 2. Rascality. 3. Journalism. 4. Politics. The story of a heartless man of ambition, who wins several women as his mistresses, schemes successfully in journalism and politics, marries to advance his fortunes, gets a divorce, and marries the daughter of his first mistress, who had loved him since childhood.

137. PIERRE AND JEAN (1888), VI. 335. 1. Character. 2. Domestic Infelicity. 3. Pathos. An elder brother suspects his brother is not his father's son, and finally proves it. He cannot restrain himself from torturing his mother and brother, and flees from home, to her sorrow, to avoid it.

PIERRE LOTI [LOUIS MARIE JULIEN VIAUD] (1850–   ), XIX. 297.

138. MADAME CHRYSANTHÈME (1887), XII. 45. 1. Japanese Life. 2. Autobiography. An account of a summer in Japan spent by a young French naval officer (the author), recounting his companionship with a Japanese girl.

ANALYSIS OF THE WORLD'S STORIES

PAUL BOURGET (1852–), XIX. 61.

139. COSMOPOLIS (1892), III. 161. 1. Character. 2. Roman Society. 3. Intrigue. 4. Tragedy. "A romance of international life," and "a drama of passion," the scene of which is laid in modern Rome.

RENÉ BAZIN (1853–), XIX. 38.

140. THE INK-STAIN (1888), II. 358. 1. Love. 2. Family Life. The course of true love, troubled by family opposition, but finally leading to peaceful waters.

AMÉLIE SCHULTZ (1870–), XIX. 363.

141. THE STORY OF COLLETTE (1887), XIV. 255. 1. Comedy. 2. Love. A young girl prays to a saint for a husband. None appears. In anger she hurls the image out of the window, where it hits a passing traveller who proves in time to be the husband desired.

SPAIN.

142. THE CID (1252–1270), IV. 413. 1. History. 2. Chivalry. 3. Patriotism. 4. Adventure. The epic story, by unknown authors, of the knightly Christian partisan leader against the Moors, Ruy Diaz, the Champion of Bivar.

DIEGO HURTADO DE MENDOZA (1503–1575), XIX. 316.

143. LAZARILLO DE TORMES (1553), XII. 280. 1. Adventure. 2. Rascality. 3. Satire. The escapades of a rascally adventurer, in which the author exposes the abuses of the times.

MIGUEL DE CERVANTES SAAVEDRA (1547–1616), XIX. 85.

144. DON QUIXOTE (1605), IV. 320. 1. Satire. 2. Humor. 3. Adventure. 4. Insanity. 5. Character. A satire on chivalry. A demented gentleman imagines himself a hero of romance, and sets out on a quest in which his hallucinations lead him into all sorts of amusing and absurd adventures. His squire is a man in whom simplicity and shrewdness combine to render him as notable a character as his master.

MATEO ALEMAN (1550–1609), XIX. 11.

145. THE LIFE AND ADVENTURES OF GUZMAN D'ALFARACHE (1599), I. 177. 1. Rascality. 2. Adventure. The escapades of a knavish adventurer.

PEDRO ANTONIO DE ALARCON (1833–1891), XIX. 8.

146. BRUNHILDE (1891), I. 121. 1. Music. 2. Love. 3. Melodrama. An orchestra leader (violinist), in love with a prima donna, is kidnapped by a rival.

BENITO PEREZ GALDOS (1845-   ), XIX. 196.

147. SARAGOSSA (1874), IX. 72. 1. History. 2. War. 3. Avarice. A vivid account of the siege of Saragossa in Spain during the Napoleonic war. A miser traffics with the enemy. An officer orders his son to shoot him. The young man refuses, for he loves the miser's daughter, who has been the heroine of the siege. Moncey and Palafox, the respective French and Spanish generals, appear in the story.

148. MARIANELLA (1878), IX. 82. 1. Blindness. 2. Love. 3. Pathos. A blind young man, wealthy, loves his guide, an ugly, dwarfish girl. His sight is restored and she shuns him. He falls in love with a beautiful girl. The dwarf attempts suicide, and is saved by the doctor only to see the repulsion in her beloved's face (that she had attempted to avoid) and to die of the hurt.

ITALY.

GIOVANNI BOCCACCIO (1313-1375), XIX. 54.

149. THE DECAMERON (1350), III. 122. 1. Pestilence. 2. Religion. 3. Rascality. 4. Adventure. 5. Love. 6. Tragedy. Four stories of the one hundred told by a party of Florentines in a country retreat during a plague. (1) The Three Rings is a parable told by a Jew to the Sultan Saladin, to inculcate tolerance in religion. (2) The Wife's Revenge is a tale of a rascal who wagers with a comrade that the comrade's wife is unfaithful, and wins his bet by trickery, whereupon the husband orders a servant to kill the wife. The wife escapes and, disguised as a man, has many strange adventures. Finally, she secures the punishment of the villain and is reunited to her repentant husband. (3) The Mistress Regained is a tale of a lover, who is separated from his mistress by a rascal monk, and who returns in disguise, thereby discovering and exposing the rascality and regaining his mistress. (4) The Lover's Heart is a tragic tale of a brutal father who murders his daughter's paramour, and sends her his heart, whereupon she mingles its blood with her tears and poison, and drinks the fatal draught.

150. LA FIAMMETTA (1341), III. 145. 1. Character. 2. Love. 3. Superstition. The emotions of a wife, unfaithful to an unsuspecting husband, and in doubt as to her paramour's fidelity. Divination by dreams plays a part in the story.

ALESSANDRO MANZONI (1785-1883), XIX. 305.

151. THE BETROTHED (1827), XII. 170. 1. History. 2. Marriage. 3. Religion. Two betrothed lovers are separated on the eve of marriage by a robber baron. The woman vows virginity to the Virgin if she escapes dishonor; she escapes, and later is absolved of her vow, and weds her lover. A plague at Milan in the early 17th century is described.

ANALYSIS OF THE WORLD'S STORIES 25

TOMMASO GROSSI (1791-1853), XIX. 237.

152. Marco Visconti (1834), IX. 287. 1. History. 2. Chivalry. 3. War. A romantic tale of Italian feuds in the Middle Ages, in which the passions of love and revenge are depicted as leading to single combats, assassinations, etc.

MASSIMO TAPARELLI D'AZEGLIO (1798-1866). XIX. 28.

153. Ettore Fieramosca; or, The Challenge of Barletta (1833), II. 12. 1. Tragedy. 2. History. The story of a combat between thirteen French and thirteen Italian knights, led up to by crimes committed against fair ladies, chiefly instigated by the infamous Cæsar Borgia.

FRANCESCO GUERRAZZI (1804-1873), XIX. 237.

154. Beatrice Cenci (1854), IX. 298. 1. History. 2. Crime. 3. Tragedy. A tragic romance, based on the crimes of Count Cenci. He is represented as slain by a protector of his own daughter from his incestuous designs. The torture of this daughter and others, and their final execution are described.

CESARE CANTU (1804-1895), XIX. 82.

155. Margherita Pusterla (1838), IV. 278. 1. History. 2. Tragedy. 3. Crime. A story of the days of the feud between Guelphs and Ghibellines, in which intrigue and lust and politics lead to various tragedies, the chief being the willing death of a son at the hands of his unwilling father, in order to revenge him upon the father.

GIOVANNI RUFFINI (1807-1881), XIX. 358.

156. Doctor Antonio (1855), XIV. 136. 1. Medicine. 2. History. 3. Love. 4. Patriotism. An English girl in Italy falls sick and is attended by an Italian physician. They come to love each other, but her people take her away to England, where she marries. Left a widow, she returns to find her lover. He has become involved in the Sicilian revolution, and is imprisoned. The Englishwoman plans to rescue him, but he refuses to be liberated while his comrades are in prison. He is transferred elsewhere, and never heard of again, and the lady dies of grief.

GIULIO CARCANO (1812-1884), XIX. 82.

157. Damiano (1840), IV. 291. 1. Poverty. 2. Family Love. A poor family struggles against adversity and intrigue, and finally attains success and a measure of happiness for its members.

ANTON GIULIO BARRILI (1836-   ) XIX. 37.

158. The Eleventh Commandment (1870), II. 334. 1. Farce-comedy. 2. Italian Society. 3. Marriage. An heiress, to escape an unwelcome marriage, assumes man's disguise, and takes refuge in a lay monastery. Her sex is suspected, and all the brothers fall in love with her. She settles the turmoil by marrying the head of the monastery, which is thereby dissolved.

(HERE MAY FOLLOW 444 AND 445.)

GIOVANNI VERGA (1840-), XIX. 412.

159. THE MALAVOGLIA (1881), XVII. 107. 1. Peasant Life and Character. 2. Poverty. 3. Pathos. The bitter struggle of a poor Italian family with misfortune, leading to tragedies of life and love.

ANTONIO FOGAZZARO (1842-), XIX. 189.

160. THE SAINT (1906), VIII. 400. 1. Religion. 2. Character. A divorced woman, an agnostic, is deserted by her lover, who has become suddenly converted by the recovery to reason at death of his insane wife. He becomes a priest and is worshipped as a saint by the people. He incurs the enmity of priests and politicians by denouncing abuses of their orders, and is worn to death in the resulting contests. He converts his former mistress to Christianity on his death-bed.

EDMONDO DE AMICIS (1846-1908), XIX. 114.

161. THE ROMANCE OF A SCHOOLMASTER (1876), VI. 221. 1. Education. 2. Italian Life. 3. Politics. 4. Character. The story of an Italian public schoolmaster, and the petty politics which caused his removal from place to place. Rural types of character are carefully portrayed.

MATILDE SERAO (1856-), XIX. 369.

162. THE CONQUEST OF ROME (1889), XV. 205. 1. Politics. 2. Character. A country member of the Italian Parliament is ruined politically by the young wife of an old man, who intrigues with him without really loving him.

(HERE MAY FOLLOW 509.)

GABRIELE D'ANNUNZIO (1864-), XIX. 15.

163. THE INTRUDER (1892), I. 248. 1. Ethics. 2. Crime. 3. Pathos. 4. Character. A woman, living with her dissipated husband, but estranged from him, bears an illegitimate child, and confesses to him her infidelity. The child is unwelcome to the husband, and he exposes it to the cold a moment, then repents and fosters it with eager care. But it dies, leaving the man in conscience-stricken agony.

164. THE TRIUMPH OF DEATH (1894), I. 258. 1. Character. 2. Tragedy. 3. Love. The tragedy of two soul-sick and world-weary lovers, to whom love is both an intoxication and an obsession, preventing all natural joys and social duties. To solve the problem they kill themselves together. The story presents pictures of death in all its phases, forming an artistic monograph, as it were, of the theme.

ENRICO ANNIBALE BUTTI (1868-), XIX. 74.

165. ENCHANTMENT (1899), IV. 221. 1. Character. 2. Love. 3. Politics. A young man who has devoted himself to the study of economics struggles against the fascination of sex in the person of a beautiful young woman of inferior mental powers to his own, but in the end succumbs to it.

GERMANY.

166. REYNARD THE FOX (1498), XIV. 26. 1. Youth. 2. Fable. 3. Animals. 4. Symbolism. 5. Satire. An animal legend in which human attributes are ascribed to beasts. The Fox symbolizes Earl Reynard, a crafty noble of the tenth century.

JOHANN WOLFGANG VON GOETHE (1749–1832), XIX. 210.

167. THE SORROWS OF WERTHER (1774), IX. 141. 1. Suicide. 2. Love. 3. Character. A young man loves the wife of a friend, and, after declaring his passion, kills himself, at the news of which expected event the woman is prostrated near to death. The special feature of the novel is its detailed presentation of the anguish of hopeless love.

168. WILHELM MEISTER'S APPRENTICESHIP (1795), IX. 149. 1. Character. 2. Adventure. 3. The Theatre. 4. Autobiography. The story of a young man's career, chiefly as a member of a travelling theatrical troupe. It is autobiographical not in events, but in the psychological development of the hero. In particular many phases of female character are presented.

169. ELECTIVE AFFINITIES (1809), IX. 160. 1. Ethics. 2. Character. 3. Love. 4. Marriage. A husband and wife live happily together with a bachelor and maiden. The husband comes to love the maiden, the wife the bachelor. A child is born to the married pair which resembles both the maiden and bachelor. All but the maiden agree to a divorce and a remating according to their affinities. The child is drowned while in charge of the maiden, and she accepts it as a divine warning. She dies, and the husband dies also, as if in psychological sympathy.

JEAN PAUL [RICHTER] (1763–1825), XIX. 351.

170. TITAN (1800–3), XIV. 65. 1. Character. 2. Ethics. 3. Magic. 4. Love. 5. Friendship. A father enjoins his son to marry his ward. The son loves another, the sister of a bosom friend, and finds that the friend loves the ward. But all things conspire to force him to accept the father's choice, even magic being brought into play to this end. His own beloved resigns him, and dies of grief, and at last he submits to the inevitable, and finds that the chosen one is really his mystical mate.

BARON DE LA MOTTE FOUQUÉ (1777–1843), XIX. 192.

171. UNDINE (1811), IX. 1 1. Imagination. 2. Magic. 3. Love. 4. Pathos. A fairy tale of a water-sprite that gained a soul upon marriage with a man—a knight. She still possesses uncanny power over the water-sprites, and her husband, in awe of her, turns for human companionship to another woman. The water-sprites, seeing Undine mistreated, take her to themselves. Her husband marries the other woman, and by fairy law Undine is compelled to kill him.

28 ANALYSIS OF THE WORLD'S STORIES

172. SINTRAM AND HIS COMPANIONS (1811), IX. 11. 1. Imagination 2. Magic. 3. Symbolism. 4. Religion. 5. Ethics. 6. Paganism. A young North German knight in the Dark Ages of the struggle between paganism and Christianity, contends with the Devil, personifying human selfishness, and with Death, by his victory over the former disarming the latter.

ADALBERT VON CHAMISSO (1781–1838), XIX. 88.

173. PETER SCHLEMIHL: THE MAN WITHOUT A SHADOW (1814), IV. 346. 1. Imagination. 2. Magic. 3. Ethics. 4. Humor. A grotesque tale of a man who sold his shadow to the devil, and of the troubles this occasioned. He refuses, however, to purchase back the shadow with his soul, and devotes himself to philanthropy, reaping in the end his reward.

BARON VON EICHENDORFF (1788–1857), XIX. 169.

174. THE HAPPY-GO-LUCKY (1824), VIII. 173. 1. Poetry. 2. Love. 3. Art. 4. Adventure. The idyl of an idler who falls in love with a lady who seems to be a countess and too high for him. After many adventures he is brought by two artists, the famous Leonardo and Reni, to a castle, where she is given to him as a bride. To his joy he learns she is as poor as himself.

WILHELM HAUFF (1802–1827), XIX. 249.

175. THE IRON HEART (1825), X. 108. 1. Imagination. 2. Magic. 3. Forest Life. 4. Symbolism. 5. Ethics. A fairy story of the Black Forest in which the supernatural characters are elves, giants, sorcerers, etc., and the human ones are lumbermen, charcoal-burners, glassmakers, etc. The purpose of the allegory is to teach humanity patience, thrift, and other good qualities.

BARONESS VON TAUTPHŒUS (1807–1893), XIX. 399.

176. THE INITIALS (1850), XVI. 261. 1. German Life and Character. 2. Love. A young Englishman is admitted by mistake into an exclusive German circle, where he makes himself most welcome. He is instrumental in saving a young woman by exposing a rascal by whom she is attracted. At first angry with him, she comes to be grateful to him and finally to love him.

FRITZ REUTER (1810–1874), XIX. 350.

177. IN THE YEAR '13 (1860), XIV. 13. 1. History. 2. German Peasant Life. A story of the troubles occasioned among the peasants by Napoleon's campaign through Germany.

FANNY LEWALD (1811–1889), XIX. 292.

178. HULDA (1875), XII. 1. 1. Psychic Phenomena. 2. The Theatre. 3. Love. A pastor's daughter is loved by a baron. But she has a presentiment that something is wrong at home, and returning thither, finds her mother dead. Her father is worked upon by the baron's sister to persuade her to give the baron up. She does so. On her father' death she becomes an actress, and later is reconciled to the baron, and marries him.

BERTHOLD AUERBACH (1812-1882), XIX, 19.

179. ON THE HEIGHTS (1865), I. 368. 1. Royalty. 2. Loyalty. 3. Intrigue. A peasant woman, wet-nurse of a prince, sees the corruption of the royal court, and by her loyalty causes the King's mistress to repent her treason to the Queen, and brings about the reconciliation of the two ladies and the King and Queen at the mistress's death-bed.

LUISE MUEHLBACH [KLARA MUNDT] (1814-1873), XIX. 326.

180. HENRY THE EIGHTH AND HIS COURT (1851), XII. 403. 1. History. 2. Religion. The story of the English royal Bluebeard and his last wife, Catherine Parr. The great lords and ladies of the court appear in the story, and the Reformation of the Church in England is touched upon.

181. BERLIN AND SANS SOUCI (1866), XII. 416. 1. History. A romance centering about Frederick the Great in his pleasure palace at Potsdam. Other royal personages are introduced, great nobles and generals, a favorite dancer and a noted adventurer. The Seven Years' War with Maria Theresa of Austria is touched upon, and Frederick's friendship with Voltaire.

182. MARIE ANTOINETTE AND HER SON (1867), XII. 429. 1. History. 2. Tragedy. A dramatic presentation of the execution of Louis XVI. and his Queen, and a romantic, non-historic tale of the escape of the young Dauphin.

FRIEDRICH WILHELM VON HACKLÄNDER (1816-1877), XIX. 239.

183. FORBIDDEN FRUIT (1850), IX. 316. 1. Love. 2. Art. A young soldier falls in love with the model of his brother-in-law, an artist. His jealous sister leads him to suppose that there is an amour between artist and model, and this leads to misunderstandings, which are finally resolved by the discovery that the bond between the suspected pair is a secret—the restoration of the model to her rightful place in society.

CHRISTOPH SCHÜCKING (1814-1883), XIX. 362.

184. PAUL BRONKHORST (1868), XIV. 244. 1. Law. 2. German Life and Character. 3. Marriage. A picture of Westphalian life and character of a century ago. The plot turns on the impairment of eligibility to clerical office by a misalliance.

GUSTAV FREYTAG (1816–1895), XIX. 195.

185. DEBIT AND CREDIT (1855), IX. 48.   1. Fidelity in Love and Business. The upward career in business of an honorable young man, who sacrifices self interest to restore the fortunes of a noble family, and is beloved by the daughter of the house; however, he remains true to a sweetheart of his own mercantile class.

EMILE ERCKMANN (1822–1899); LOUIS G. C. A. CHATRIAN (1826–1890); XIX. 172.

186. THE CONSCRIPT (1865), VIII. 258.   1. History.   2. Horrors of War. A conscript's story of the horrors of the last campaign of Napoleon I. before his exile to Elba. Ney, Blucher, Bernadotte, Moreau, and Metternich also appear in the story. The battles of Lützen, Leipzig, and the Elster are described.

GOLO RAIMUND (BERTHA FREDERICH) (1825–1882), XIX. 349.

187. A NEW RACE (1880), XIII. 333.   1. Love.   2. Restitution.   A young man is despoiled of his estate by a rich old man, and is embittered against him and his granddaughter. But she discovers the wrong, and, hearing the young man has become blind, attends to him, under an assumed name. When she comes into her property, she offers the betrothed of the young man an estate, in recompense of the wrong done him. The young man forbids his betrothed to accept a gift from one of the hated race. She refuses to obey him, and the engagement is broken. He recovers his sight and discovers that the giver is his companion, whereupon he falls in love with her and they marry.

E. MARLITT [EUGENIE JOHN] (1825–1887), XIX. 312.

188. THE OLD MAM'SELLE'S SECRET (1868), XII. 180.   1. Crime.   2. Heroism.   3. Music.   A rich old woman, a recluse, forms a secret friendship with a dependent girl. The recluse dies, and a fanatic woman destroys her chiefest treasures, priceless autograph music scores. The young girl knows of the vandalism, but forbears to reveal it and another secret, viz., that the vandal's son is innocently living on stolen money. The woman boldly confesses and justifies her crime, the son bravely repudiates the fortune, and marries the girl.

189. A LITTLE MOORLAND PRINCESS (1875), XII. 192.   1. Love.   2. Ambition.   3. Numismatics.   A girl of Jewish descent, brought up among the moors by her father, a collector of coins, is introduced into society where pride of birth is a ruling passion. She takes a dislike to a merchant who declares that coins found by her father in a mound are counterfeit. She cruelly reminds him of a duel he had fought in his youth in which he killed his opponent. Later she finds that his judgment on the coins is correct, and that his duel was justified, and marries him.

FRIEDRICH VON SPIELHAGEN (1829-   ), XIX. 382.

190. HAMMER AND ANVIL (1869), XV. 376. 1. Smuggling. 2. Imprisonment. 3. Manufacturing. 4. Social Reform. A young man is involved with smugglers, and is imprisoned. He foils a plot to murder the wardens, and is pardoned. He enters a factory, and by his ability becomes in time a partner in the business. He inaugurates reforms, such as profit-sharing and co-partnership of workingmen.

PAUL HEYSE (1830-   ), XIX. 255.

191. IN PARADISE (1875), X. 240. 1. Artist Life. 2. Love. 3. Philosophy. A tale of artist life in Munich, in which several love affairs are complicated by misunderstandings about models, former marriage, etc., and finally resolved by an explanation of these complications. Epicureanism is presented as the philosophy of life.

LUDWIG HARDER (1835-1880).

192. A FAMILY FEUD (1877), IX. 390. 1. Enmity. 2. Love. A man, who had adopted a boy, marries afterward, and has a daughter, who becomes his heiress. His sister tries to create discord between the children. The little girl is kidnapped, and suspicion falls on the youth. The outrage is traced to the aunt, and the young people are reconciled and marry each other.

GEORGE EBERS (1837-1898), XIX. 164.

193. UARDA (1877), VIII. 117. 1. History. 2. Archæology. 3. Mythology. 4. Witchcraft. A romance of ancient Egypt (under Rameses II.). The customs, mythology, superstitions, etc., of the time are set forth, and war with the Hittites is described.

194. HOMO SUM (1878), VIII. 108. 1. Religion. 2. Character. 3. Love. 4. Tragedy. A man of the world, a lover, an athlete, etc., becoming converted to Christianity from paganism, takes the vows of an anchorite. His struggles to subdue natural human desires form the tragedy of the story.

E. JUNCKER [ELISABETTA SCHMIEDEN] (1841-1896), XIX. 280.

195. MARGARETHE (1870), XI. 183. 1. Love. 2. Marriage. 3. Medicine. 4. Heroism. A story of courtship and wedded life. A husband, alienated from his wife, saves her life by the transfusion of his blood, and, later, she is reconciled to him by his heroism in rescuing life in an inundation.

EVA HARTNER [EMMA VON TWARDOWSKA] (1850-   ), XIX. 249.

196. SEVERA (1880), X. 99. 1. Youth. 2. Love. An orphan girl discovers that her guardian had been rejected by her mother for a vagabond actor, and, being in love with the guardian, she tries to run away from him. He, however, stays her by declaring his love for her.

PORTUGAL.

LUIZ DE CAMOËNS (1524-1580). XIX. 79.

197. THE LUSIAD (1572), IV. 273. 1. History. 2. Mythology. 3. Naval Adventure. An epic in the classic manner celebrating the exploits of Vasco da Gama.

GREAT BRITAIN.

APHRA BEHN (ENGLAND, 1640-1689), XIX. 45.

198. OROONOKO: OR, THE ROYAL SLAVE (1658), II. 418. 1. Humanitarianism. 2. Heroism. 3. Love. A romance of two enslaved negro lovers, a prince and princess, in which the cruelty of their masters is depicted in black contrast to their own bravery and constancy.

DANIEL DEFOE (ENGLAND, 1661-1731), XIX. 116.

199. ROBINSON CRUSOE (1719), VI. 245. 1. Adventure. 2. Invention. 3. Loyalty. 4. Cannibalism. 5. Mutiny. A sailor is cast on a desolate island, where he makes life comfortable by many devices. He saves an Indian from being eaten by cannibals, and the man becomes his faithful servant. They escape from the island by overpowering mutineers who have landed on the island, and rescuing their captain whom they were about to kill.

JONATHAN SWIFT (IRELAND, 1667-1745), XIX. 397.

200. GULLIVER'S TRAVELS (1726-1727), XVI. 224. 1. Satire. 2. Imagination. 3. Adventure. 4. Philosophy. 5. Animals. Imaginary voyages to marvellous countries, of mites, of giants, of visionary philosophers, and of rational horses, in all of which the author takes occasion to satirize the human race as a whole: in its chief vocations—the government, law, medicine, science, invention, philosophy; in countries and cities, such as France and England, Paris and London; and in individuals, Charles II., James II., William III., and Bolingbroke being obscurely referred to.

SAMUEL RICHARDSON (ENGLAND, 1689-1761), XIX. 350.

201. PAMELA (1740), XIV. 32. 1. Ethics. A servant girl resists the seductions of her infatuated master, until he proposes honorable marriage, which she accepts.

202. CLARISSA HARLOWE (1747-8), XIV. 43. 1. Ethics. 2. Pathos. A young girl is pursued by a libertine, who ruins her against her will. She dies, and he repents and is killed by her cousin in a duel.

203. SIR CHARLES GRANDISON (1753), XIV. 54. 1. Ethics. 2. Religion. An heiress, abducted by a villain, is rescued by the hero. They fall in love. But he is in honor bound to an Italian girl, a very devout

Catholic, who has been trying to convert him to her faith. Finding her efforts vain, she gives him up, and, thus released, he marries the English girl.

HENRY FIELDING (ENGLAND, 1707-1754), XIX. 177.

204. THE ADVENTURES OF JOSEPH ANDREWS (1742), VIII. 319. 1. Satire. 2. Adventure. 3. Character. 4. Love. A satire on Richardson's "Pamela" (201) who is represented as the hero's sister. Joseph, under temptation, proves to be a marvel of chastity. He and a penniless parson, whose portrait is the distinctive feature of the book, have interesting adventures together on the road. Joseph falls in love with a poor girl; it appears that she is his sister, then, later, not so. It transpires that Joseph is well-born; the two marry, and their troubles are at an end.

205. JONATHAN WILD (1743), VIII. 328. 1. Satire. 2. Crime. A burlesque of the heroic apotheosis of criminals. The career of a low, mean thief is depicted as worthy of admiration. He is represented as picking the pocket of the parson at his hanging—and getting a corkscrew.

206. TOM JONES (1749), VIII. 339. 1. Adventure. 2. Humor. 3. Character. A country gentleman adopts a foundling. He incurs the jealous hatred of the heir, a lad of his own age. They both covet the same young lady. After much intrigue and misunderstanding, it developing that the hero is the nephew of the man who adopted him, Tom wins the girl.

207. AMELIA (1752), VIII. 356. 1. Law. 2. Imprisonment. 3. Intrigue. 4. Marriage. A soldier is witness of an assault, and, being too poor to bribe the constables, is thrown into prison. Here he becomes intimate with a dissolute woman. Through her he is released. He rejoins his wife and shuns his prison mistress. She is jealous and involves him in a duel and other complications, which are finally resolved to his credit and benefit.

SAMUEL JOHNSON (ENGLAND, 1709-1784), XIX. 276.

208. RASSELAS (1759), XI. 139. 1. Philosophy. 2. Ethics. 3. Imagination. A romance of an Abyssinian prince who seeks the secret of happiness, and finds it in "neither youth nor age, solitude nor society, affluence nor poverty, high station nor humble birth, learning nor ignorance, marriage nor celibacy."

LAURENCE STERNE (ENGLAND, 1713-1768), XIX. 387.

209. TRISTRAM SHANDY (1759-1767), XV. 462. 1. Humor. 2. Medicine. 3. Satire. 4. Education. 5. Character. 6. Autobiography. The hero has a succession of misfortunes, happening (1) in his geniture (2) to his nose, (3) in his christening, and (4) in his education, the author taking opportunity thereby to poke good-natured fun at fathers and

mothers, doctors, physiognomists, teachers, etc. The chief feature of the book is its delineation of types of character, notably a preacher (whose original was the author himself) and a retired veteran.

210. A SENTIMENTAL JOURNEY (1768), XV. 475. 1. Travel. 2. Humor. 3. Sentiment. 4. Adventure. Adventures of a sentimental philosopher, rather amorously inclined, on a journey through France and Italy, with his quaint reflections upon subjects suggested thereby, love, liberty, religion, etc.

HORACE WALPOLE (ENGLAND, 1717-1797), XIX. 417.

211. THE CASTLE OF OTRANTO (1765), XVII. 148. 1. Melodrama. 2. Magic. 3. Ethics. A romance of a mediæval castle, a seat of magical horrors, in which are involved villains and their intended victims, lovers, etc. In the end, crime is punished and virtue rewarded.

TOBIAS GEORGE SMOLLETT (SCOTLAND 1721-1771), XIX. 379.

212. RODERICK RANDOM (1748), XV. 310. 1. Autobiography. 2. Sea Life. 3. Adventure. 4. Character. 5. Satire. The career of an apprentice who goes out into the world to seek his fortune. He meets with many adventures, becoming in time a surgeon's assistant on a man-of-war. Here the story becomes autobiographical. The author's experiences as a surgeon in the attack on Carthagena is described, with satirical comments on the mismanagement of the expedition. Later, the hero enters the French army and fights at Dettingen. He returns to England, marries his sweetheart, finds his father whom he had supposed dead, and ends his life in prosperity. Various types of mariners are delineated in semi-caricature.

213. PEREGRINE PICKLE (1751), XV. 323. 1. Adventure. 2. Politics. 3. Authorship. 4. Character. The career of a young man of a satirical turn of mind which involves him in trouble with his sweetheart, and both injures and aids him in his political fortunes. Queer characters, an old sea-dog in particular, are delineated.

214. FERDINAND, COUNT FATHOM (1753), XV. 334. 1. Rascality. 2. Adventure. The adventurous career of a sharper, ending in jail, whence he is generously liberated by a friend whom he had grievously misused.

215. LAUNCELOT GREAVES (1761), XV. 345. 1. Adventure. 2. Satire. 3. Insanity. An imitation of Don Quixote (**144**). The hero becomes insane on the subject of knight-errantry, and, clothed in armor, rides forth through the country seeking romantic adventures. In time he lands in an insane asylum, wherein he finds that his lady love is also confined. Both are rescued, and, cured of his delusion, he settles down with her to a happy married life.

216. HUMPHRY CLINKER (1771), XV. 356. 1. Humor. 2. Travel. 3. Character. The story of a stupid, faithful servant of a squire on a tour with his family through various cities and resorts of **England**.

ANALYSIS OF THE WORLD'S STORIES

OLIVER GOLDSMITH (ENGLAND, 1728-1774), XIX. 226.

217. The Vicar of Wakefield (1766), IX. 182. 1. Family Life. 2. Intrigue. 3. Rascality. 4. Love. 5. Character. The story of an English vicar and his family, especially a daughter who is abducted by a villain, who also persecutes the good vicar. She is rescued by a good man who truly loves her, and all ends happily.

JOHN MOORE (SCOTLAND, 1729-1802), XIX. 321.

218. Zeluco (1789), XII. 357. 1. Crime. 2. Character. 3. Insanity. The adventures of a brilliant but criminal and debased man. In a jealous frenzy he murders his child, and drives his wife insane temporarily. She recovers her mind at sight of a picture in which is shown a soldier murdering a child. The wife's defender kills Zeluco in a duel, and marries her.

HENRY MACKENZIE (SCOTLAND, 1745-1831), XIX. 303.

219. The Man of Feeling (1771), XII. 117. 1. Sentiment. 2. Character. 3. Adventure. 4. Love. 5. Pathos. A sentimental young man is made the dupe of clever rogues and politicians, and, recognizing that he is unfit to cope with the world, and win a livelihood for himself and the woman with whom he is in love, dies of melancholy.

HANNAH MORE (ENGLAND, 1745-1833), XIX. 323.

220. Cœlebs in Search of a Wife (1809), XII. 374. 1. Marriage. 2. Character. 3. Education. A didactic novel treating of the proper mating of people, education of children, etc. Various types of English society are presented.

FRANCES BURNEY (ENGLAND, 1752-1840), XIX. 73.

221. Evelina (1778), IV. 211. 1. Character. 2. Society. 3. Love. The heroine is a girl of obscure birth who is thrust into polite society ignorant of its manners. The mistakes she makes supply largely the incidents of the story and form the critical situations of the plot. The mystery of her birth is cleared, and her love romance terminates happily.

WILLIAM GODWIN (ENGLAND, 1756-1836), XIX. 208.

222. Caleb Williams (1794), IX. 135. 1. Character. 2. Crime and its Punishment. 3. Remorse. A secretary ferrets out the secret that his employer is guilty of a murder for which he has permitted an innocent man to be hanged. Yet in other respects the employer is a noble man. The secretary denounces him to the police, then, in remorse, tries to save him. The murderer refuses to be saved, admits his guilt, charges his former cowardice to an overpowering fear of public degradation, and dies, leaving his secretary the victim of immedicable remorse.

WILLIAM BECKFORD (ENGLAND, 1759–1844), XIX. 40.

223. VATHEK: AN ARABIAN TALE (1786), II. 382. 1. Magic. 2. Imagination. 3. Extravaganza. A story in imitation of the Arabian Nights Entertainment, employing the same machinery of the supernatural and fantastic.

(HERE MAY FOLLOW 517.)

ANNE RADCLIFFE (ENGLAND, 1764–1823), XIX. 348.

224. THE ROMANCE OF THE FOREST (1791), XIII. 308. 1. Crime. 2. Melodrama. A high-born Frenchman flees from punishment for his many crimes. A highwayman forces him to take along a beautiful young girl. He takes up his residence in a deserted abbey said to be haunted. He aids the designs of a wicked marquis to marry her, but she is rescued, after enduring unspeakable terrors in the haunted abbey, and marries a brave young soldier.

225. THE MYSTERIES OF UDOLPHO (1794), XIII. 318. 1. Crime. 2. Melodrama. The hair-raising adventures of a girl in a castle which is a den of thieves, and fitted by them with terrifying machinery to give it the name of being haunted. She is rescued and reunited to her lover, and the villains are punished.

REGINA MARIA ROCHE (IRELAND, 1765–1845), XIX. 354.

226. THE CHILDREN OF THE ABBEY (1798), XIV. 108. 1. Melodrama. 2. Crime. A romantic tale of ladies mistreated by villains, of stolen fortunes, and of lovers united and heirs righted in the end.

MARIA EDGEWORTH (IRELAND, 1767–1849,) XIX. 165.

227. CASTLE RACKRENT (1800), VIII. 132. 1. Irish Life and Character. 2. Rascality. The memoirs of a fictitious Irish family, told by a loyal retainer, who reveals the successful plot of his own rascally son to get possession of the property.

228. THE ABSENTEE (1812), VIII. 138. 1. Anglo-Irish Life and Character. 2. Social Reform. 3. Rascality. Owing to the social ambition of the wife, an Irish landed family live in England, where the husband is unhappy, and the wife ridiculed. The son goes to Ireland, sees the deplorable condition of some of their tenants, frustrates the plot of a rascally agent, and persuades his parents to return home, and become model landlords.

WALTER SCOTT (SCOTLAND, 1771–1832), XIX. 364.

229. WAVERLEY (1814), XIV. 273. 1. History. 2. Love. 3. Adventure. The adventures of an English officer among Highlanders in the war with the Pretender, Charles Stuart, and his love complications with two Scotswomen.

230. GUY MANNERING (1815), XIV. 286. 1. Adventure. 2. Character. 3. Astrology. 4. History. A romance of the middle of the 18th century, depicting characters of the time, a gipsy, a smuggler, and the

ANALYSIS OF THE WORLD'S STORIES

author's tutor. The titular hero pretends to be an astrologer, and casts the horoscope of the real hero, which is singularly verified by his romantic career.

231. THE ANTIQUARY (1816), XIV. 300. 1. Character. 2. Antiquarianism. 3. Love. 4. History. A tale of the closing years of the 18th century, in which are presented the quaint characters of an antiquarian and a royal bedesman or beggar. There is a love plot which turns upon the recognition of a natural son.

232. THE BLACK DWARF (1816), XIV. 313. 1. Character. 2. History. 3. Love. The story of a deformed recluse during the war of the Pretender James. He prevents a girl sacrificing herself in marriage to save her father.

233. OLD MORTALITY (1816), XIV. 323. 1. History. 2. Character. 3. Religion. 4. Love. A romance of the rising of the Covenanters in 1679–1690. Their leader is the chief character of interest. Colonel Claverhouse and the Duke of Monmouth appear in the story. With the historical narrative is entwined a love romance.

234. ROB ROY (1817), XIV. 337. 1. History. 2. Character. 3. Love. A story of the chief of the Macgregor clan, during the Revolution of 1715. Various types of Scotch character are depicted, and a love romance is intertwined with the historical narrative.

235. THE HEART OF MIDLOTHIAN (1818), XIV. 350. 1. History. 2. Bravery. 3. Character. A romance of the Porteous Riot in Edinburgh. A girl condemned to death for infanticide is saved by her sister walking to London and procuring a pardon from Queen Caroline through intercession of the Duke of Argyle.

236. THE BRIDE OF LAMMERMOOR (1819), XIV. 363. 1. Tragedy. 2. Character. 3. Poverty. The family of the beloved of a poor gentleman separates her from him, and cause her to marry another. She becomes insane, and kills her husband on the wedding night. The lover, riding to a duel with her brother, is swallowed up in a quicksand. His servant is a quaint character, who adopts ludicrous expedients to conceal his master's poverty.

237. A LEGEND OF MONTROSE (1819), XIV. 374. 1. History. 2. Character. 3. Adventure. A Scotch mercenary who had served under Gustavus Adolphus of Sweden, enlists under the Earl of Montrose, commander of the Royalist forces in Scotland in the Revolution against Charles I. Captured and imprisoned, he escapes with a Highland chief. A love story is intertwined with the narrative of adventure.

238. IVANHOE (1819), XIV. 386. 1. History. 2. Adventure. 3. Chivalry. 4. Character. 5. Witchcraft. A romance of chivalric adventure in the days of Richard I. and his regent John. Robin Hood, the outlaw, is a character in the book. The titular hero is beloved by a Jewess who succors him in prison. He becomes her champion when she is tried for witchcraft.

239. The Pirate (1820), XIV. 399. 1. Piracy. 2. History. 3. Magic. The love romance of a gallant pirate and a Shetland girl. Goffe, a famous pirate, appears in the story. A sibyl plays a leading part in the plot.

240. The Monastery (1820), XIV. 413. 1. History. 2. Magic. 3. Literature. 4. Religion. A tale of Elizabethan days in Scotland, when the Reformed religion was supplanting the Catholic. A tutelary spirit of a family plays a magical part in the plot. An interesting character is a follower of Lyly, the English dramatic poet who introduced "Euphuism," or affected speaking, into the royal court.

241. The Abbot (1820), XIV. 427. 1. History. 2. Religion. A sequel to the "Monastery," containing an account of the imprisonment of Queen Mary of Scotland.

242. Kenilworth (1821), XV. 1. 1. History. 2. Tragedy. The story of the murder of the wife of the Earl of Leicester, at his instigation. Queen Elizabeth and her courtiers appear in the story.

243. The Fortunes of Nigel (1822), XV. 16. 1. History. 2. Business. The career of George Heriot, founder of Heriot's Hospital in Edinburgh, who rose to be the King's goldsmith and banker. With this is implicated a love romance concerning his god-daughter. King James I. and his courtiers appear in the story.

244. Peveril of the Peak (1823), XV. 32. 1. History. 2. Religion. Founded on the alleged conspiracy of the Roman Catholics to murder Charles II. and re-establish their Church in England. These matters separate two lovers, who are reunited by the king.

245. Quentin Durward (1823), XV. 46. 1. History. 2. Love. 3. Character. The hero is a Scots soldier in the service of Louis XI. of France during his trouble with the Duke of Burgundy. By his bravery he wins the hand of a princess. Delineation of the character of Louis XI. is notable.

246. St. Ronan's Well (1823), XV. 62. 1. Tragedy. 2. Character. The scene is laid at a watering-place, where various types of character are assembled. A wronged girl dies, and her brother kills her undoer in a duel.

247. Red Gauntlet (1824), XV. 74. 1. History. 2. Loyalty. A tale of the loyalty of a family to the Pretender, Charles Edward.

248. The Betrothed (1825), XV. 88. 1. History. 2. Love. A knight goes to the Crusades leaving his betrothed in charge of his nephew. Though loving each other each remains true to the trust. The knight returns and confutes the scandal that a villain has spread abroad. The villain is slain by an assassin in error for the knight. The knight unites the lovers.

ANALYSIS OF THE WORLD'S STORIES

249. THE TALISMAN (1825), XV. 102. 1. History. 2. Chivalry. 3. Character. A tale of the Crusades in which the contrast between Oriental and Occidental character is presented. The hero is David, Prince Royal of Scotland. Richard I. of England and Saladin, the Saracen, appear in the story.

250. WOODSTOCK (1826), XV. 116. 1. History. A tale of the English Revolution, immediately after the defeat of Charles II. by Cromwell at the battle of Worcester. The King is saved from capture by a loyal subject who impersonates him, and who is condemned to death by Cromwell, and saved upon reconsideration.

251. THE FAIR MAID OF PERTH (1828), XV. 130. 1. History. 2. Heroism. A young armorer defends his sweetheart from David, son of Robert III. of Scotland, who would carry her away. He afterward takes part as a substitute in a duel between two Highland clans, and refuses knighthood and wealth which the Black Douglas would confer on him for his bravery.

252. ANNE OF GEIERSTEIN (1829), XV. 144. 1. History. 2. Loyalty. 3. Adventure. The adventures of a young Englishman among the Swiss at the time of their war with the Duke of Burgundy. The hero wins the love of a daughter of a Swiss noble, who sanctions their marriage on the eve of his parting on a dangerous quest—the killing of the Duke of Burgundy at the command of the Vehmegericht, or Secret Tribunal.

253. COUNT ROBERT OF PARIS (1831), XV. 159. 1. History. 2. Adventure. 3. Animals. A knight of the First Crusade has many adventures at the court of Alexius Comnenus of Constantinople. Cast into a dungeon, he kills a tiger that he finds therein and subdues an orang-utan. He fights in single combat with Hereward, the English patriot and outlaw, and spares his life at the request of his wife's attendant, who is in love with Hereward.

254. CASTLE DANGEROUS (1831), XV. 174. 1. History. 2. Chivalry. Robert Bruce is battling against Edward I. of England. An English knight enters into single combat with Sir James Douglas for the possession of Douglas Castle, and of the lady love of the Englishman. Only on hearing of Bruce's victory does he yield to Douglas, and then he is ordered to surrender himself to his beloved.

MATTHEW GREGORY LEWIS (ENGLAND, 1775-1818), XIX. 293.

255. THE MONK (1795), XII. 11. 1. Magic. 2. Religion. 3. Melodrama. A monk yields to temptation, and becomes a monster of hypocrisy, lust, and murder. He sells his soul to the devil, who requires it in person.

JANE AUSTEN (ENGLAND, 1775-1817), XIX. 21.

256. SENSE AND SENSIBILITY (1811), I. 377. 1. Character. 2. Marriage. 3. Love. 4. Family Life. A story of English country gentry, presenting shrewd studies of character, especially in relation to affairs of the heart, in which the common-sense attitude is contrasted with the emotional.

257. PRIDE AND PREJUDICE (1813), I. 387. 1. Character. 2. Marriage. 3. Love. 4. Family Life. A story of the love affairs of two sisters which are complicated by pride of birth and prejudice against character in the parties themselves and their relatives.

258. MANSFIELD PARK (1814), I. 398. 1. Character. 2. Marriage. 3. Love. 4. Family Life. A story in which traits of character are exhibited in family relations, pleasant and unpleasant, and in marriages, happy and unhappy.

259. EMMA (1815), I. 408. 1. Character. 2. Marriage. 3. Love. 4. Family Life. A story of English country gentry, in which a number of interinvolved love affairs are presented, that of the heroine remaining to the last, because dependent on the straightening out of all the others.

260. PERSUASION (1818), I. 418. 1. Character. 2. Marriage. 3. Love. 4. Family Life. A story of English country gentry, in which a number of love affairs are involved. The heroine has been persuaded to break her engagement to a young man because both families object to the alliance. Later, these objections are removed, and the marriage takes place.

261. NORTHANGER ABBEY (1818), I. 427. 1. Character. 2. Love. 3. Family Life. Fashionable life at Bath and home life at a country seat are depicted. There are several love affairs, the principal one being complicated by the objections of the man's father, which are finally removed.

JANE PORTER (ENGLAND, 1776-1850), XIX. 343.

262. THADDEUS OF WARSAW (1803), XIII. 248. 1. History. 2. Melodrama. A Polish noble who has fought unsuccessfully to free his country from the tyranny of Catherine of Russia, flees to England, where he falls in love. Discovering, as he thinks, that a disreputable English nobleman is his father, he discontinues his suit. Later, he finds that his father is another English lord, of high character. The lord recognizes him as his son and he marries the lady of his love.

263. THE SCOTTISH CHIEFS (1810), XIII. 260. 1. History. 2. Tragedy. A love romance founded on the career of William Wallace, the hero of Scotland. He marries the heroine on the day of his execution, and she dies of grief of remembrance on the day Robert Bruce is crowned.

THOMAS MOORE (IRELAND, 1779-1852), XIX. 322.

264. THE EPICUREAN (1827), XII. 368. 1. Philosophy. 2. Archæology.

3. Religion. A recreation of Egyptian life and customs in the early days of Christianity when it was in conflict with Greek pagan philosophy, especially that of Epicurus.

JOHN GALT (SCOTLAND, 1779-1839). XIX. 197.

265. LAWRIE TODD (1832), IX. 88. 1. Pioneer Life. 2. Labor. 3. History. The experiences of a Scotch settler in the Genesee valley of New York State about 1800. He rears a family, develops a nail-making industry and other enterprises at Rochester, visits Scotland, and, though almost a dwarf in stature, and of middle age, brings home a fine young widow as his wife, thereby disappointing an aged spinster.

GEORGE CROLY (IRELAND, 1780-1860). XIX. 107.

266. SALATHIEL (1827), VI. 49. 1. Legend. 2. History. 3. Adventure. 4. Religion. 5. Magic. The romance of the Wandering Jew, who, assuming the responsibility for Jesus's death, was condemned to roam the earth till the Second Coming. He meets with many adventures: is at the burning of Rome by Nero; leads the revolt of the Jews of Palestine against Rome, and beholds the fall of Jerusalem, and the triumph of Titus; leads Alaric the Goth against Rome; inspires Mohammed to avenge the Jews, maltreated by the Christians, and brings the Crusaders to expell the Saracens from the Temple at Jerusalem which they had polluted. He is seized with the passions of invention and discovery, becoming an alchemist, and one of the first printers, and a companion of Columbus. He becomes a poet with Petrarch, an artist with Angelo, a reformer with Luther, etc.

JAMES J. MORIER (ENGLAND, 1780-1849). XIX. 324.

267. THE ADVENTURES OF HAJJI BABA OF ISPAHAN (1824), XII. 383. 1. Persian Life. 2. Adventure. The wandering adventures of a clever, unscrupulous young Persian, who finally achieves a brilliant success.

CHARLES MATURIN (IRELAND, 1782-1824). XIX. 314.

268. MELMOTH THE WANDERER (1820), XII. 249. 1. Madness. 2. Magic. 3. The Inquisition. 4. Hindu Mythology. 5. Tragedy. A wild tale of a madman, of whom the devil had prophesied that he would become insane. He describes the horrors of the Inquisition, and the murderous worship of the Hindu goddess Kali, and the story ends with his self murder.

SUSAN E. FERRIER (SCOTLAND, 1782-1854). XIX. 175.

269. THE INHERITANCE (1824), VIII. 290. 1. Wealth. 2. Love. 3. Character. The troubles of a headstrong girl who has become heir of a rich estate. Her mother, her betrothed, who is a fortune-hunter, and her guardian, who truly loves her, order her life and affairs contrary to her liking, the mother and betrothed for the worse, the guardian for

the better. At last she disobeys her mother's commands to bear the insolence of a strange man, and he reveals himself as her father. She loses her wealth, her betrothed jilts her, and her guardian proposes to her. It then transpires that her putative father is an impostor, and all ends happily.

THOMAS LOVE PEACOCK (ENGLAND, 1785–1886), XIX. 338.

270. HEADLONG HALL (1816), XIII. 189. 1. Character. 2. English Country Life. A study of eccentric types of character gathered together in an English country house.

THOMAS DE QUINCY (ENGLAND, 1785–1859), XIX. 128.

271. THE AVENGER (1853), VI. 366. 1. Crime. 2. Tragedy. 3. Love. A French officer is captured and tortured to death by a jailer in a German town. His wife, a Jewess, is subjected to inhuman treatment by the citizens. Years after their son comes incognito to the town and wreaks terrible vengeance on their abusers, even killing one man with whose granddaughter he had fallen in love.

MICHAEL SCOTT (SCOTLAND, 1789–1835), XIX. 363.

272. TOM CRINGLE'S LOG (1833), XIV. 264. 1. Sea Life and Character. 2. History. 3. Adventure. The log of a British sailor during the War of 1812 with the United States.

FREDERICK MARRYAT (ENGLAND, 1792–1848), XIX. 313.

273. JAPHET IN SEARCH OF A FATHER (1836), XII. 214. 1. Adventure. 2. Gipsy Life. The story of a foundling's many and varied adventures—among gipsies and high society—undertaken to find his father, which he finally does among the aristocracy.

274. MR. MIDSHIPMAN EASY (1836), XII. 226. 1. Sea Life. 2. Satire. 3. Adventure. A story of the adventures of a young naval officer. The author satirizes the democratic doctrine of equal natural rights by showing the hero in his ridiculous attempts to assert them on shipboard.

275. THE LITTLE SAVAGE (1848), XII. 237. 1. Youth. 2. Adventure. 3. Religion. 4. Animals. The story of a boy Crusoe, who grows up in savagery, obeying his natural impulses until taught better things by a woman missionary. A pet seal is one of the interesting features of the story.

WILLIAM CARLETON (IRELAND, 1794–1869), XIX. 83.

276. WILLY REILLY (1855), IV. 301. 1. Religious Persecution. 2. Love. 3. Insanity. The love of a Catholic man and a Protestant girl during the religious strife in Ireland. The heroine becomes insane over the conviction of her lover, but recovers her reason on his release from prison.

MARY WOLLSTONECRAFT SHELLEY (ENGLAND, 1797-1851, XIX. 372.

277. FRANKENSTEIN (1816), XV. 238. 1. Imagination. 2. Allegory. 3. Magic. A man endows a human monster whom he has formed, with life, and this pursues its creator to his death.

SAMUEL LOVER (IRELAND, 1797-1868), XIX. 298.

278. HANDY ANDY (1842), XII. 52. 1. Humor. 2. Irish Character. The amusing bulls and blunders of a raw young Irishman.

JOHN BANIM (IRELAND, 1798-1842), XLX. 33.

279. BOYNE WATER (1826), II. 287. 1. History. 2. Patriotism. 3. Love. 4. Tragedy. 5. Divination. A romance of civil war in Ireland (James II. vs. William III.). A Protestant brother and sister love a Catholic sister and brother respectively, but are divided by the war. A witch foretells a tragic outcome for one match and a happy one for the other, which prophecy is realized. Historic characters introduced are: Generals Kirke, Schomberg, and Sarsfield.

LEITCH RITCHIE (SCOTLAND, 1800-1865), XIX. 352.

280. THE ROBBER OF THE RHINE (1833), XIV. 77. 1. History. 2. Crime. A romance founded on the career of the famous bandit Schinderhannes.

G. P. R. JAMES (ENGLAND, 1801-1860), XIX. 272.

281. HENRY MASTERTON (1832), XI. 85. 1. History. 2. Adventure. 3. Love. The romantic adventures in love and war, in England and France, of a Cavalier in the English Revolution. Generals Ireton and St. Maur appear in the story.

HARRIET MARTINEAU (ENGLAND, 1802-1876), XIX. 314.

282. THE HOUR AND THE MAN (1840), XII. 203. 1. History. 2. Heroism. 3. Slavery. A romance of the career of Toussaint L'Ouverture, the heroic liberator of San Domingo. Napoleon I. appears in the story.

EDWARD GEORGE EARLE BULWER-LYTTON (ENGLAND, 1803-1873), XIX. 71.

283. FALKLAND (1827), III. 335. 1. Melodrama. 2. Psychic Phenomena. A man of compelling will, who has tempted beyond her resistance a married woman to elope with him, meets her ghost at the assignation.

284. PELHAM: OR, ADVENTURES OF A GENTLEMAN (1827), III. 340. 1. Gambling. 2. Melodrama. 3. Society. A titled gambler betrays a girl and her lover plots his ruin. The gambler is murdered, and the teller of the story believes his enemy has killed him. Being in love with the sister of the suspected assassin, the story-teller avoids her and him, whereupon the suspect proves his innocence.

285. THE DISOWNED (1828), III. 355. 1. Melodrama. 2. Society. A son whose mother had eloped after his birth with a lover, is disowned by his putative father. The young man, after various vicissitudes, attains a position in society, and falls in love. The girl's parents, however, object to him because of his unknown antecedents, and favor another suitor. The lover discovers that his rival is his half brother, and suffers the imputation of cowardice rather than fight him. Then the "Disowned" is acknowledged as his son and heir by his father, and all is made right.

286. DEVEREUX (1829), III. 365. 1. Adventure. 2. Melodrama. 3. History. A tale of enmity between twin brothers, each of whom loves a third younger brother. The younger lad falls under the influence of a priest, who is scheming for the restoration of the Stuarts, and contrives the villainy which one twin supposes practised against him by the other. Lord Bolingbroke enters as a character into the story.

287. PAUL CLIFFORD (1830), III. 378. 1. Crime. 2. Melodrama. The hero is a robber, who is represented as possessed of an heroic and even tender nature. He is reclaimed from his evil life.

288. EUGENE ARAM (1832), III. 391. 1. Crime. 2. History. 3. Character. A novelization of a real murder, in which the character of the criminal, a man of education, is made the subject of special presentation.

289. GODOLPHIN (1833), III. 406. 1. Character. 2. Love. 3. Astrology. 4. Politics. 5. The Theater. 6. Tragedy. The hero is a young man swayed by various influences and interests, astrology, politics, the theater, etc., chiefly represented in the persons of women. His end is tragic.

290. THE LAST DAYS OF POMPEII (1834), III. 415. 1. History. 2. Archæology. 3. Love. 4. Tragedy. A novel based upon the tragic historic event of the destruction by earthquake of Pompeii. A blind girl is the distinctive character of the story.

291. RIENZI: THE LAST OF THE TRIBUNES (1835), IV. 1. 1. History. 2. Tragedy. 3. Love. The principal and titular character is an historic personage, a mediæval dictator of Rome who strove to save the state from the feuds of the houses of Orsini and Colonna. The interest of romance is added to that of history by developing the part played by his wife in the situation which culminated in his assassination.

292. ERNEST MALTRAVERS (1837), IV. 13. 1. Melodrama. 2. Crime. 3. Love. A daughter of an assassin saves the life of a handsome young traveller, and he takes her into his household and educates her. She loves him, but he is in love with a high-born lady. This woman is done to death by two villains, one of whom becomes a maniac, after shouldering the sole responsibility of the villainy.

293. ALICE; OR, THE MYSTERIES (1838), IV. 26. 1. Melodrama. 2. Crime. 3. Love. A sequel to "Ernest Maltravers." The hero is about to wed a young girl, when he is told that she is his child by the assassin's

ANALYSIS OF THE WORLD'S STORIES 45

daughter, who had been stolen away from him. He finds the mother and learns the story is untrue, and they are united over the grave of the true child. The chief of the villains who separated them, now become a lord, is strangled by his tool, the maniac, who thereupon drowns himself.

294. LEILA; OR, THE SIEGE OF GRANADA (1838), IV. 40. 1. History. 2. Love. 3. Religious Persecution. 4. Magic. A romance based upon the Spanish conquest of the Moors. The heroine is a beautiful Jewess, beloved by Muza, the chief general of Boabdil, the Moorish king. Her father, a sorcerer, gives her as a hostage for the Jews to Ferdinand, the Spanish king. Through Queen Isabella and Torquemada she is converted to Christianity. Her father slays her as she is about to take the nun's veil, and he is torn in pieces by the mob.

295. NIGHT AND MORNING (1841), IV. 51. 1. Melodrama. 2. Crime. 3. Character. 4. Love. Two brothers are robbed of their inheritance by their uncle. The elder, a high-strung and bold spirit, refuses to compound for the injury, while the younger, a weaker soul, does so. They love the same woman, and the elder resigns her to the younger; he is rewarded, however, by the realization that his benevolence to an outcast girl has insensibly grown into love.

296. ZANONI (1842), IV. 61. 1. Magic. 2. Love. 3. History. 4. Tragedy. The hero is a Rosicrucian who barters supernatural power for love, substituting himself for his wife as the victim of the guillotine in the Reign of Terror. Robespierre, Desmoulins, Nicot, and René Dumas appear as characters in the story.

297. THE LAST OF THE BARONS (1843), IV. 73. 1. History. 2. Invention. 3. Politics. 4. Love. 5. Magic. A love romance founded on the War of the Roses. It is democratic in spirit. One of the characters is an inventor who is looked upon as a wizard. King Edward IV. is represented in an evil light, and Warwick, the King-maker, the titular hero, in a favorable one. Richard of Gloucester, the Duke of Clarence, Margaret of Anjou, Henry VI., Friar Bungay, the necromancer, and other historic personages appear in the story.

298. LUCRETIA; OR, THE CHILDREN OF THE NIGHT (1847), IV. 155. 1. Crime. 2. Insanity. 3. Tragedy. The titular character by intrigue attains social position, and by murder attempts to retain it. She is exposed, however, by a man whom she has poisoned to close his mouth, and who proves to be her own son, upon the discovery of which she goes mad.

299. HAROLD (1848), IV. 84. 1. History. 2. Love. 3. Magic. A love romance founded on the Norman Conquest. Astrology, and sorcery play an important part in the mechanism of the plot. Edward the Confessor, William the Conqueror, Earl Godwin and his sons, especially Harold, who is the titular hero, and other historic personages, are characters in the story.

300. THE CAXTONS (1849), IV. 95. 1. Character. 2. Humor. 3. Business. 4. Rascality. Various types of character in a family, the absent-minded scholar, who is the father, the sanguine promoter, who is the uncle, the rascal cousin, who is reclaimed, etc., presented in a humorous vein.

301. MY NOVEL (1853), IV. 106. 1. Character. 2. Humor. 3. Melodrama. 4. Politics. 5. Journalism. 6. Love. A novel in diverse veins, containing humorous sketches of village characters, such as a doctor, an Italian exile who is restored at the end to his noble rank at home; an idyllic romance of a poor poet and an outcast girl; studies of journalism and politics, all woven into a somewhat conventional melodramatic plot of mistaken identity disclosed, and villainy unmasked.

302. WHAT WILL HE DO WITH IT? (1858), IV. 122. 1. Character. 2. Melodrama. 3. Love. 4. Crime. A study of English domestic life, with a melodramatic plot, in which one character stands out with distinction —a woman who frustrates the plans of her villainous lover, to keep him in her power.

303. A STRANGE STORY (1862), IV. 134. 1. Magic. 2. Medicine. 3. Crime. An Englishman murders an Arabian sorcerer, and gains possession of an elixir imparting youth and magical powers. Returning to England, he uses his black arts to attach to himself a girl of mediumistic temperament. Her lover, however, a doctor, frustrates him.

304. THE COMING RACE (1871), IV. 163. 1. Science. 2. Imagination. 3. Sociology. A mining engineer penetrates into an underworld, inhabited by people who have advanced far beyond our race in science, industry, and social organization. They have especially developed the power of the will into a force called *vril*, which is an agent of either destruction or construction.

305. KENELM CHILLINGLY (1872), IV. 144. 1. Character. 2. Love. 3. 3. Renunciation. 4. Art. The hero is a young man of strong though eccentric personality. He renounces a girl, whose love he had won, to her benefactor, an artist, whose inspiration she is. The girl dies, before her marriage, with a broken heart.

306. THE PARISIANS (1873), IV. 171. 1. Parisian Society. 2. Politics. 3. Love. A love romance dealing with typical characters in Parisian society and politics during the Second Empire, and the Franco-Prussian War.

307. PAUSANIAS THE SPARTAN (1875), IV. 179. 1. History. 2. Love. 3. Tragedy. An historical romance based on the story of the Spartan regent who slew by mistake his beloved, as she stole by night to his couch.

GERALD GRIFFIN (IRELAND, 1803-1840), XIX. 235.

308. THE COLLEGIANS (1828), IX. 274. 1. Tragedy. 2. Character. A young Irish gentleman, spoiled by his mother, secretly marries a peasant girl; later he is dragged by his mother into marriage with a woman of his rank. He orders his servant to get his real wife out of the way, which the servant interprets as an order for her murder. This man kills her and is assaulted by the husband. The servant denounces him to the police, and he is apprehended for the crime, and, despite his mother's protest, confesses it. The mental torture of the husband is admirably portrayed.

GEORGE HENRY BORROW (ENGLAND, 1803-1881), XIX. 60.

309. LAVENGRO: THE SCHOLAR—THE GIPSY—THE PRIEST (1851), III. 151. Gipsy Life. 2. Adventure. 3. Autobiography. 4. Authorship. 5. Religious Fanaticism. 6. Boxing. A semi-autobiographical romance of rambling adventure in Scotland, Ireland, and Wales, chiefly among gipsies. The hero is about to be killed by a mad gipsy woman when he is rescued by a Welsh preacher, a fanatic. He beats a bully in a fist fight and wins the admiration of a woman of the bully's following, who becomes the hero's companion.

BENJAMIN DISRAELI, EARL OF BEACONSFIELD (ENGLAND, 1805-1881), XIX. 153.

310. VIVIAN GREY (1826), VII. 133. 1. Autobiography. 2. Politics. 3. History. 4. Gambling. 5. Love. A romance of a young man's career in love and politics. The hero is a portrait of the author, and the following personages of the time are represented under assumed names: Wellington, Prince Esterhazy, the rich Mrs. Coutts, Prince Gortschakoff, the Marquis of Hertford, Theodore Hook, and Lord Brougham. Gambling at a German watering-place is vividly described.

311. THE YOUNG DUKE (1831), VII. 147. 1. English Nobility. 2. Politics. 3. Love. A romance of titled folk, dealing with intrigues in love and politics. The triumph in Parliament of the hero is strangely prophetic of the author's subsequent career.

312. CONTARINI FLEMING (1832), VII. 158. 1. Travel. 2. Psychic Phenomena. 3. Authorship. 4. Autobiography. A young German noble, son of an Italian woman, visits Italy—where he snatches from the altar a girl about to become a bride of the church—Spain, the Holy Land, and other countries. The places he visits he has anticipated in dreams. The romance is semi-autobiographical in its account of the hero's novel-writing.

313. ALROY (1833), VII. 169. 1. History. 2. Adventure. 3. Magic. 4. Religion. 5. Tragedy. A romance, partly historical, partly imaginative, of a Jewish "Prince of the Captivity," telling of the hero's battles, mystical adventures, unfortunate love, and tragic death.

314. HENRIETTA TEMPLE (1836), VII. 182. 1. English Aristocracy. 2. Love. A romance of the upper English classes, in which love is represented as an immediate and intuitive perception of affinity which knows no barrier of disparity of age.

315. VENETIA (1837), VII. 192. 1. History. 2. Authorship. 3. Love. 4. Tragedy. A story of tragic love, founded on the true romances of Byron and Shelley, who, with Byron's uncle and mother, Shelley's daughter (the heroine), Bishop Wilberforce, and others, are represented under assumed names.

316. CONINGSBY (1844), VII. 203. 1. Politics. 2. Social Reform. 3. History. 4. Love. The career of a young statesman, intent on improving social conditions. He is beloved and aided by noblewomen, and he has brilliant men as political foes and allies. Among these may be mentioned the following statesmen appearing under assumed names: Gladstone, Bright, Baron de Rothschild, and the Marquess of Hertford, Baron von Humboldt, and Theodore Hook are also found thinly disguised in its pages.

317. SYBIL (1845), VII. 217. 1. Politics. 2. Social Reform. 3. History. 4. Labor. 5. Love. The events cover the period of industrial depression in England from 1837 to 1842. The hero, a member of Parliament, leads an agitation for the relief of the workingmen. These rise in riots, incited by the hero's rival in love, who is killed. The hero saves his sweetheart from the rioters.

318. TANCRED (1847), VII. 227. 1. Religion. 2. Magic. 3. History. 4. Adventure. 5. Love. A romance of Oriental love and adventure, tinged with mysticism, intended to harmonize Christianity and Judaism. Baron de Rothschild and other of the author's contemporaries appear in the story under fictitious names.

319 LOTHAIR (1870), VII. 235. 1. Religion. 2. History. 3. English Aristocracy. A novel based on the Anglican movement toward Roman Catholicism, and the Italian Revolution under Garibaldi. The chief characters are members of the English aristocracy. Lothair, the hero, represents in character the Marquis of Bute; other persons in real life represented are Cardinal Manning, Professor Goldwin Smith, Monsignore Capel, etc.

320. ENDYMION (1880), VII. 249. 1. Autobiography. 2. History. 3. Politics. A romance founded on the author's own rise to the premiership. Public characters represented under fictitious names are: the Rothschilds, Queen Hortense of Belgium, Napoleon III., Bismarck, the Earl of Derby, Lord Palmerston, Cardinal Wiseman, Harcourt, Lady Burdett-Coutts, Richard Cobden, Dickens, Thackeray, et al.

WILLIAM HARRISON AINSWORTH (ENGLAND, 1805–1882), XIX. 6.

321. THE TOWER OF LONDON (1840), I. 94. 1. History. 2. Tragedy. Story of the execution of Lady Jane Grey.

322. JACK SHEPPARD (1845), I. 106. 1. Crime. 2. Melodrama. 3. History. Romantic version of the career of a noted English criminal.

CHARLES LEVER (IRELAND, 1806–1872), XIX. 291.

323. CHARLES O'MALLEY (1841), XI. 401. 1. Adventure. 2. History. 3. Character. The adventures in love and war of a devil-may-care young Irishman. He fights under Wellington in Spain, and in the Waterloo campaign, where he is brought before Napoleon I. as a prisoner.

324. TOM BURKE OF OURS (1844), XI. 411. 1. Adventure. 2. History. 3. Love. The adventures of an Irish soldier in the French army under Napoleon I., and his love for a maid of honor to the Empress Josephine.

HENRY COCKTON (ENGLAND, 1807–1853), XIX. 96.

325. VALENTINE VOX, THE VENTRILOQUIST (1840), V. 7. 1. Ventriloquism. 2. Humor. 3. Rascality. A ventriloquist creates many amusing situations by his art. He wins the love of a fine girl whose putative father turns out to be a rascal, shortly after which her real father is discovered. The rascal has lovable traits, and the delineation of his character is the worthiest feature of the story.

SAMUEL WARREN (ENGLAND, 1807–1877), XIX. 421.

326. TEN THOUSAND A YEAR (1841), XVII. 198. 1. Law. 2. Character. 3. Crime. A mean-spirited shop-clerk inherits a great fortune and makes himself ridiculous in dissipating it. A legal sharper gets hold of him and robs him. It is found that there is a flaw in the inheritance, and, after a suit at law, the rightful owners come into possession; whereupon the sharper commits suicide and the false heir dies of debauchery in a debtors' prison.

(HERE MAY FOLLOW 156.)
(HERE MAY FOLLOW 176.)

ELIZABETH GASKELL (ENGLAND, 1810–1865), XIX. 199.

327. CRANFORD (1853), IX. 96. 1. Village Life. 2. Character. 3. Humor. A novel of English village life, with special study of feminine characteristics. There is an affecting romance of an old maid saved from poverty by the return of a lost brother, and a partially humorous, partly pathetic tale of a traveling conjurer.

WILLIAM M. THACKERAY (ENGLAND, 1811–1863,) XIX. 401.

328. CATHERINE (1840), XVI. 293. 1. Crime. 2. Satire. Based on the burning of a woman for the revolting murder of her husband in 1726. A realistic story of vice and crime, written to satirize a contemporary habit among novelists of investing these subjects with romance.

329. BARRY LYNDON (1844), XVI. 304. 1. Rascality. 2. Adventure. 3. Gambling. 4. Satire. The career of a despicable Irish adventurer and card-sharper in Dublin, London, and European courts. He marries an heiress and ruins her life. The story was written in burlesque of Bulwer-Lytton's "Pelham," which is a romantic treatment of the same sort of a man.

330. PENDENNIS (1848), XVI. 316. 1. Character. 2. Youth. 3. Love. The career of a thoughtless, spoiled young man, who involves himself in debts, scrapes with actresses, etc., from which his mother rescues him at great sacrifice, and through all of which a girl who loves him patiently awaits his coming to a realization of the true meaning of life.

331. VANITY FAIR (1848), XVI. 332. 1. Rascality. 2. Character. 3. History. The career of an adventuress among English aristocracy. The delineation of character is the chief feature of the story. The battle of Waterloo is its central event.

332. HENRY ESMOND (1852), XVI. 346. 1. History. 2. Character. 3. Love. A romance of the days of the Pretender James. The hero is a legitimate son of a gentleman by a low-born wife, whom he allows to be thought illegitimate. He is taken into the household of his uncle, where he becomes devoted to the wife and daughter. The latter is a coquette, and, as the years pass, leads him a pretty dance. The former is a noble woman, and sides with him against her daughter. Finally, on her becoming a widow, and his breaking the daughter's spell, they marry, and settle in Virginia.

333. THE NEWCOMES (1855), XVI. 359. 1. Paternal Love. 2. Character. 3. Youth. 4. Banking. An Indian officer devotes himself to his motherless boy, standing by him in his foolish expenditures, his love troubles, etc. To gain money for him he enters into speculation, and is ruined by the failure of his bank. He sacrifices everything to his creditors and dies a noble type of gentleman and father.

334. A SHABBY-GENTEEL STORY (1857), XVI. 370. 1. Character. 2. Comedy. The love affairs, social intrigues, etc., of various types of character in a boarding house.

335. THE VIRGINIANS (1859), XVI. 379. 1. History. 2. Character. 3. Brotherly Love. A sequel to "Henry Esmond" (**332**). Esmond's two grandsons return to England, where one enters the army. He is a spendthrift, and his brother pays his debts, involving himself in trouble. The American Revolution breaks out, and they take opposite sides, but remain good friends. Generals Wolfe and Washington appear in the story.

336. LOVEL THE WIDOWER (1860), XVI. 390. 1. Character. 2. Comedy. A stage dancer becomes governess of a widower's children. She attracts a number of men, and so when her former career is revealed there is instant denunciation from their women of the circle, which is stilled by the widower marrying her.

337. THE ADVENTURES OF PHILIP (1862), XVI. 400. 1. Family Relations. 2. Character. 3. Journalism. A doctor deceives a poor girl with a mock marriage, and elopes with a rich one. His son by the second woman learns of these facts, and, breaking with his father, strikes out in an independent career as a journalist. The father embezzles the son's inheritance, but the young man bravely endures poverty, and wins the love of a young girl, and finally, inherits wealth.

CHARLES DICKENS (ENGLAND, 1812–1870), XIX. 185.

338. PICKWICK PAPERS (1837), VI. 400. 1. Humor. 2. Character. 3. Adventure. 4. Law. 5. Imprisonment. A humorous tale of a group of eccentric characters, of which the chief are the titular hero and his servant, Sam Weller, who is remarkable for his witticisms. Mr. Pickwick gets into awkward situations with ladies eligible for matrimony, from which Sam does his best to extricate him. However, he loses a suit against him for breach of promise, and suffers imprisonment rather than pay damages, and is released by paying the costs.

339. OLIVER TWIST (1838), VI. 410. 1. Youth. 2. Poverty. 3. Crime. 4. Tragedy. A foundling passes from the workhouse into apprenticeship, and escapes from ill treatment to be taken up by thieves. He is rescued by a gentleman, retaken by the thieves, and by the aid of a woman escapes again with clues which reveal his parentage. The woman is murdered by her lover, who kills himself by accident in attempting to escape from the police. The hero is adopted by the gentleman who first rescued him.

340. NICHOLAS NICKLEBY (1839), VI. 420. 1. Education. 2. Youth. 3. Rascality. 4. Character. 5. Adventure. A cruel money-lender gets rid of his dead brother's son by securing him a place as teacher in a private school, where unfortunate children are "taken in and done for" for the money their heartless parents supply to have them out of sight. He beats the wicked schoolmaster, and runs away with a simple-minded waif, and after various adventures returns home to find his sister made the prize of the uncle's dealings with scoundrels. The uncle's designs are frustrated; the simpleton is revealed as his son, and he hangs himself.

341. THE OLD CURIOSITY SHOP (1840), VII. 1. 1. Youth. 2. Rascality. 3. Character. 4. Adventure. 5. Pathos. 6. Gambling. An old gambler and his granddaughter escape from the toils of a villainous usurer by flight. The usurer hunts for them as well as the gambler's brother, who wishes to aid them. The fugitives have many adventures with eccentric people. The usurer is foiled, and is accidentally drowned, and the brother finds the gambler with brain distracted by the death of the grandchild.

342. BARNABY RUDGE (1841), VII. 11. 1. History. 2. Crime and its Detection. 3. Character. 4. The Raven. A story dealing with the "No Popery" riots of 1780. The mysterious perpetrator of an old murder is discovered, proving to be the father of the hero, a half-witted boy, who has an impish raven as a pet. A character study of Lord Chesterfield is made in the person of one of the characters.

343. Martin Chuzzlewit (1844), VII. 22. 1. Character. 2. Rascality. 3. Crime. 4. Love. 5. Humor. A rich old man believes his relatives are all hypocrites. His grandson makes love to his ward, which leads to a quarrel between him and the old man. The grandson is taken up by a rascally cousin, who cuts him adrift when he learns of his quarrel with the grandfather. The young man goes to America and the rascal makes love to the ward. The young man, taught humility by misfortune, returns to ask his grandfather's forgiveness. The rascal attempts to foil this purpose, but is unmasked by the grandfather. A would-be parricide is arrested, and commits suicide. Other rascals in the family are exposed. Eccentric humorous characters are introduced.

344. Dombey and Son (1846), VII. 33. 1. Youth. 2. Pathos. 3. Love. 4. Business. 5. Rascality. A merchant, engrossed in business, is left with a motherless boy and girl. The boy dies a victim to his father's ambition to force him ahead. The father marries an adventuress, who is redeemed by love for her step-daughter. Both are abused by the merchant, and, to get away, the wife elopes with a rascally manager, and the daughter marries a poor man. The merchant finds himself ruined by the absconding manager, and is about to kill himself when his daughter returns to care for him.

345. David Copperfield (1849), VII. 44. 1. Character. 2. Melodrama. 3. Love. 4. Autobiography. The author's own career in school, and as stenographer and author, is set forth in the experiences of the hero, around whom are grouped a world of lifelike characters. He wins and loses by death a "child-wife," and is comforted by a woman who had loved him all the while, and who proves to be his soul mate. The chief plot, however, relates to the seduction of a fisher girl by an aristocratic youth, and the resultant tragedy.

346. Bleak House (1853), VII. 54. 1. Law. 2. Character. 3. Satire. 4. Youth. 5. Melodrama. An indictment of the law's delay, showing the tragedies it produces, especially on young lives. There is incidental satire of foreign missions. Certain characters have been identified with contemporaries of the author: Landor, Leigh Hunt, et al. There is a melodramatic sub-plot in which one of the actors is modeled on a real murderess.

347. Hard Times (1854), VII. 65. 1. Labor. 2. Politics. 3. Crime. 4. Pathos. A rich man, a member of Parliament, has no place for idealism or love in his philosophy. As a result, his son turns out to be a thief, and his daughter a loveless wife, fleeing to him to escape forbidden love. Central heroic figures are a mechanic oppressed by employers on one side and the trades unions on the other, and the woman who loves him but cannot marry him because of their poverty.

348. Little Dorrit (1857), VII. 74. 1. Law. 2. Rascality. 3. Insanity. 4. Love. An indictment of red tape in public business, and of imprisonment for debt. An old prisoner for debt is left a fortune. His family are surrounded by rogues and hypocrites, and lose their money, the father becoming an imbecile. The daughter, the heroine, is, however, united to her true love.

349. A TALE OF TWO CITIES (1860), VII. 84. 1. History. 2. Drama. 3. Description. A dramatic romance founded on the French Revolution. The fall of the Bastile is described. The hero, a dissolute man, loves a woman who is in love with another, and he takes the place of the favored one when he is condemned to the guillotine.

350. GREAT EXPECTATIONS (1860), VII. 94. 1. Youth. 2. Character. 3. Crime. 4. Insanity. 5. Love. A boy feeds an escaping convict. Later, he is chosen by an eccentric woman to be a playmate for her adopted daughter. Still later he is told that a fortune has been placed in trust for him. He thinks it is from the lady who has chosen him to marry her daughter, but the girl rebukes his presumption. He discovers his benefactor is the convict, who is shortly afterward arrested, and, dying of his wounds, is bereft by the state of his wealth. The hero rescues the old lady from her burning house and she repents that she misled him to love her daughter. But the girl's heart turns to him at last and they are united.

351. OUR MUTUAL FRIEND (1865), VII. 104. 1. Avarice. 2. Comedy. 3. Crime and its Detection. 4. Love. A girl who has repulsed a lover because he is poor, is taught a lesson by her guardian, who pretends to be avaricious, and mistreats the poor lover, thus causing the girl to come to his defence. The young man proves to be the heir to a fortune the desire for which has tempted others to crime.

352. THE MYSTERY OF EDWIN DROOD (1870), VII. 114. 1. Crime and its Detection. 2. Opium Habit. Two young men are rivals in love. One disappears, and a third young man, an opium-eater, tries to force the girl to marry him by threatening to fix the murder of the absent on the present lover. A man of unknown antecedents enters the story evidently as a detective. Here the MS. ends.

CHARLES READE (ENGLAND, 1814–1884), XIX. 349.

353. PEG WOFFINGTON (1840), XIII. 340. 1. History. 2. The Theatre. A romance of the stage in which the famous actress, Margaret Woffington, uses her histrionic ability to help a poor artist by putting her head in a frame, and confounding the critics of the supposed portrait who declare it a bad one, by jeering at them at the close of their remarks. After they are gone, the wife of the actress's lover appears and pleads with the supposed portrait to give him back to her. The actress is moved by the plea and brings about a reconciliation of husband and wife.

354. CHRISTIE JOHNSTONE (1855), XIII. 349. 1. Heroism. 2. Love. 3. Fishing. 4. Art. A Scotch fisher lass and an artist form a comradeship that leads to love. The artist's mother objects to his sweetheart's low condition, and the proud girl breaks the engagement. The girl saves the artist from drowning and the mother begs her forgiveness. It transpires that the mother had been a cook, and was the wife of a green grocer.

355. IT IS NEVER TOO LATE TO MEND (1856), XIII. 356. 1. Prison Reform. 2. Mining. 3. Australian Life. 4. Crime and its Discovery. A man, condemned for theft, suffers great hardships in prison, which the chaplain tries to mitigate, and is transported to Australia, where he chums with an English farmer. They discover gold. They return rich to England, where it is found that the real thief is the villain who has separated the farmer and his sweetheart, his exposer being a Jew whom he had robbed and cursed.

356. WHITE LIES (1857), XIII. 364. 1. Ethics. 2. Self-sacrifice. A French girl obeys her mother and sends her lover away to the wars and marries a man she respects but does not love. Her husband goes to the wars also, and is reported dead. The lover returns and marries the girl. Then she learns that her first husband is not dead and she dismisses the lover. The husband returns, and finding a child of an age to indicate his wife's infidelity, is about to kill her, when her sister claims the child as hers, even at the cost of losing her own lover. The husband sends the seeming betrayer into a desperate charge, in which he is reported killed. Then the wife confesses the truth, whereupon the first husband renounces his claim in favor of the dead man. But this one was not killed, and returns to claim her as his wife, the first husband remaining as the friend of both, and the sister becoming reconciled to her lover.

357. LOVE ME LITTLE, LOVE ME LONG (1859), XIII. 374. 1. Love. Two guardians of an heiress select different husbands for her, but she chooses a ship's mate for herself, and, amid the contest of the guardians, slips away and marries him.

358. THE CLOISTER AND THE HEARTH (1861), XIII. 381. 1. Adventure. 2. Love. 3. Travel. A mediæval romance of the parents of Erasmus, in which the hero, separated by guile from his betrothed, travels from Holland to Italy, meeting many adventures and becoming a monk. He returns to find himself a father, to confute the enemies of himself and betrothed, and to live in friendship with her, both engaged in holy works.

359. HARD CASH (1863), XIII. 400. 1. Insanity. 2. Law. 3. Crime. The sequel of "Love Me Little, Love Me Long" (**357**). A rascally banker shuts up his son in a private insane asylum to prevent him disclosing the father's embezzlement of the funds of the father of the girl that the son is about to marry. There he meets the man who has been robbed, a sea-captain, and escapes with him. The captain is mad, but recovers his reason, the young man brings his father to terms, and all ends happily.

ANALYSIS OF THE WORLD'S STORIES 55

360. GRIFFITH GAUNT (1866), XIII. 407. 1. Jealousy. 2. Medicine. An insanely jealous husband suspects his wife's relations with a priest and assaults him. Whereupon he flees and marries a farmer's daughter. His true wife proves her innocence, and he returns, leading a double life. This, the second wife discovers. The man disappears and his first wife is accused of his murder. He returns and exonerates her. She falls sick and he saves her by transfusion of blood, hearing of which she forgives him. A former suitor of the wife marries the second wife of the jealous man.

361. FOUL PLAY (1868), XIII. 418. 1. Crime. 2. Love. 3. Insurance. A young merchant commits forgery, and fastens the crime on a friend, who is transported to Australia. As a ticket-of-leave man, he becomes gardener to the betrothed of his enemy and comes to love her. He takes the same ship with her for England. Ignorant that it bears his betrothed, the merchant wrecks it for insurance. The convict saves the girl, and they live together on a desolate island. He contrives their rescue, and, on their return to England, exposes the forger and murderer, and marries the girl.

362. PUT YOURSELF IN HIS PLACE (1870), XIII. 426. 1. Labor. 2. Invention. 3. Love. 4. Crime. An ingenious young mechanic is fought by the trades unions because of his inventions, and is undermined in love by a villainous rival, but overcomes both of these enemies.

363. A TERRIBLE TEMPTATION (1871), XIII. 437. 1. Ethics. To outwit an enemy a wife descends to deceit, and palms off as her son one who is not the child of her husband. Whether or not she has been faithful to her husband, or is justified in her deceit, are the problems of the story.

364. A SIMPLETON (1873), XIII. 447. 1. Medicine. 2. Mining. 3. Marriage. 4. Crime. A struggling physician marries a spoiled girl, and is forced to give up practice because of her extravagance. He goes to South Africa and is reported dead. He discovers diamonds, and sends his partner back to the settlements with gems to sell, and with word for his wife. The partner is a rascal and goes to England, where, with the backing of his father he woos the supposed widow. The husband returns just in time to stop their marriage and is reconciled to his wife.

365. A WOMAN-HATER (1878), XIII. 456. 1. Woman's Rights. 2. Medicine. 3. Music. 4. Love. 5. Gambling. A prima donna is the secret wife of a blackleg, who is courting another woman. But he hears that his wife has won a fortune at the gaming table, and so plays fast and loose with both women. Now the brother of the second woman, though a professed woman-hater, comes to love the singer through their common devotion to music. She reveals to him her husband's rascality and they save the sister from him, with the aid also of a woman who has struggled against heavy odds to establish herself as a physician.

MRS. HENRY WOOD (ENGLAND, 1814–1887), XIX. 425.

366. EAST LYNNE (1861), XVII. 259. 1. Melodrama. 2. Pathos. A wife, by her folly, runs away from her husband and little children. For love of the child she returns in disguise and takes service in her husband's house. After years of agonizing love, she dies, her secret being disclosed while she is on her death-bed, and her husband forgiving her.

ANTHONY TROLLOPE (ENGLAND, 1815–1882), XIX. 407.

367. THE WARDEN (1855), XVII. 1. 1. The Clergy. 2. Reform. A clergyman comes into a sinecure at the expense of the recipients of a charity. A suitor for his daughter is one of the reformers who attack him, with a resultant complication of the love affair. In the end the clergyman resigns his sinecure and the lovers are married. Thomas Carlyle is the original of one of the characters.

368. BARCHESTER TOWERS (1857), XVII. 9. 1. The Clergy. A sequel to "The Warden." The story relates to complications in love matters arising from strife about church preferment.

369. ORLEY FARM (1861), XVII. 20. 1. Farming. 2. Crime. 3. Law. A widow commits forgery of a deed to retain a farm for her son. She confesses the crime to her lover and son who stand by her. She is acquitted and the farm is then given to the rightful owner. The son's mercenary sweetheart then jilts him, and the mother refuses to marry her suitor.

370. CAN YOU FORGIVE HER? (1864), XVII. 32. 1. Politics. 2. Character. An heiress has two suitors, one with moral imperfections and winning ways, the other too good to be attractive. She becomes engaged now to one, now to the other. The weak man, who has political aspirations, uses her money to aid his ambition, and, as a result, is opposed by his rival and defeated in the end.

371. THE SMALL HOUSE AT ALLINGTON (1864), XVII. 42. 1. Love. 2. Pathos. The complicated love affairs of two sisters, ending happily for one and sadly for the other.

372. HE KNEW HE WAS RIGHT (1869), XVII. 52. 1. Psychology. 2. Pathos. The tragedy of a husband and wife, resulting from the latter's folly and the former's conviction that he can never be mistaken, and his almost insane insistence on having his own way.

CHARLOTTE BRONTË [CURRER BELL] (ENGLAND, 1816–1855), XIX. 65.

373. JANE EYRE (1847), III. 230. 1. Character. 2. Melodrama. 3. Insanity. 4. Love. A governess is about to wed a man when she discovers that he has a maniac wife. Although she appreciates the misery of his position and his need of her, she remains true to principle, and declines to marry him, and convinces him of his duty toward his wife. The maniac sets fire to the house and her husband is crushed and blinded in a vain attempt to rescue her. Then the governess marries him. The depiction of the powerful passionate character of the husband is the striking feature of the novel.

374. SHIRLEY (1849), III. 241. 1. Renunciation. 2. Love. 3. Labor. 4. Business. A poor girl in love with a mill-owner, ruined by the American embargo and the resultant labor difficulties, resigns him to a wealthy girl. This one, however, learns to love a teacher whom she had at first looked down upon, and the mill-owner, ashamed of his mercenary motives, returns to his first love.

375. VILLETTE (1853), III. 252. 1. Education. 2. Love. 3. Character. A semi-autobiographical story of an English girl's experience in a Belgian school, and her love for a fellow instructor, a Belgian of marked individuality.

376. THE PROFESSOR (1857), III. 263. 1. Education. 2. Love. 3. Character. The story of an Englishman, teaching in Belgium, and his love for one of his pupils. Delineation of types of character among the hero's fellow teachers is the special feature of the novel.

GRACE AGUILAR (ENGLAND, 1816–1847), XIX. 4.

377. HOME INFLUENCE (1847), I. 45. 1. Youth. 2. Education. 3. Home Life. 4. Pathos. An orphan girl, adopted by a good aunt, lays herself under evil imputations to save her wayward brother from disgrace.

378. THE MOTHER'S RECOMPENSE (1850), I. 57. 1. Education. 2. Home Life. 3. Love. A sequel to "Home Influence." A mother's influence solves the love complications of her children, especially of a wayward daughter.

CHARLES WILLIAM SHIRLEY BROOKS (ENGLAND, 1816–1874), XIX. 67.

379. THE GORDIAN KNOT (1868), III. 285. 1. Marriage. 2. Ethics. A husband and his wife are estranged by the ghost of his evil past rising between them, the appearance of her scapegrace father on the scene, and the machinations of a defeated suitor for her hand. The wife nurses the former mistress of her husband, and beside the dying bed of the penitent outcast is united again to her husband.

EMILY BRONTË [ELLIS BELL] (ENGLAND, 1818–1849), XIX. 65.

380. WUTHERING HEIGHTS (1847), III. 273. 1. Psychic Phenomena. 2. Character. The story of a strange affinity between a neglected adopted boy and a bright girl, repeated after their death in the son of the boy's persecutor and the girl's daughter. The ghost of the mother haunts the house of the man to whom she was spiritually bound.

CHARLES KINGSLEY (ENGLAND, 1819–1875), XIX. 282.

381. ALTON LOCKE (1850), XI. 222. 1. Labor. 2. Authorship. The life story of a poor poet who took up the side of the workingmen in the Chartist agitation, and suffered imprisonment, dying in jail.

382. HYPATIA (1853), XI. 233. 1. History. 2. Philosophy. 3. Religion. 4. Tragedy. 5. Psychology. A romance based on the conflict in Egypt of Christian asceticism with Neo-Platonism, of which the heroine is the chief expounder. She is torn to pieces by a mob. Racial characteristics are clearly differentiated, Jews, Greeks, Romans, and even Goths being portrayed in typical representations.

383. WESTWARD HO! (1855), XI. 244. 1. Adventure. 2. History. 3. Heroism. A tale of adventures of Englishmen at sea, and in South America, during the reign of Elizabeth. The defeat of the Spanish Armada forms the climax. Sir Richard Grenville, Sir Humphrey Gilbert, Sir John Hawkins, and other great captains appear in the story.

384. TWO YEARS AGO (1857), XI. 265. 1. Love. 2. History. 3. Heroism. 4. Slavery. The hero, an Englishman, helps a beautiful slave girl in Louisiana to escape; he is wrecked on the coast of England, and robbed of his money. Suspicion of the theft falls on the schoolmistress who rescues him. She discovers that her mother is the thief, and, taking the belt of money, follows vainly after the Englishman, who has gone to the Crimean War. They meet in his father's home, where the story ends with their marriage.

385. THE WATER-BABIES (1863), XI. 276. 1. Youth. 2. Imagination. 3. Natural History. A little chimney-sweep falls into a stream, and finds himself changed into a tiny water-baby. Here he learns the habits of water-animals, and moral lessons about behavior to one's fellows.

386. HEREWARD THE WAKE (1866), XI. 255. 1. History. 2. Adventure. 3. Heroism. A tale of the "Last of the English," who heroically resisted the Normans under William the Conqueror, after the defeat of King Harold at Hastings. Lady Godiva is the hero's mother.

GEORGE ELIOT [MARY ANN EVANS CROSS] (ENGLAND, 1819–1880), XIX. 170.

387. ADAM BEDE (1859), VIII. 182. 1. Seduction. 2. Infanticide. 3. Religion. A mechanic is betrothed to a light-minded girl, who is seduced by a young gentleman. She kills the child, and is about to be hanged for it, when her seducer secures a reprieve for her. The mechanic marries an evangelist, who had befriended her.

388. THE MILL ON THE FLOSS (1860), VIII. 191. 1. Family Life. 2. Youth. 3. Tragedy. A stern brother and brilliant sister are devoted to each other. She loves the son of the man who has ruined her father, and the brother forbids their meeting. The betrothed of a girl friend entraps the sister into a compromising situation with himself, and she is harshly treated therefor by her brother. But brother and sister are united in death by flood.

ANALYSIS OF THE WORLD'S STORIES 59

389. SILAS MARNER (1861), VIII. 201. 1. Avarice. 2. Parenthood. 3. Labor. An avaricious weaver is robbed of his hoard. In its place he finds a child, whom he adopts. Sixteen years later the money is recovered and the rich father of the foundling appears, to take her away. But she is betrothed to a workingman, and refuses to change her lot.

390. ROMOLA (1863), VIII. 212. 1. History. 2. Character. 3. Crime. 4. Religion. 5. Tragedy. A romance connected with the tragic death of Savonarola, the religious reformer of Florence. The heroine is married to a bigamist who is also a thief and in intention a parricide. Inspired by the teaching and example of Savonarola, upon the death of her husband and the exposure of his crimes, she does not shirk her duty, but cares for his other wife and their children.

391. FELIX HOLT, THE RADICAL (1866), VIII. 223. 1. Politics. 2. Social Reform. 3. Labor. 4. Love. The hero is a social reformer, who, by force of circumstances becomes a leader in a labor riot. The heroine exonerates him and refuses wealth to put herself on his plane, whereupon they marry and continue their reform work together.

392. MIDDLEMARCH (1872), VIII. 234. 1. Marriage. 2. Character. 3. Love. 4. Crime. An elderly, jealous husband, dying, wills his wife his property on condition that she does not marry a certain young man who is her admirer. A relative of the admirer is discovered to be a criminal, whereupon the heroine marries the young man in order to share the odium of the disgrace, and her private fortune with him. The study of the jealous husband's character is the distinctive feature of the novel.

393. DANIEL DERONDA (1876), VIII. 245. 1. Zionism. 2. Search for Lost Relatives. 3. Jewish Life and Character. 4. Religion. A young English gentleman, in searching for the relatives of a Jewess he has rescued from suicide, discovers he himself is a Jew. He thereupon enters the Zionist movement with the Jewess's brother, who is an enthusiast in it, and, the brother dying, and the father proving a rascal, betroths the Jewess.

MRS. JAMES SADLIER (IRELAND, 1820–1903), XIX. 359.

394. BESSIE CONWAY (1861), XIV. 154. 1. Irish Life and Character. 2. Ethics. 3. Religion. A wild, sacrilegious young man of the Irish gentry is in love with a peasant girl going to America and steals on board the vessel. She is protected from him by lads of her own class, and after several years returns to Ireland to aid her parents with her earnings. She finds her lover there repentant of his sacrilege and immorality, and she forgives him and marries him.

JEAN INGELOW (ENGLAND, 1820–1897), XIX. 268.

395. OFF THE SKELLIGS (1872), XI. 36. 1. Ethics. 2. Love. 3. Youth. 4. Sea-Life. 5. Social Reform. The heroine, precocious in youth,

and clever and self-supporting in womanhood, is beloved by a man with whom she is yachting. But he learns that his young step-brother is in love with her, and steps aside, to her wonder and dismay. The step-brother, however, transfers his affections elsewhere and all ends happily. The heroine aids poor people to help themselves.

ANNE BRONTË [ACTON BELL) (ENGLAND, 1821-1849), XIX. 65.

396. AGNES GREY (1847), III. 214. 1. Love. 2. English Society. 3. Character. The love romance of a governess and a curate, with which her eldest pupil, a coquette, attempts to interfere, but fails to do so.

397. THE TENANT OF WINDFELL HALL (1848), III. 222. 1. Character. 2. Mystery. 3. Love. A woman, apparently a widow, of whose antecedents nothing is known, comes into a country district. A man of the neighborhood is in close touch with her. Another man falls in love with her, and wins her friendship through her child, proposes marriage, but is refused. Jealous of her friend, the lover assaults him. Later he discovers that the woman's husband is alive, but is a brute, from whom her brother, the apparent friend, has separated her. The husband drinks himself to death, whereupon the widow marries her lover.

JAMES GRANT (SCOTLAND, 1822-1887), XIX. 230.

398. BOTHWELL (1851), IX. 204. 1. History. 2. Tragedy. A romance of the assassination of Lord Darnley, husband of Mary, Queen of Scots.

THOMAS HUGHES (ENGLAND, 1822-1896), XIX. 264.

399. TOM BROWN'S SCHOOL DAYS (1857), X. 377. 1. Youth. 2. Sport. 3. Education. 4. Ethics. A story of life at Rugby, an English school directed by Dr. Thomas Arnold. Moral as well as physical courage is portrayed in the acts of the chief characters. Football and other sports are described.

MARMION W. SAVAGE (IRELAND, 1823-1872), XIX. 362.

400. THE BACHELOR OF THE ALBANY (1847), XIV. 224. 1. Humor. 2. Love. 3. Archery. A bachelor desires to live an independent life, but he is put under obligations to a fine woman who saves him from a fire, and beats him at archery. He gallantly proposes marriage and is accepted.

CHARLOTTE M. YONGE (ENGLAND, 1823-1901), XIX. 427.

401. THE HEIR OF REDCLYFFE (1853), XVII. 282. 1. Character. 2. Ethics. A prig is intolerant of his cousin, an amiable man with human frailties. His attitude is the cause of the cousin's death, and his accession to the estate of which the cousin was the heir. Remorse causes him to change his character, and he becomes humble and charitable.

ANALYSIS OF THE WORLD'S STORIES

WILLIAM WILKIE COLLINS (ENGLAND, 1824–1889), XIX. 97.

402. ANTONINA (1852), V. 13. 1. History. 2. Character. 3. Religion. A romance of the time of Honorius, Emperor of Rome. The contest of the Romans and Goths and that of Christianity and Paganism supply the incidents and the contrasting types of character. Alaric, the Gothic King, is introduced as one of the characters.

403. THE WOMAN IN WHITE (1860), V. 24. 1. Crime and its Detection. 2. Character. 3. Love. 4. Mistaken Identity. In order to possess her property, a villain, preyed upon by another villain, the portrayal of whose character is the chief feature of the book, contrives the death of his wife's double, and incarcerates the wife in her place in a madhouse. Her sister rescues her and a former suitor ferrets out the crime. The husband is burned to death while attempting to hide a forgery, and his accomplice is slain by a member of a political brotherhood whose cause he had betrayed.

404. NO NAME (1862), V. 58. 1. Law (Marriage). 2. Crime and its Detection. 3. Rascality. 4. Love. Through misadventure, for which the law does not have a remedy, an orphan girl is left illegitimate and penniless. Her lover repudiates her. She becomes an adventuress, and by the aid of a precious rascal, marries the owner of the property that is morally though not legally hers. Her husband's housekeeper, a shrewd woman, exposes her deception. He dies and she is again left penniless. She is redeemed by a good man's love, and enriched by the discovery of a secret trust fund left by her father.

405. ARMADALE (1866), V. 35. 1. Crime. 2. Mistaken Identity. 3. Character. 4. Tragedy. A woman of middle age makes herself appear young by aid of a "beauty doctor" and becomes an adventuress, committing forgery, theft, and even murder, to advance her fortunes. She marries one of two men having the same name, intending to kill the other and claim his property as his widow, but by mistake finds she is about to kill her husband, whereupon she kills herself.

406. THE MOONSTONE (1868), V. 69. 1. Crime and its Detection. 2. Hypnotism. 3. Tragedy. Hindu priests recover a stolen jewel by the aid of hypnotism and murder. Before its recovery a number of English people are involved in its fortunes, one man stealing it while under the influence of opium, and a girl who loved him and who thought him a conscious thief, committing suicide.

407. MAN AND WIFE (1870), V. 48. 1. Law (Marriage). 2. Crime. 3. Athletics. 4. Insanity. A man, brutalized by devotion to athletics, has ruined a woman, and by a trick, makes a friend marry her, unknown to either. But the athlete has overreached himself, and in the negotiations called the woman his wife, which is marriage by Scotch law. She claims him as her husband, and he accepts her as such, threatening her life. He is about to use an insane woman to accomplish his purpose, when he is stricken by paralysis.

GEORGE MACDONALD (SCOTLAND, 1824-1905), XIX. 302.

408. David Elginbrod (1862), XII. 108. 1. Religion. 2. Education. 3. Hypnotism. A devout Scotch steward is an influence for good in the education of a young man. The young man circumvents a villain who had acquired hypnotic control of a young girl, and he marries the girl.

MRS. ALEXANDER [MRS. ALEXANDER HECTOR, NÉE ANNIE FRENCH] (ENGLAND, 1825-1902), XIX. 12.

409. Which Shall It Be? (1866), I. 188. 1. Love. 2. Melodrama. A poor girl, dependent on cruel and socially ambitious relatives, is about to be forced into marriage to a villain. She escapes, and is loved in her poverty by a good man. She comes into wealth, and her lover, too proud now to woo her, withdraws himself. The villain, become a maniac for love of her, attempts to kill her and himself, and she is rescued by her true love.

410. The Wooing O't (1873), I. 197. 1. Love. 2. Friendship. A poor girl among rich people becomes a good comrade of a boyish lord. A mature man, his unofficial guardian, suspects that she is a fortune-hunter. She undeceives him and he falls in love with her and marries her.

WILLIAM DODDRIDGE BLACKMORE (ENGLAND, 1825-1900), XIX. 53.

411. Lorna Doone: A Romance of Exmoor (1869), III. 112. 1. Love. 2. Adventure. 3. English Life and Scenery. A romance of Devonshire in the 17th century. A yeoman loves a daughter of an outlaw, and wins her after heroic adventures with her people in their retreat. The hero is concerned in the rebellion of Monmouth, and Judge Jeffreys appears in the story.

DINAH MARIA MULOCK [CRAIK] (ENGLAND, 1826-1887), XIX. 326.

412. John Halifax, Gentleman (1857), XIII. 1. 1. Character. 2. Business. 3. Family Life. The life story of a boy of sterling character who rose from a tan-yard worker to a great manufacturer. The love affairs of his children, as well as of himself, are the features of chief interest. Their family life is contrasted with that of dissolute aristocracy.

413. A Brave Lady (1870), XIII. 12. 1. Character. 2. Heroism. 3. Marriage. A character study of a noble wife of a shallow, selfish husband.

CUTHBERT BEDE [EDWARD BRADLEY] (ENGLAND, 1827-1889), XIX. 42.

414. The Adventures of Mr. Verdant Green (1853), II. 395. 1. English University Life. 2. Humor. 3. Love. A lively story of the experiences at Oxford of an unsophisticated youth, and of his love-making during vacations.

ANALYSIS OF THE WORLD'S STORIES

GEORGE MEREDITH (ENGLAND, 1828–), XIX. 317.

415. The Ordeal of Richard Feverel (1859), XII. 287. 1. Love. 2. Youth. 3. Education. A gentleman's son marries a farmer's niece. His father refuses to see him "on principle." The young man, in disgrace, succumbs to the wiles of a siren and is involved in a duel. Before it occurs he is reconciled to his wife. He is badly wounded in the duel and his wife dies of the shock. Her father-in-law, however, fails to see in her death the results of his system of moral training.

416. The Egoist (1879), XII. 299. 1. Character. A study of a selfish and self-opinionated man, who alienates in turn the woman whom he thinks he loves, and her who had thought she loved him.

417. Diana of the Crossways (1885), XII. 310. 1. Biography. 2. Character. 3. Authorship. 4. Politics. The original of the heroine was Mrs. Caroline Norton, the poetess. She is represented as a brilliant author and a meddler in politics, in the latter part, complicating her love affairs, from which, however, she happily emerges in the end.

ELIZABETH RUNDLE CHARLES (ENGLAND, 1828–1896), XIX. 89.

418. The Schönberg-Cotta Family (1862), IV. 360. 1. History. 2. Religion. The records of a Protestant family during the Reformation. The character and history of Luther are intimately described.

MARGARET OLIPHANT (SCOTLAND, 1828–1897), XIX. 331.

419. Salem Chapel (1863), XIII. 104. 1. English Middle Class Life. 2. Religion. A bachelor preacher of a church of shop-keepers is attracted by a woman of the higher classes, leading to troubles with his congregation. His sister is ensnared by a villain, who is murdered. Suspicion falls on her; she is saved by her brother, who retires from the ministry.

420. A House in Bloomsbury (1894), XIII. 114. 1. English Middle Class Life. Domestic tragedies in the life of the family of a librarian in the British Museum. A long-lost mother returns and dies, a young man is claimed as her son by a woman who had posed as a maiden lady and he marries the daughter of the librarian.

LAURENCE OLIPHANT (ENGLAND, 1829–1888), XIX. 330.

421. Altiora Peto (1883), XIII. 94. 1. Character. 2. Love. 3. Business. A study of marked and contrasting personalities, English and American, especially in the relation of lovers. Rascally promoters, impecunious aristocrats, a romantic heiress who poses as a poor girl, an intellectual girl whose heart is late in developing, etc., form the characters.

ELIZABETH SARA SHEPPARD (ENGLAND, 1830–1862), XIX. 374.

422. CHARLES AUCHESTER (1853), XV. 245. 1. Music. 2. Love. 3. Biography. The love story of a musician, the original of whom was Felix Mendelssohn-Bartholdy.

HENRY KINGSLEY (ENGLAND, 1830–1876), XIX. 283.

423. RECOLLECTIONS OF GEOFFRY HAMLIN (1859), XI. 284. 1. Australian Life. 2. Crime. 3. Tragedy. A forger and gambler flees to Australia and becomes a bush-ranger. His wife follows after with their son. Grown to manhood, the son has a fight with the rangers in which he is killed by his father.

424. RAVENSHOE (1862), XI. 296. 1. Law. 2. Religion. 3. Intrigue. A story dealing with the intrigue of a Catholic priest to keep a Protestant child from his inheritance.

JAMES PAYN (ENGLAND, 1830–1898), XIX. 337.

425. LOST SIR MASSINGBERD (1864), XIII. 177. 1. Youth. 2. Melodrama. A monster of wickedness, who oppresses his ward and uses his estate, strangely disappears, and his body is found years after, like Longfellow's arrow, "in the heart of an oak."

CHARLES HAMILTON AIDE (ENGLAND, 1830–   ), XIX. 5.

426. RITA: AN AUTOBIOGRAPHY (1864), I. 69. 1. English Society. 2. Home Life. 3. Rascality. 4. Love. The domestic troubles of a girl with a scamp of a father, and her subsequent complications in love owing to her clouded name. The author's father was the original of the heroine's father. Other well-known characters of Mid-Victorian society are portrayed under fictitious names.

427. A VOYAGE OF DISCOVERY (1875), I. 82. 1. American Society. 2. Love. Love affairs of an English girl traveling in America in the seventies.

AMELIA B. EDWARDS (ENGLAND, 1831–1892), XIX. 166.

428. IN THE DAYS OF MY YOUTH (1872), VIII. 148. 1. Parisian Student Life. 2. Love. The story of the dissipations, love, intrigues, etc., of an English student in the Latin Quarter of Paris.

(HERE MAY FOLLOW 597.)

GEORGE MANVILLE FENN (ENGLAND, 1831–   ), XIX. 174.

429. THE MASTER OF THE CEREMONIES (1886), VIII. 279. 1. Character. 2. Crime. 3. Paternal Love. A social functionary is hard put to keep up appearances. He resists the temptation to substitute paste diamonds for real ones, owned by a rich lodger in arrears of rent. But they are stolen by one whom he believes to be his son. The son, while denying the crime to his father, plans to save the old man who is charged with the theft. The son is a soldier. He flogs his superior officer, who has tempted his sister to elope, and purposely gets himself shot by attempting to escape from guard, and, dying, takes the crime on himself. But it transpires that the major is the criminal, having impersonated the private soldier.

BENJAMIN L. FARJEON (ENGLAND, 1833-1903), XIX. 173.

430. JOSHUA MARVEL (1872), VIII. 268. 1. Youth. 2. Love. 3. The Sea. 4. Disguise. One of a group of young people goes to sea. On his return he is wounded by an enemy. A girl saves his life. He marries another girl and returns to sea, to find that his rescuer through love of him and in ignorance of his marriage has shipped in disguise on the vessel. They are wrecked on a desolate island, but live like brother and sister. She dies and he is rescued.

SABINE BARING-GOULD (ENGLAND, 1834-1906), XIX. 35.

431. GRETTIR THE OUTLAW (1860), II. 298. 1. History. 2. Heroism. 3. Supernaturalism. The transcription of the saga of an Icelandic outlaw, describing his feats of bravery and strength. He contends too successfully with a ghost, and, receiving its curse, wastes in strength and meets with disaster and ultimate defeat.

PHILIP GILBERT HAMERTON (ENGLAND, 1834-1894), XIX. 242.

432. WENDERHOLME (1869), IX. 369. 1. Youth. 2. Love. 3. Business. A boy rises by his industry from a childhood of cruel usage to be the owner of a fine country estate, and the husband of the daughter of its former proprietor, who has been ruined by extravagance.

JOSEPH H. SHORTHOUSE (ENGLAND, 1834-1903), XIX. 374.

433. JOHN INGLESANT (1881), XV. 256. 1. Religion. 2. History. 3. Philosophy. The career of an English partisan of Archbishop Laud, who becomes a Catholic, and takes part in the Roman insurrection of Molinos. He is a mystic in his philosophy, and ends his life as a Quietist in religion.

GEORGE DU MAURIER (ENGLAND, 1834-1896), XIX. 163.

434. PETER IBBETSON (1892), VIII. 86. 1. Psychic Phenomena. 2. Love. 3. Music. 4. Art. 5. Travel. 6. Crime. 7. Imprisonment. 8. Youth. 9. Insanity. A man kills the traducer of his mother, and is imprisoned for life. He and a lady, who had been childish sweethearts, make a pact to join each other in their dreams. So they live by night in a world of beautiful music, art, scenery, etc., more real than their waking existence. The death of the lady drives the man insane, and on his recovery he communes with her spirit, and by longing rapidly passes into the spirit world to join her.

435. TRILBY (1894), VIII. 97. 1. Hypnotism. 2. Parisian Student Life. 3. Love. 4. Pathos. 5. Music. 6. Art. 7. Friendship. Three English artists live together in the Latin Quarter of Paris. One falls in love with a model, and his people come and take him away from her.

She has a glorious voice but is tone-deaf. A man, vile in looks and character, but a musical genius in soul, though without a voice, hypnotizes her, marries her, and sings to the world through her voice. The three artists, attracted by the fame of the new singer, go to a concert, recognize her as their old model; the hypnotist suddenly dies, and, relieved from the spell, she breaks down. Broken in health, she dies, singing a swan song, under the spell of a picture of the hypnotist.

WILLIAM MORRIS (ENGLAND, 1834–1896), XIX. 324.

436. CHILDE CHRISTOPHER (1895), XII. 393. 1. Youth. 2. Legend. A romance in the style of mediæval legends, telling of the love of a prince and a princess, who became good and beloved king and queen.

BESANT AND RICE: WALTER BESANT (ENGLAND, 1836–1901); JAMES RICE (ENGLAND, 1846–1882); XIX. 48.

437. READY-MONEY MORTIBOY (1871), III. 34. 1. Avarice. 2. Rascality. 3. Character. The story of a miser robbed by his own son, who, though a precious rascal, exhibits strong elements of character, such as courage, resourcefulness, and loyalty.

WALTER BESANT (ENGLAND, 1836–1901), XIX. 48.

438. ALL SORTS AND CONDITIONS OF MEN (1884), III. 41. 1. Social Reform. 2. Love. A romance in which the lovers are brought together in a plan for aiding the poor by establishing an institution of amusement and instruction in the East Side of London (The People's Palace).

439. HERR PAULUS (1888), III. 47. 1. Charlatanry (Spiritualism). 2. Character. 3. Love. An exposé of the tricks of spiritualism, and a study of the psychology of charlatanism, with incidental love romance.

MARY ELIZABETH BRADDON [MRS. JOHN MAXWELL] (ENGLAND, 1875–   ), XIX. 62.

440. LADY AUDLEY'S SECRET (1862), III. 181. 1. Melodrama. 2. Insanity. 3. Crime. The story of the unmasking of a partially demented adventuress who has committed bigamy to attain social position, and who commits arson and attempts homicide to evade detection.

441. JOHN MARCHMONT'S LEGACY (1863), III. 192. 1. Melodrama. 2. Insanity. 3. Crime. 4. Jealousy. A jealous step-mother, partially demented, and an envious cousin separate by intrigue and crime a wife from her husband. Believing his wife dead, the husband is about to remarry, when the step-mother repents and reveals to him that his wife is alive.

ANNE THACKERAY [RITCHIE] (ENGLAND, 1838–   ), XIX. 401.

442. THE VILLAGE ON THE CLIFF (1865), XVI. 282. 1. French Life and Character. 2. Art. 3. Love. An unsuccessful English artist in Normandy falls in love with his peasant model. His people recall him

to England to separate the pair. An English governess learns to love him, and to get her out of the way also, the artist's friends succeed in persuading her to marry a Frenchman. This man and the artist go to rescue a wrecked crew. The Frenchman is drowned. Then the widow realizes she had learned to love him, and encourages the artist to remain true to his peasant love, although his friends are now desirous that he make up to the rich widow.

WALTER PATER (ENGLAND, 1839-1894), XIX. 336.

443. MARIUS, THE EPICUREAN (1885), XIII. 167. 1. Religion. 2. Philosophy. A Roman disciple of Epicurus is converted to Christianity and, being imprisoned, dies of exposure.

OUIDA [LOUISE DE LA RAMÉE] (ENGLAND, 1840-1908), XIX. 333.

444. UNDER TWO FLAGS (1867), XIII. 134. 1. Melodrama. 2. Self-Sacrifice. An English nobleman is ruined by the forgeries of his brother and enlists as a soldier of France in Algiers. He refuses to reveal his identity even when his brother succeeds to the title that is rightfully his own, and he resigns the woman he loves to another. In defence of her honor he strikes his commander and is sentenced to death, from which he is saved at the cost of her life by a woman of the regiment.

445. FRIENDSHIP (1878), XIII. 145. 1. Autobiography. 2. Character. 3. Pathos. Said to be founded on a love affair of the author. A woman false friend comes between the heroine, an Englishwoman, and her lover, an Italian nobleman, who proves too weak to contend against circumstances; and the lovers are doomed to live, the man in self-reproaching despair and the woman in resigned melancholy.

RHODA BROUGHTON (ENGLAND, 1840-   ), XIX. 68.

446. GOOD-BYE, SWEETHEART! (1872), III. 293. 1. Pathos. 2. Love. A coquette offends her lover beyond power of reconciliation. He marries another and she dies on his wedding day.

447. NANCY (1873), III. 304. 1. Love. 2. Jealousy. A young girl marries a man of middle age, and, hearing he had been engaged to an attractive widow, becomes jealous, and flirts with another man. However, she repents of her conduct, and is rewarded by learning that she is her husband's only love.

THOMAS HARDY (ENGLAND, 1840-   ), XIX. 244.

448. FAR FROM THE MADDING CROWD (1874), X. 1. 1. Rustic Life. 2. Tragedy. 3. Love. A farmer woos a poor girl, who refuses him because of the inequality of the match. Later, their positions are reversed; she inherits a farm and he becomes her shepherd. He refuses to make love to her and she throws herself away on an adventurer, who is killed by another of her lovers. Finally, she indicates to the shepherd her preference for him.

449. THE RETURN OF THE NATIVE (1878), X. 11. 1. Rustic Life. 2. Tragedy. 3. Intrigue. A wife, fascinated by an old lover, himself married to a woman loving another man, neglects her mother-in-law, thereby causing her death, and finally is drowned with her lover. Her husband becomes an evangelist, and the wife of the dead man marries her lover.

450. THE MAYOR OF CASTERBRIDGE (1885), X. 22. 1. Village and Rustic Life. 2. Tragedy. A drunken rustic sells his wife and child to a sailor. The rustic forswears drink, and rises to be mayor of a town. His wife returns, the sailor having died, with her little daughter. The mayor accepts the wife, annulling his marriage to another woman. His rival in trade falls in love with the daughter and is rejected by the mayor. On his wife's death the mayor learns that the girl is not his daughter, and recalls his objections to her lover. But the lover has transferred his affections to the woman discarded by the mayor, and shortly marries her. The mayor fights his rival, but forgoes his revenge when he has him at his mercy. The mayor and his rival's wife die, and the rival marries the sailor's daughter.

451. TESS OF THE D'URBERVILLES (1891), X. 32. 1. Tragedy. 2. Rustic Life. 3. Character. A country girl is betrayed by a man of an old family. Later she marries a cultured man who has voluntarily put himself in the farming class. On their wedding night, he confesses his lapses from chastity, and she tells of her fall. But he does not condone her fault, and separates himself from her. She is then sought out by her betrayer, and, urged by her needy family, she becomes his mistress. Her husband returns repentant, and she kills her betrayer, and suffers death for the murder.

MARY CECIL HAY (ENGLAND, 1840–1886), XIX. 253.

452. OLD MYDDLETON'S MONEY (1874), X. 203. 1. Crime and its Detection. 2. Comedy. A miser has been murdered; his nephew disappears, and is charged with the crime, but is at last exonerated by the discovery of the real criminal, and brought back to be the heir. There is a secondary plot, in which a rich old lady disguises herself as a poor one, and by her reception by her kinsfolk, picks out the one deserving to inherit her wealth.

KATHERINE MACQUOID (ENGLAND, 1840–   ), XIX. 304.

453. AT THE RED GLOVE (1885), XII. 138. 1. Character. 2. Swiss Life. A study of middle class life and character in Berne, Switzerland, dealing especially with matrimonial scheming and love affairs.

WILLIAM BLACK (SCOTLAND, 1841–1898), XIX. 52.

454. THE MONARCH OF MINCING LANE (1871), III. 86. 1. English Society. 2. Love. A rich man, in order to prevent his son marrying a poor girl, contrives to have her marry a drunken rascal. The son is a good comrade of a high-born girl whom his father intends him to marry;

ANALYSIS OF THE WORLD'S STORIES 69

and, when her father becomes embarrassed for funds, proposes to marry her. They are saved from this mistake by the young man becoming independent of his father through a legacy, the return of the high-born girl's sweetheart, and the death of the poor girl's drunken husband.

455. THE STRANGE ADVENTURES OF A PHAETON (1872), III. 92. 1. Character. 2. Love. A German officer is a member of an English party driving for pleasure over England. A young lady in the party, prejudiced against him at first, learns to appreciate his fine traits of character, which favorably contrast with the boorish manners of an English suitor, and becomes engaged to him at the end of the drive.

456. A PRINCESS OF THULE (1873), III. 98. 1. Scottish Life. 2. Love. 3. Character. A Londoner marries a girl of the Hebrides Islands, and takes her to London, where her husband tires of her because of her primitive habits. She flees from him; he repents his cruelty, changes his idle habits for industrious, and becomes at last united to her in her Highland home.

457. MACLEOD OF DARE (1878), III. 105. 1. Scottish Life. 2. The Theatre. 3. Tragedy. 4. Character. A raw, high-born Highlander falls in love with a London actress, and they become affianced. She visits his home and is dismayed at the desolate life in prospect. Returning to London, she breaks the engagement. Crazed by this, the Highlander kidnaps her on his yacht and both go down in a storm.

ROBERT BUCHANAN (ENGLAND, 1841–1901), XIX. 70.

458. GOD AND THE MAN (1881), III. 327. 1. Melodrama. 2. Adventure. The dramatic tale of a man who pursues another who had injured him, and, when thrown with him on a desert isle, forgets his thirst for revenge and succors him.

CLARK RUSSELL (ENGLAND, 1844–), XIX. 358.

459. THE WRECK OF THE GROSVENOR (1878), XIV. 147. 1. Sea Life. 2. Adventure. Sailors mutiny against a cruel captain and mate and kill them. They scuttle the ship and desert it, leaving on it the second mate, the boatswain, and an old man and his daughter, who had been picked up from a wreck. These contrive to keep the ship afloat until they are rescued.

ADA CAMBRIDGE (ENGLAND, 1844–), XIX. 78.

460. THE THREE MISS KINGS (1891), IV. 263. 1. Australian Life. 2. Love. 3. Character. The love affairs of three Australian girls. Their characters and their lovers' are clearly differentiated.

ANDREW LANG (SCOTLAND, 1844–), XIX. 289.

461. A MONK OF FIFE (1895), XI. 371. 1. History. 2. Adventure. The romantic experiences of a Scotsman in France at the time of Joan of Arc.

HUGH CONWAY [FREDERICK JOHN FARGUS] (ENGLAND, 1847–1885), XIX. 99.

462. CALLED BACK (1883), V. 93. 1. Crime and its Detection. 2. Blindness. 3. Music. 4. Psychic Phenomena. A blind man is the "witness" of a murder. He recovers his sight afterward, and marries a girl to whom the past is a blank. Later, under the spell of music, she reproduces the scene of the murder, of which she also had been a witness, and its perpetrators are thereby discovered.

DAVID CHRISTIE MURRAY (ENGLAND, 1847–1907), XIX. 327.

463. THE WAY OF THE WORLD (1884), XIII. 35. 1. Journalism. 2. Love. A love romance centering about a newspaper venture.

WILLIAM E. NORRIS (ENGLAND, 1847–   ), XIX. 329.

464. THE ROGUE (1888), XIII. 56. 1. Character. A story in which the interest is cleverly fixed upon the question of just how much of a rascal the chief character may be.

FLORA ANNIE STEEL (ENGLAND, 1847–   ), XIX. 384.

465. ON THE FACE OF THE WATERS (1896), XV. 408. 1. History. 2. Heroism. A romance of thrilling rescues and hair-breadth escapes of English men and women in the Sepoy Rebellion.

(HERE MAY FOLLOW 634, 635, AND 636.)

ROBERT LOUIS STEVENSON (SCOTLAND, 1850–1894), XIX. 389.

466. TREASURE ISLAND (1883), XVI. 1. 1. Youth. 2. Adventure. 3. Piracy. A boy's story of an expedition after buried treasure in a Pacific island, and of a contest for it with pirates.

467. PRINCE OTTO (1885), XVI. 12. 1. Adventure. 2. Loyalty. 3. Love. A sentimental king of a mythical country has a brilliant queen who does not realize how much she loves him until by the machinations of his enemies, who play upon her high opinion of her own abilities, he is deposed. Then she does not accept his renunciation of her, but begins life over with him as a humble citizen.

468. THE STRANGE CASE OF DR. JEKYLL AND MR. HYDE (1886), XVI. 24. 1. Psychic Phenomena. 2. Allegory. 3. Imagination. 4. Tragedy. 5. Chemistry. A physician with a longing for lawless pleasure discovers a chemical which enables him to separate himself into two personalities; one, a respectable doctor, the other, a vicious criminal. On the exposure of this double life, he kills himself, leaving a confession of his misdeeds. The story is an allegory of the debasing effects of self-indulgence.

469. THE MASTER OF BALLANTRAE (1889), XVI. 32. 1. Kinship. 2. Adventure. 3. Oriental Craft. The story of a feud between a wicked elder brother and a younger, to whom he has forfeited his inheritance. The elder pursues the younger with persecutions, and the younger's

wife with attentions, even to America. The villain seeks buried treasure in the Adirondacks. To escape death at the hands of his partner in the enterprise, his Oriental servant buries him alive, returning, however, too late to resuscitate him.

470. KIDNAPPED (1886), XVI. 44. 1. Youth. 2. Adventure. 3. History. An heir is kidnapped by order of his wicked uncle, to be sold to labor in the Carolinas. The ship is wrecked on the Scots island of Mull, and the hero escapes with a Highland gentleman, outlawed for his part in the rebellion of 1745. After many adventures they return to the lad's home, and successfully plot the undoing of the wicked uncle.

471. THE BLACK ARROW (1888), XVI. 54. 1. Youth. 2. History. 3. Adventure. A juvenile romance of the War of the Roses. An heiress runs away, disguised as a boy, from a young husband that is to be forced upon her by a wicked guardian. She falls in with the very lad, and, he being ignorant of her sex, they become good comrades, and have many exciting adventures, chiefly with a band of outlaws who are enemies of the guardian. Finally the villain is discomfited and the comrades are converted into lovers.

472. DAVID BALFOUR (1893), XVI. 67. 1. Adventure. 2. Love. A sequel to "Kidnapped" (**470**). The hero is drawn into further adventures by his outlaw comrade. He becomes the protector of the daughter of an infamous perjurer, a noble girl who repudiates her father, and in the end he marries her.

473. WEIR OF HERMISTON (1894), XVI. 77. 1. Tragedy. 2. Character. A young man kills the seducer of a girl who had been his own sweetheart. His father, as a criminal-judge, condemns him to death. The girl's brothers rescue him forcibly from jail, and he escapes with the girl to America. But the father had died of grief over sentencing his son.

474. ST. IVES (1894), XVI. 90. 1. Adventure. 2. History. 3. Love. French soldiers of Napoleon are imprisoned in Edinburgh. A girl visits the prisoners and buys their trinkets. An officer among them kills a fellow prisoner in a duel for insulting her. He escapes, and is harbored by her. At the end of the war he returns and marries her.

JESSIE FOTHERGILL (ENGLAND, 1851-1891), XIX. 191.

475. THE FIRST VIOLIN (1877), VIII. 420. 1. Music. 2. Love. An English girl flees from a rich and rascally suitor, who is being forced on her, to Germany, where she studies music. She falls in love with a fellow traveller, a seeming gentleman, but whom she next sees as a fiddler in an orchestra. In her confusion she cuts him. He assumes that this is done purposely and refuses to accept her explanations. He saves her life while out skating and reveals his own love, but perversely tries to make her hate him. The reason for this becomes apparent when a story is spread about that he is a thief, disowned by his highborn family, and he does not deny it. The English girl sets to work and finds that he is shielding the real thief, who was his wife, now **dead**. The two lovers marry and he is restored to his former social position.

MRS. HUMPHRY WARD (ENGLAND, 1851–   ), XIX. 418.

476. LADY ROSE'S DAUGHTER (1903), XVII. 168. 1. Biography. 2. Character. 3. Politics. The original of the heroine was Julie de Lespinasse, a Parisian who, in the middle of the 18th century, conducted a famous literary salon. The author has removed the scene to London, and the time to the present, and made the heroine intrigue in politics for the sake of her lover. He is a selfish man and she is saved from him and the consequences of her own folly, by the daring of a true-hearted man.

HALL CAINE (ENGLAND, 1853–   ), XIX. 77.

477. THE DEEMSTER (1887), IV. 252. 1. Melodrama. 2. Religion. 3. Love. A dramatic tale of the Isle of Man, in which a man kills his cousin, repents, and heroically loses his life in saving the community that has cast him out. His old sweetheart teaches the dying man to pray.

GEORGE MOORE (IRELAND, 1853–   ), XIX. 320.

478. ESTHER WATERS (1894), XII. 336. 1. Service. 2. Racing. 3. Realism. The life of a servant girl of racing people, written in realistic manner.

479. EVELYN INNES (1898), XII. 347. 1. Music. 2. Character. 3. Religion. A study of the musical temperament. A prima donna is pulled about by the emotions of love, music, and religion.

STANLEY WEYMAN (ENGLAND, 1855–   ), XIX. 422.

480. A GENTLEMAN OF FRANCE (1893), XVII. 210. 1. History. 2. Adventure. The romantic adventures of a poor nobleman in the service of Henry III. in his relations with Henry of Navarre, afterward Henry IV.

SARAH GRAND [FRANCES CLARKE McFALL] (IRELAND, 1855–   ), XIX. 229.

481. THE HEAVENLY TWINS (1893), IX. 193. 1. Education. 2. Ethics. 3. Marriage. 4. Disguise. A novel dealing with the higher education of women and the ethics of marriage. A young wife disguises herself as her twin brother, and forms Platonic relations with a tenor, which leads to his death and the anguish of her husband, with whom, however, she becomes reconciled.

GEORGE BERNARD SHAW (IRELAND, 1856–   ), XIX. 371.

482. THE IRRATIONAL KNOT (1880), XV. 217. 1. Ethics. 2. Marriage. 3. Business. An electrical inventor marries an aristocratic woman. Their ideals and habits of life are incompatible, and she elopes with a man of her class. She repents, and is reconciled to her husband, but they agree that to live apart is the wisest course.

483. Cashel Byron's Profession (1882), XV. 227. 1. Prize-fighting. 2. Marriage. An intellectual woman marries a prize-fighter, who is nothing more than a splendid animal. This union of opposites, or, rather, complements, proves a most happy one.

F. ANSTEY [THOMAS ANSTEY GUTHRIE] (ENGLAND, 1856–   ), XIX. 16.

484. Vice Versa (1882), 1. 269. 1. Youth. 2. Comedy. 3. Magic. By the influence of an amulet a father and son exchange places and bodies, but not minds, one going to school, where he is persecuted for his airs by his fellows, and the other to the office, where he plays hob with business.

485. The Giant's Robe (1883), I. 280. 1. Authorship. 2. Rascality. 3. The Love. 4. Heroism. An author succumbs to the temptation to let the novel of a friend, supposed to be dead, pass as his own. The secret is discovered by a rejected suitor of the author's sweetheart, who plots to revenge himself by promoting their marriage and then exposing the author's crime. The wedding takes place, the true author returns, and, being in love himself with the wife, frustrates the charge against the husband by assuming responsibility for the literary forgery, thus incurring the contempt of the wife. The husband reveals the truth, however, when the true author is dying.

486. The Tinted Venus (1885), I. 292. 1. Magic. 2. Comedy. A London barber puts a ring on the finger of a statue of Venus, which is thereby endowed with life, and also with love for the barber, causing him no end of trouble with his sweetheart.

487. A Fallen Idol (1886), I. 300. 1. Magic. 2. Comedy. 3. Love. The idol of a mischief-making East Indian god comes into the possession of an artist, and plays hob with his affairs, especially his love-making.

H. RIDER HAGGARD (ENGLAND, 1856–   ), XIX. 240.

488. King Solomon's Mines (1886), IX. 328. 1. Adventure. 2. Melodrama. 3. Wealth. The strange adventures of an English party in South Africa, searching for the lost mines of King Solomon. They are saved from death by the self-sacrifice of a negro girl, and suffer imprisonment in the mines, whence they escape with pockets full of diamonds.

489. She (1887), IX. 338. 1. Magic. 2. Melodrama. English explorers in South Africa meet a female chief who seems to have immortal youth and beauty. She recognizes one traveller as the incarnation of an ancient lover. She takes him to a flame streaming up from earth's centre, which is a fountain of immortality, and, to persuade him to bathe in it, steps herself within,—and is turned to a withered hag, old in appearance as her 2,000 years, dying in agonies of love and shame.

OSCAR WILDE (IRELAND, 1856-1900), XIX. 423.

490. THE PICTURE OF DORIAN GRAY (1890), XVII. 236. 1. Ethics. 2. Imagination. 3. Magic. 4. Art. 5. Crime. 6. Tragedy. 7. The Theatre. A beautiful young man has his portrait painted, and, under the influence of a tempter, who tells him youth and beauty are the only desirable things in life, wishes that the portrait grow old and ugly, and that he remain through life as he is. His wish is magically granted. He plunges into vice and crime, without visible effect on himself, causing an actress to kill herself for him, and ending with murdering the artist and destroying the painting in a maniacal rage, after which he falls dead, and is found, old and hideous, at the foot of the portrait restored to its pristine youth and beauty.

FIONA MACLEOD [WILLIAM SHARP] (Scotland, 1856-1905), XIX. 370.

491. PHARAIS (1894), XII. 128. 1. Insanity. 2. Imagination. 3. Pathos. A young husband of the Hebrides goes mad with temperamental melancholy, and he and his wife resolve to drown themselves to prevent the evil passing to their unborn child. They are rescued, each believing the other dead. The child is born blind. The parents are united. The child dies, and his death is followed by the mother's, the father lapsing into a state of mild lunacy.

(HERE MAY FOLLOW 690.)

EDNA LYALL [ADA ELLEN BAYLY] (ENGLAND, 1859-1903), XIX. 299.

492. DONOVAN (1882), XII. 73. 1. Religion. 2. Character. The story of an atheist, persecuted for his honest convictions, who becomes a broad minded Christian.

A. CONAN DOYLE (SCOTLAND, 1859-   ), XIX. 158.

493. A STUDY IN SCARLET (1887), VII. 280. 1. Detection of Crime. 2. Character. 3. Mormonism. The detection, by clues, of a murder of a Mormon, in vengeance for his crimes. The intellectual powers of the detective are the distinctive feature of the story.

494. THE WHITE COMPANY (1890), VII. 286. 1. History. 2. Adventure. 3. Chivalry. An historical romance of the time of Edward III., describing the deeds of an English troop of knights and archers in Spain, in behalf of King Pedro. The character of the doughty captain of the troop is of chief interest. Edward, the Black Prince, and Du Guesclin appear in the story.

MARY CHOLMONDELEY (ENGLAND, 1859-   ), XIX. 93.

495. RED POTTAGE (1889), IV. 389. 1. Tragedy. 2. Love. A husband and his wife's paramour draw lots as to which shall kill himself by a certain date. The paramour is chosen. He falls in love with a girl in the interim, and, on the death by accident of his fellow "duellist," fails to fulfill the pact. He confesses his dishonor to the girl, and she spurns him. Then he kills himself.

JEROME K. JEROME (ENGLAND, 1859–), XIX. 274.

496. PAUL KELVER (1902), XI. 122. 1. Autobiography. 2. Authorship. 3. The Theatre. 4. Friendship. A semi-autobiographical tale of an author's career; he is entrapped into an engagement with a barmaid, involved in a literary theft by a collaborating playwright, passes through calf-love, but comes out all right in the end, sustained by the good comradeship of a sensible woman.

MAXWELL GRAY [MARY G. TUTTIETT] (England, 18– ––––), XIX. 233.

497. THE SILENCE OF DEAN MAITLAND (1886), IX. 229. 1. Crime and its Punishment. 2. Tragedy. A clergyman seduces a girl and in self-defence murders her father. He is dressed, for disguise, in the clothing of a friend, who is accused, convicted, and imprisoned for the crime. At the expiration of his sentence he hears the clergyman deliver an eloquent sermon against the Judas type of man. The preacher sees him, is convicted of his sin, and confesses his crime, falling dead in the pulpit.

JAMES MATTHEW BARRIE (SCOTLAND, 1860–), XIX. 36.

498. A WINDOW IN THRUMS (1889), II. 320. 1. Biography. 2. Character. 3. Family Love. 4. Pathos. 5. Humor. A story of a Scotch woman, a cripple, the original of which was the author's mother, and of her husband, a born "humorist." The joys and sorrows of motherhood are depicted.

499. THE LITTLE MINISTER (1891), II. 327. 1. Love. 2. Religion. 3. Character. 4. Melodrama. The love romance of a young Scotch minister and a wild gipsy girl, with resultant soul tragedy, and, because of the machinations against the girl of a fanatic member of the minister's congregation, a melodramatic ending.

SAMUEL RUTHERFORD CROCKETT (SCOTLAND, 1860–), XIX. 107.

500. THE LILAC SUNBONNET (1894), VI. 40. 1. Love. An idyllic story of two sweethearts, who are each tricked at their tryst by lovers they had spurned, and whose union is opposed by the minister, on the ground that the girl was illegitimate, he being her father. Despite such opposition the two lovers marry.

MAY SINCLAIR (ENGLAND, 1860–), XIX. 377.

501. THE DIVINE FIRE (1904), XV. 288. 1. Authorship. 2. Love. 3. Business. 4. Character. The career of a book-store clerk, who becomes a poet. He falls in love with an intellectual woman of social position, with whom his business puts him upon a false footing. A false friend creates further trouble between them; but she is brave enough to overlook appearances and put aside conventional prejudice and let him know she loves him.

MAURICE HEWLETT (ENGLAND, 1861–   ), XIX. 254.

502. THE FOREST LOVERS (1898), X. 220. 1. Chivalry. 2. Love. 3. Adventure. A tale in the mode of mediæval romance, in which a true knight combats with a false one, a wicked lady gets the good knight in her toils, etc., and virtue triumphs in the end.

503. RICHARD YEA-AND-NAY (1900), X. 229. 1. History. 2. Character. 3. Adventure. 4. Chivalry. A character study of Richard I. of England, especially in his relations with women. Many adventures are described, especially those of the Crusades.

EDEN PHILLPOTTS (ENGLAND, 1862–   ), XIX. 341.

504. SONS OF THE MORNING (1900), XIII. 221. 1. Love. 2. Self-Sacrifice. 3. Nature. A woman thinks herself in love with two men, who are drawn together in a common love for nature. One, feeling the other the better man, goes away, and is reported dead. She marries the other. Number one returns and becomes a comrade of the wife. The husband then effaces himself, committing suicide as if he died by accident, whereupon the widow realizes that she had loved him truly. She marries, however, the other man from a sense of duty to him.

ARTHUR T. QUILLER-COUCH (ENGLAND, 1863–   ), XIX. 347.

505. THE SPLENDID SPUR (1889), XIII. 302. 1. History. 2. Adventure. 3. Love. An Oxford student, a partisan of the king, is entangled in the English Revolution. He escapes from the Roundheads with a girl disguised as a boy. Another girl loves him and, assuming the love is returned, causes trouble between him and the girl in disguise, whom alone he loves. But the unloved one dies after aiding him to escape, and all is made right between him and the other.

ANTHONY HOPE [HAWKINS] (ENGLAND, 1863–   ), XIX. 262.

506. THE PRISONER OF ZENDA (1894), X. 337. 1. Adventure. 2. Love. 3. Disguise. 4. Ethics. An Englishman is the physical double of a king of a mythical Balkan state, in which he is a tourist. A revolution breaks out. The king is captured. The Englishman, in the king's interest, assumes the throne, representing himself as the king himself. A princess, betrothed to the king, but who had not loved him, is charmed with this new revelation of his personality, as it seems to her. When the king is restored to his throne, the Englishman has the choice presented him of keeping or resigning the princess. In the higher interests of duty, they both renounce their love, and each goes his appointed way.

MAX PEMBERTON (ENGLAND, 1863–   ), XIX. 339.

507. THE FOOTSTEPS OF A THRONE (1900), XIII. 200. 1. Russian Life. 2. Gambling. An Englishman loves a Russian princess, who is rapidly

ANALYSIS OF THE WORLD'S STORIES 77

impoverishing herself by her inherited passion for gambling. The paternal Russian government interferes with their proposed marriage, but he cleverly foils the governor who has her in charge, and the lovers escape to England.

W. W. JACOBS (ENGLAND, 1863–   ), XIX. 271.

508. AT SUNWICH PORT (1902), XI. 62. 1. Humor. 2. Character. 3. Sea Life. Intrigues of parents and lovers in a village of active and retired sailors. An old sea-captain who intends to get his son kidnapped, to save him from marrying his enemy's daughter, finds himself "crimped."

MARIE CORELLI [MINNIE MACKAY] (ENGLAND, 1864–   ), XIX. 104.

509. A ROMANCE OF TWO WORLDS (1886), VI. 8. 1. Magic. 2. Imagination. 3. Electricity. 4. Tragedy. A phantasmagoria of mysticism, in which electricity is represented as the divine power of the universe. An adept in its use is the chief character. His sister is his subject, and her death by lightning forms the tragic climax of the story.

ISRAEL ZANGWILL (ENGLAND, 1864–   ), XIX. 428.

510. CHILDREN OF THE GHETTO (1892), XVII. 292. 1. Jewish Life and Character. 2. Authorship. A story of life in the poor Jewish quarter of London, depicting the career of a girl who gains fame as an author, and wins the love of an Oxford graduate.

ROBERT HICHENS (ENGLAND, 1864–   ), XIX. 256.

511. THE GREEN CARNATION (1894), X. 251. 1. Satire. 2. Humor. 3. Character. A humorous satire upon Oscar Wilde's æsthetic philosophy, in which the personalities of Wilde and a typical disciple of his are portrayed in exaggerated form.

512. THE GARDEN OF ALLAH (1905), X. 263. 1. Geography. 2. Character. 3. Love. 4. Religion. A liberal Catholic woman meets a strange, unsophisticated sort of a man on an oasis in the Sahara. They are mutually attracted and marry. It transpires that he is an emancipated Trappist monk. He repents the breaking of his vows, and his wife sends him back into the church.

RUDYARD KIPLING (ENGLAND, 1865–   ), XIX. 284.

513. THE LIGHT THAT FAILED (1890), XI. 307. 1. Journalism. 2. Art. 3. Comradeship. 4. Love. 5. Heroism. A journalist and artist become chums in the Soudanese war. Returning to London, the artist blocks his model's designs on the journalist. In revenge she destroys his masterpiece. But the artist has become blind, and is not cognizant of the loss, which his sweetheart conceals from him. The lovers become estranged and the blind man goes to the Soudan and throws himself into a fight where he is killed.

514. CAPTAINS COURAGEOUS (1897), XI. 321. 1. Youth. 2. Sea-Life. 3. Ethics. A rich man's son, spoiled and insolent, falls overboard from an Atlantic liner, and is picked up by a Yankee fishing-smack, where he is put to work, and so is made a man of.

515. THE JUNGLE BOOK (1894), XI. 330. 1. Youth. 2. Animals. The story of a were-wolf, a boy adopted by wolves, who becomes the master of the beasts of the forest.

**ELLEN THORNEYCROFT FOWLER (ENGLAND, 1873–   ),
XIX. 193.**

516. A DOUBLE THREAD (1899), IX. 20. 1. Impersonation. 2. Love. An heiress, to encourage her lover too proud to propose, impersonates her twin sister, a poor girl, and as such weans him away from her rich self. She contrives that her poor self is under suspicion of theft. He comes forward to the defence, and she then reveals the deception. He is angered and goes away. She tries to love another, but fails to do so. The report of her refusal brings her old lover to her side.

UNITED STATES OF AMERICA

SUSANNA ROWSON (ENGLAND, 1761–1824), XIX. 357.

517. CHARLOTTE TEMPLE (1790), XIV. 127. 1. Biography. 2. Betrayal. 3. Pathos. A true story of a woman now buried in Trinity churchyard, New York, who was betrayed by her lover.

WASHINGTON IRVING (1783–1859), XIX. 269.

518. RIP VAN WINKLE (1819), XI. 46. 1. Legend. 2. Magic. 3. History. 4. Character. 5. Humor. A legend of the Catskills during Colonial and Revolutionary times. The hero, a lovable, lazy, henpecked husband, meets a goblin crew, and, drinking their brew, falls asleep for twenty years. Awaking, he finds wonderful changes in his village, the pleasantest of which is the demise of his shrewish wife.

519. THE LEGEND OF SLEEPY HOLLOW (1819), XI. 53. 1. Legend. 2. Humor. 3. Character. 4. Magic. A Yankee schoolteacher and a New York Dutchman are rivals for the hand of a farmer's daughter at Tarrytown, N. Y., in Colonial days. The Dutchman scares the Yankee away from the neighborhood, by representing the part of a Headless Horseman, a legendary spirit.

JAMES FENIMORE COOPER (1789–1851), XIX. 100.

520. PRECAUTION (1820), V. 101. 1. English Society. 2. Mistaken Identity. 3. Love. A love romance in aristocratic English circles, which is complicated by a mistake in the identity of the lover, and its satisfactory explanation.

ANALYSIS OF THE WORLD'S STORIES

521. THE SPY (1821), V. 113. 1. History. 2. Patriotism. 3. Love. A love romance complicated by the events and animosities of the Revolutionary war. The titular character is a private spy of General Washington, who endures the odium of treason for his country's good.

522. THE PIONEERS (1823), V. 124. 1. Pioneer and Indian Life and Character. 2. Heroism. 3. Pathos. 4. Love. The fifth of the "Leatherstocking Tales." In it the hero and his comrade, the Mohegan chief, Chingachgook, endure the one imprisonment, the other death, to protect the person and secret of the senile owner of an estate, held by others. The old man's grandson, on the revelation of the secret, becomes the accepted lover of a girl to whom he had hitherto been too modest to pay court.

523. THE PILOT (1823), V. 138. 1. Sea Life and Character. 2. History. 3. Love. A conventional love romance in a maritime setting, which is the distinctive feature of the novel. An old coxswain, Long Tom Coffin, is the most original character. The titular character is understood to represent John Paul Jones, the sea hero of the American Revolution.

524. LIONEL LINCOLN (1825), V. 148. 1. History. 2. Melodrama. 3. Insanity. A romance whose scene is laid in Boston at the beginning of the Revolutionary War. The hero is a British soldier, whose life is saved at Lexington and Concord by an old Continental lunatic and a simpleton, who prove afterward to be his father and half brother. Their deaths are tragic, but clear the way for the success in love and advancement in society of the hero.

525. THE LAST OF THE MOHICANS (1826), V. 161. 1. Pioneer and Indian Life and Character. 2. Adventure. 3. Tragedy. 4. History. The second of the "Leatherstocking Tales." The chief characters are Leatherstocking, the pioneer, and the Indian father and son, Chingashgook and Uncas. They perform prodigies of valor in the war of 1756, in conveying a white party through hostile Indian country, Uncas meeting a tragic death in vainly trying to save one of the ladies.

526. THE RED ROVER (1827), V. 171. 1. Sea Life. 2. Piracy. 3. History. A maritime romance of the days preceding the American Revolution. The titular hero is a gallant slaver and pirate, who saves from his wild crew a captain who had won his respect by a brave resistance.

527. THE PRAIRIE (1827), V. 181. 1. Frontier and Indian Life. 2. Tragedy. The fifth and the last of the "Leatherstocking Tales." The hero, grown old, has become a trapper in the West. He is instrumental in detecting a murder and an abduction among a party of emigrants. Warfare between two Indian tribes and a duel between their chiefs are described.

528. THE WEPT OF WISH-TON-WISH (1829), V. 193. 1. History. 2. Pioneer and Indian Life. 3. Tragedy. A tale of early New England, in which the Indian chiefs King Philip and Canonche figure. An

Indian captive, a boy, saves the children of a pioneer from massacre. One child is captured by the Indians, and years after meets her mother and dies in her arms. A regicide of Charles I. aids the pioneers in their fight against the Indians.

529. THE WATER WITCH (1830), V. 205. 1. Sea Life. 2. Piracy. 3. Heroism. 4. History. A pirate leads a British cruiser a pretty chase in New York waters in colonial days. The cruiser is attacked by two French vessels, whereupon the pirate comes to its rescue.

530. THE BRAVO (1831), V. 212. 1. Melodrama. 2. Crime. 3. Heroism. A romance intended to illustrate in all its phases the tyranny of the doges of Venice.

531. THE HEIDENMAUER (1832), V. 226. 1. History. 2. Religion. A tale of the contest between the German barons and monks in the days of Luther. A famous drinking-bout between the champions of the two classes, held at Hartenburg, is described.

532. THE HEADSMAN (1833), V. 239. 1. Social Prejudice. 2. Crime. 3. The Dog. A romance based on the prejudice against the public executioner. He is represented as a man of noble nature, with a fair daughter and brave son, about whose proposed marriages troubles arise because of their father's calling. The betrothed of the girl repudiates her, and is afterward murdered. The crime is charged against a stranger, who saves himself by revealing himself as the son of the Doge of Genoa. But the true son is found to be the reputed son of the headsman. The heroic act of a St. Bernard dog in saving life is described, and it plays an important part in the crime and its detection.

533. THE MONIKINS (1835), V. 251. 1. Satire (Political and Social). The hero defers marriage until he has made every possible conquest in man's world, that of business and politics, when he finds his lady love is not quite ready for him, still having a few conquests to make in her woman's world of admiration. Various monkeys are introduced in the story in satire of human foibles.

534. HOMEWARD BOUND AND HOME AS FOUND (1837), V. 259. 1. Sea Life. 2. Character. 3. Family Life. 4. Autobiography. A novel and its sequel, relating the adventures on the sea of an American family returning from Europe. The author makes a special effort to depict types of character, that of the sea-captain being the best. One character is intended to portray the author himself.

535. THE PATHFINDER (1840), V. 270. 1. Pioneer and Indian Life and Character. 2. Adventure. 3. Love. 4. History. The third of the "Leatherstocking Tales." The hero and Chingachgook perform valorous deeds in the war of 1756, chiefly on behalf of a lady with whom Leatherstocking is in love. He has a rival in her affections, who is falsely accused of treachery, and to him Leatherstocking resigns her.

ANALYSIS OF THE WORLD'S STORIES 81

536. Mercedes of Castile (1841), V. 283. 1. History. 2. Love. A companion of Columbus, in love with a lady of the court of Ferdinand and Isabella, is attracted by an Indian princess who resembles his sweetheart, and saves her life and brings her to Spain. The sweetheart is jealous, but the lover proves his fidelity. The Indian becomes a Christian and dies contented that she was second in the Spaniard's affection.

537. The Deerslayer (1841), V. 295. 1. Pioneer and Indian Life and Character. 2. Adventure. 3. Love. The first of the "Leatherstocking Tales." The hero and his Indian comrade, Chingachgook save a pioneer family from the Iroquois. Leatherstocking gives himself up as a hostage to them, and is about to be slain, when one of the pioneer's two daughters interposes to delay the execution, until Chingachgook arrives with a rescue party.

538. The Two Admirals (1842), V. 305. 1. Sea Life and Character. 2. History. 3. Loyalty. A story of the reign of George II., when France was supporting the cause of the Pretender, Charles Edward. An admiral who sympathizes with the Stuart cause, delays aiding a fellow admiral in fight with the French, until he sees him hard beset, when he comes to the rescue, losing his life.

539. Wing and Wing (1842), V. 312. 1. Sea Life and Character. 2. History. A story of clever manœuvering by a French privateer in the Napoleonic war. The captain of the craft and an American sailor are the chief characters. Lord Nelson appears in the story.

540. Wyandotte (1843), V. 320. 1. Indian Character. 2. Pioneer Life. 3. Tragedy. 4. History. A pioneer family, during the Revolution, are attacked by Indians. An Indian supposed to be friendly kills one of the party who had insulted him, and is badly wounded saving others who trusted him.

541. Satanstoe (1844), V. 333. 1. Pioneer Life. 2. History. 3. Indian Character. 4. Love. The first of the Littlepage Manuscripts. Rivalry of two men for one woman. There is a thrilling account of a sleigh-ride on the Hudson River while the ice is breaking up. The operations against Ticonderoga are described. An Indian revenges himself on a negro who had flogged him.

542. Afloat and Ashore (1844), V. 344. 1. Sea Life. 2. Adventure. 3. Piracy. 4. History. The second of the Littlepage Manuscripts. Encounters with pirates and French vessels in the war with France after the Revolution.

543. Miles Wallingford (1844), V. 353. 1. Sea Life. 2. Adventure. 3. History. The third of the Littlepage Manuscripts. The sequel of "Afloat and Ashore." Sea fights during the War of 1812.

544. The Chainbearer (1845), V. 364. 1. Pioneer Life and Character. 2. Love. 3. Tragedy. The fourth of the Littlepage Manuscripts.

82 ANALYSIS OF THE WORLD'S STORIES

An ignorant, but brave, true-hearted surveyor's assistant, gives up his life for the girl he loves, in a fight with a timber-stealing squatter.

545. The Redskins (1846), V. 377. 1. History. 2. Pioneer Life. 3. Labor. The fifth of the Littlepage Manuscripts. The story relates to the Anti-Rent disturbances in New York State in the forties, when squatters, disguised as Indians, attacked the landlords. They are captured by real Indians.

546. The Crater (1847), V. 390. 1. Sea Life. 2. Adventure. 3. Physical Geography. Adventures of a castaway on a volcanic island appearing and later disappearing in the sea.

547. Jack Tier (1848), V. 402. 1. Sea Life. 2. Adventure. 3. Piracy. 4. Disguise. A law-breaking sailing vessel is pursued by a U. S. steamer (gunboat). The captain has been followed to sea by his wife disguised as a sailor. She prevents him abducting another man's sweetheart.

548. The Oak Openings (1848), V. 411. 1. Pioneer and Indian Life and Character. 2. History. 3. Bee-hunting. The scene is in the Michigan woods at the outbreak of the War of 1812. A bee-hunter is the chief character. He has befriended an Indian who saves him and his wife from massacre.

549. The Sea Lions (1849), V. 423. 1. Sea Life. 2. Adventure. 3. Hidden Treasure. A race between two Long Island whaling ships, each named "The Sea Lion," for hidden treasure.

550. The Ways of the Hour (1850), V. 431. 1. Law. 2. Crime and its Detection. A story intended to show the inadequacy of the jury system, especially in criminal cases. A woman is arrested for murder. She refuses to escape by bribery, and is convicted on circumstantial evidence, but is freed later, by the appearance of the man supposed to have been murdered.

JOHN P. KENNEDY (1795–1870), XIX. 281.

551. Horseshoe Robinson (1835), XI. 208. 1. History. 2. Love. A love romance based on the warfare between Whigs and Tories in the Revolution, in southern Virginia and the Carolinas.

DANIEL P. THOMPSON (1795–1868), XIX. 405.

552. The Green Mountain Boys (1840), XVI. 421. 1. History. A romance of the controversy between New Hampshire and New York over Vermont, and of the Revolution. The characters have originals in history. Ethan Allen and Benedict Arnold appear in the story.

ROBERT MONTGOMERY BIRD (1803–1854), XIX. 50.

553. Nick of the Woods (1837), III. 55. 1. Melodrama (Indian Warfare). 2. Pioneer life in America. A sensational romance of a mad Quaker, who massacres Indians under the guise of a spirit.

ANALYSIS OF THE WORLD'S STORIES

NATHANIEL HAWTHORNE (1804–1864), XIX. 251.

554. FANSHAWE (1828), X. 130. 1. Character. 2. Tragedy. A college student, doomed by disease to an early death, is ready to sacrifice his life to save his sweetheart from a ruffian. The ruffian perishes by accident, and the lover resigns the girl to a young man in health, and dies.

555. The SCARLET LETTER (1850), X. 141. 1. Tragedy. 2. Religion. 3. Character. 4. Ethics. An adulteress bears a mark of her lapse from chastity, concealing the name of the man equally guilty with her. This man is the clergyman. Unable to bear the reproaches of his conscience, at last he publicly acknowledges his guilt.

556. THE HOUSE OF THE SEVEN GABLES (1851), X. 152. 1. New England Life and Character. 2. Tradition. 3. Discovered Treasure. A judge, a rich heir, persecutes a poor brother and sister, his fellow heirs, supposing the brother, who is a lunatic, knows of the location of treasure belonging to the estate. The judge falls dead, a victim to an ancient curse. His death is charged to the lunatic, but it and the treasure myth are explained by a young photographer, the lover of a cousin of the family.

557. THE BLITHEDALE ROMANCE (1852), X. 162. 1. Philosophy. 2. Character. 3. History. 4. Love. A love romance dealing with the farm community founded by the Trancendentalists, some of whom appear under fictitious names in the story, Margaret Fuller and the author in particular.

558. THE MARBLE FAUN (1860), X. 171. 1. Character. 2. Imagination. 3. Sculpture. 4. Roman Scenery. 5. Tragedy. A young Italian is admitted into a circle of American artists in Rome. He is a reincarnation in mind and form of the classic man-animal, the faun. He loves an American artist, and for her sake and with her consent commits a murder. He is imprisoned and she suffers in soul for the crime.

559. SEPTIMIUS FELTON (1871), X. 181. 1. History. 2. Magic. 3. Tradition. 4. Botany. A minute man in the American Revolution kills a red-coat, who, dying, gives him the recipe of an Elixir of Life. The sweetheart of the English soldier plans revenge. One ingredient of the elixir is a magic flower. So she mixes in the draught a flower of death. But she has learned to love the American, and drinks the potion herself.

WILLIAM GILMORE SIMMS (1806–1870), XIX. 376.

560. THE YEMASSEE (1835), XV. 279. 1. North American Indian. 2. History. A romance dealing with the salvation of the colony of South Carolina from Indians and Spaniards by Governor Charles Craven.

CHARLES FENNO HOFFMANN (1806–1884), XIX. 257.

561. GREYSLAER (1840), X. 275. 1. History. 2. Adventure. 3. Crime and its Detection. A romance founded on the conflict of the American Revolutionists with the Mohawks under Joseph Brant. Many exciting scenes are depicted, the abduction and rescue of young ladies, the trial of the hero for the murder of a man, who is found to be alive, etc.

HENRY W. LONGFELLOW (1807-1882), XIX. 295.

562. HYPERION (1839), XII. 39. 1. Travel. 2. Love. 3. Pathos. 5. Literature. A young American travels through scenes in Europe reminiscent of great men in literature and historic deeds. He falls in love with a talented Englishwoman, who does not respond to his passion, and he returns home in melancholy.

EDGAR ALLAN POE (1809-1849), XIX. 341.

563. THE NARRATIVE OF ARTHUR GORDON PYM (1838), XIII. 232. 1. Adventure. 2. Mysticism. A voyage to the unknown South Polar regions, where strange adventures are had with natives who have a mystical fear of everything white.

564. THE FALL OF THE HOUSE OF USHER (1839), XIII. 239. 1. Tragedy. 2. Mysticism. 3. Insanity. 4. Music. 5. Medicine. A brother and a sister, living alone in their ancient house, have a strange affinity with it. The sister is buried while in a catalepsy. She revives and bursts her tomb, whereupon her brother goes mad; the house, in sympathy with the tragedy, falls in ruin, and buries him. The psychic effects of music are discussed, and the philosophy of the sentience of inanimate objects.

TIMOTHY SHAY ARTHUR (1809-1885), XIX. 17.

565. TEN NIGHTS IN A BARROOM (1850), I. 330. 1. Temperance. 2. Tragedy. 3. Pathos. A story of crime incited by drink, and of its resultant misery.

OLIVER WENDELL HOLMES (1809-1894), XIX. 259.

566. ELSIE VENNER (1861), X. 297. 1. Medical Science. 2. Character. 3. Snakes. A story of prenatal influence by which a girl has been endowed with some of the characteristics of a rattlesnake, and with power over the serpent tribe. She falls in love with a young doctor and saves him from the rattlesnakes; he, however, does not respond to her love, though under stress of it she casts off the serpent influence, dying in the struggle.

567. THE GUARDIAN ANGEL (1868), X. 307. 1. Character. 2. Crime and its Detection. 3. Love. A retired scholar watches over the interests of a young girl, an heiress, who has inherited strong powers of character for good or evil. He guides her love affairs successfully, and frustrates a plot to rob her of her property.

568. A MORTAL ANTIPATHY (1885), X. 318. 1. Medical Science. 2. Character. 3. Education. A young man who was injured by the carelessness of a beautiful young lady in his babyhood, has a physical antipathy to blooming young womanhood. He is attracted from afar by the sight of the students of a woman's college winning a rowing race with students of a man's college. He falls ill; the house takes fire, and the leader of the oarswomen rescues him, thereby breaking the spell, and engendering mutual love in rescuer and rescued.

FANNY FERN [SARAH PAYSON PARTON] (1811-1872), XIX. 174.

569. RUTH HALL (1868), VIII. 285. 1. Autobiography. 2. Authorship. 3. Marriage. A young couple are nagged by the man's parents, and move away from them, thereby becoming estranged from the old folks. The husband dies and the wife resorts to writing to make a living for herself and children. Though discouraged by her brother, a famous author and editor, she persists and wins success. She marries a kindly editor and triumphs over her discouragers. This is a semi-autobiographical story, the author's brother, N. P. Willis, standing for the portrait of the heroine's brother.

HARRIET BEECHER STOWE (1812-1896), XIX. 393.

570. UNCLE TOM'S CABIN (1852), XVI. 134. 1. Slavery. 2. Pathos. A tale of American negro slavery depicting all its evils, the separation of families, concubinage, torture, hounding of fugitives, etc.

571. THE MINISTER'S WOOING (1859), XVI. 160. 1. History. 2. Character. 3. Religion. 4. Slavery. A story of New England types of character late in the eighteenth century. Aaron Burr and Dr. Hopkins appear as leading characters, the amours of the former being narrated, and the anti-slavery views of the other expressed. The plot springs from the reported death of a young man, whose mother thereupon inveighs against God's cruelty, and whose sweetheart agrees to marry another suitor, the preacher, although without love. The young man's return, and the minister's resignation to him of the maiden, end the story.

572. AGNES OF SORRENTO (1861), XVI. 171. 1. Italian Life and Character. 2. History. 3. Religion. 4. Love. A young girl, destined for the church, is beloved by one of Savonarola's adherents. He rescues her from the clutches of the Borgias, and, upon a friar's assurance that marriage was a sacrament as well as holy orders she is persuaded to become his wife.

573. OLDTOWN FOLKS (1869), XVI. 149. 1. Character. 2. Religion. 3. Ethics. A story of New England life and character, especially in their religious and ethical aspects. A bride, discovering that her husband has a child by a mistress, adopts it, and acts a wifely part till relieved by the death of her rascally husband.

ANN SOPHIA STEPHENS (1813-1886), XIX. 385.

574. FASHION AND FAMINE (1854), XV. 443. 1. Melodrama. 2. Crime. 3. Punishment. A seducer of women and a forger is unmasked by

the lover of a girl he had ruined, who has taken service with him to bring about his exposure. The villain learns that his daughter is living with her mother's father. He visits the old man to get the girl to use as a pledge against his conviction. He is foiled; whereupon he kills himself. The old man is held for the murder, but dies before the trial. The granddaughter, a flower-girl, marries the son of a benefactor and lives in happy ignorance of her criminal father.

HENRY WARD BEECHER (1813–1887), XIX. 43.

575. NORWOOD (1867), II. 406. 1. New England Life. 2. History. 3. Character. 4. Love. A story of life in a country and in a college town of New England, in which types of Yankee character are presented, and a romance developed of the clash between love and patriotism during the Civil War period.

RICHARD B. KIMBALL (1816–1892), XIX. 282.

576. ST. LEGER (1835), XI. 214. 1. Legend. 2. Melodrama. A tale of the fulfilment of a prophecy of evil through the revenge of a servant against a villain who had wronged his master.

ELIZABETH PAYSON PRENTISS (1818–1878), XIX. 344.

577. STEPPING HEAVENWARD (1869), XIII. 271. 1. Religion. 2. Youth. 3. Married Life. The diary of a woman from youth through married life, expressing her religious emotions, her love, and her devotion to husband and children.

HERMAN MELVILLE (1819–1891), XIX, 315.

578. TYPEE (1846), XII. 259. 1. Travel. 2. Adventure. A sailor's adventures among the savages of the Marquesas islands in the Pacific.

579. MOBY DICK (1851), XII. 269. 1. Sea-Life. 2. Adventure. 3. Magic. The story of the pursuit of a white whale which seemed to have a supernatural power to cause disaster.

SUSAN WARNER (1819–1885), XIX. 420.

580. THE WIDE, WIDE WORLD (1851), XVII. 191. 1. Farm Life. 2. Ethics. 3. Racial Characteristics. An orphan, brought up in the arduous life of a farm, is adopted by a kind family. But she discovers that her parents had wished her to join relatives in Scotland. Her conscience compels her to obey this wish. She is well received by the Scots people, but, prejudiced against America, they strive to wean her from her old friends. Her adopted brother comes to visit her, breaks down this prejudice, and marries her with everybody's approval.

JOSIAH GILBERT HOLLAND (1819–1881), XIX. 258.

581. SEVENOAKS (1875), X. 288. 1. Crime and its Detection. 2. Invention. 3. Law. A capitalist robs an invalid inventor of his patents, and has him sent as a lunatic, with his boy, to the poorhouse. A woodsman rescues them and hides them in his camp. A lawyer on his vacation meets them, and takes up the inventor's case, and prosecutes the capitalist, cleverly convicting him of forgery.

IK MARVEL [DONALD G. MITCHELL] (1822–1908), XIX. 320.

582. DOCTOR JOHNS (1866), XII. 326. 1. Religion. 2. Character. 3. Youth. A Calvinistic preacher has his severe theological opinions modified by a little French girl who comes to live with him.

RICHARD MALCOLM JOHNSTON (1822–1898), XIX. 278.

583. PEARCE AMERSON'S WILL (1898), XI. 162. 1. Law. 2. Georgia Life and Character. 3. Crime. A story of ante-bellum days in Georgia, the plot of which centers about a disputed will, which is found to be a forgery.

SYLVANUS COBB, JR. (1823–1887), XIX. 96.

584. THE GUNMAKER OF MOSCOW (1860), V. 1. 1. Melodrama. 2. History. A melodramatic love romance in which Peter the Great is introduced as a character.

ELIZABETH B. STODDARD (1823–1902), XIX. 392.

585. THE MORGESONS (1862), XVI. 123. 1. Youth. 2. Character. A story of school-girl life and love, in which strong characters are depicted in contrasting contest.

GEORGE WILLIAM CURTIS (1824–1892), XIX. 109.

586. TRUMPS (1856), VI. 71. 1. New York Society. 2. Business. 3. Politics. 4. Youth. 5. Rascality. Showing how traits of character indicated in youth, display themselves in manhood and womanhood. The chief character is that of a crook in business and politics.

BAYARD TAYLOR (1825–1878), XIX. 400.

587. JOHN GODFREY'S FORTUNES (1864), XVI. 273. 1. Journalism. 2. Authorship. 3. Love. 4. Autobiography. A semi-autobiographic sketch of a journalistic and literary career. The hero saves a country girl from ruin; the action is misrepresented by a rival to his sweetheart, who thereupon cuts his acquaintance. All is made right in the end.

MARIA SUSANNA CUMMINS (1827–1866), XIX. 108.

588. THE LAMPLIGHTER (1854), VI. 60. 1. Youth. 2. Melodrama. 3. Love. A lamplighter adopts a girl, a waif, and educates her for a teacher. She has many thrilling and amazing experiences, is the heroine of a fire at sea, discovers her father, and is united at last to her childhood's lover.

J. T. TROWBRIDGE (1827–   ), XIX. 410.

589. NEIGHBOR JACKWOOD (1857), XVII. 63. 1. Slavery. 2. Love. A Vermont farmer hides a fugitive quadroon slave girl from her pursuers, and protects her from a libertine, and assists her love affair with a young man whose mother is bitterly opposed to the match.

590. CUDJO'S CAVE (1863), XVII. 75. 1. Slavery. 2. History. A romance of the Civil War. Outrages of the Tennessee secessionists upon Union men are described. The latter take refuge in a cave discovered and defended by negroes, and finally escape to the North.

LEW WALLACE (1827–1905), XIX. 416.

591. BEN HUR (1880), XVII. 157. 1. Religion. 2. History. 3. Adventure. 4. Horse Racing. A tale of the Christ, treating of the conflict between Rome and Jewry in general, and of one Roman and a Jew (the hero), who becomes a Christian, in particular. The Jew's victory over the Roman in a chariot race is described. Jesus cures the hero's mother and sister of leprosy.

CHARLES DUDLEY WARNER (1829–1900), XIX. 419.

592. THE GOLDEN HOUSE (1894), XVII. 181. 1. Character. 2. Marriage. 3. Social Reform. A picture of high life in New York; of money-grubbing husbands, and wives who make fads of improving the condition of the poor, patronizing art, etc., but who sacrifice these causes for their own selfish pleasure. The title refers to the golden house of Nero, a pleasure palace blazing with gold and gems.

MARION HARLAND [TERHUNE] (1831–   ), XIX. 246.

593. ALONE (1853), X. 54. 1. Youth. 2. Religion. 3. Ethics. 4. Love. The story of relations of love between members of a group of young people, in which the obligations of religion and morality are emphasized.

REBECCA HARDING DAVIS (1831–   ), XIX. 112.

594. WAITING FOR THE VERDICT (1867), VI. 204. 1. The Negro. 2. History. 3. Heroism. A story of the Civil War. A mulatto doctor, who is thought to be white, renounces the love of a white girl, and gives up his high position in his profession, to work among the negroes. While thus engaged he is assassinated.

JANE GOODWIN AUSTIN (1831–1894), XIX. 22.

595. A NAMELESS NOBLEMAN (1881), II. 1. 1. Love. 2. Royalty. A French nobleman, deceived by his sweetheart and disgusted with the intrigues of the court (of Louis XIV.), departs for Canada, and is shipwrecked on the New England coast, where he is succored by a young Quakeress, whom he marries under an assumed name. He refuses to return to France to his repentant French sweetheart, and the rank awaiting him there.

HELEN HUNT JACKSON (1831-1885), XIX. 270.

596. RAMONA (1884), XI. 73. 1. North American Indian Life and Character. 2. Pathos. A pathetic tale of the ill-treatment by the whites of Indians in southern California.

AMELIA EDITH BARR (ENGLAND, 1831-   ), XIX. 36.

597. A Bow of Orange Ribbon: A Romance of New York (1886), II. 308. 1. History. 2. Love. 3. Racial Antipathy. The romance of a Knickerbocker girl in colonial times, and her English sweetheart, who is objected to by the girl's parents.

LOUISA M. ALCOTT (1832-1888), XIX. 9.

598. Moods (1864), I. 152. 1. Character. 2. Love. A woman of varying moods allows remembrance of an early love to come between herself and husband.

599. Little Women (1868), 1. 142. 1. Youth. 2. Home Life. 3. Love. 4. Autobiography. A semi-autobiographical story of four sisters, their parents, and boy friends.

FRANK R. STOCKTON (1834-1902), XIX. 392.

600. The Casting Away of Mrs. Lecks and Mrs. Aleshine: The Dusantes (1886-1888), XVI. 112. 1. Humor. 2. Character. 3. Adventure. A party of Americans are wrecked on a Pacific island containing a summer residence, whose owners are away. Two rural widows in the party accept the situation in a matter-of-fact way, and run the place as a boarding house. They aid a young man in his love affair with the daughter of a selfish missionary, and defeat the missionary's designs upon the "board money" by tracing the owners, and, after various adventures, finding them.

HARRIET PRESCOTT SPOFFORD (1835-   ), XIX. 383.

601. Azarian (1864), XV. 388. 1. Art. 2. Medicine. 3. The Theater. 4. Music. 5. Love. A girl, an artist, is compelled by her lover, a physician who is a wonderful musician, to choose between him and her friend, an actress. She chooses the physician. He wounds her by his selfishness, and, finding that he requires her only as a plaything, she seeks out the actress, and lives with her, happy in her career and her love of two orphan boys she has adopted.

602. The Thief in the Night (1872), XV. 398. 1. Medicine. 2. Marriage. 3. Ethics. 4. Panama Canal. A man discovers a letter written by his wife to his friend and guest, revealing her love and begging him to go away. The husband opens his veins to leave the lovers free to marry. She then discovers that she really loves her husband, and by transfusion of blood from her veins, restores him to life and happiness. Incidentally, a ship canal across the Isthmus of Panama is proposed.

THOMAS BAILEY ALDRICH (1836-1907), XIX. 10.

603. THE STORY OF A BAD BOY (1869), I. 153. 1. Youth. 2. Humor. A largely autobiographical story of boyish pranks.

604. THE STILLWATER TRAGEDY (1880), I. 162. 1. Crime. 2. Labor. 3. Love. A story, founded on fact, of a murder resulting from labor troubles, of a false accusation, of the detection of the real criminal, and of the loyalty of the accused man's sweetheart.

EDWARD EGGLESTON (1837-1902), XIX. 167.

605. THE CIRCUIT RIDER (1874), VIII. 153. 1. Religion. 2. Pioneer Life and Character. 3. Love. 4. Gambling. A story of pioneer days in Ohio. A young man, converted at a religious revival, becomes an itinerant preacher, which leads to trouble in his love affair, first with the girl, and then with the girl's father. There is further complication owing to the acts of an elder brother, who has become a gambler and highwayman. But the girl is also converted, her father relents, and the man's brother repents, and all ends well.

WILLIAM DEAN HOWELLS (1837-   ), XIX. 263.

606. A MODERN INSTANCE (1883), X. 356. 1. Character. 2. Ethics. 3. Journalism. 4. Politics. The story of a noble woman married to a rascally newspaper man, and beloved by a good man, to whom the husband is perfectly willing to resign her. The presidential campaign of Hayes and Tilden is referred to.

607. THE RISE OF SILAS LAPHAM (1884), X. 367. 1. Ethics. 2. Character. 3. Love. 4. Business. A scion of an aristocratic Boston family becomes intimate with a "new rich" family of a paint manufacturer. Beloved by each of the two daughters, the younger and prettier, who is a spoiled child, assumes that she is to have him. The elder tries to sacrifice herself, but the young man will not have it, for he loves the higher mind and soul of the elder girl. The younger girl rises nobly to bear the blow. Then the father meets business reverses, which he refuses to avert by dishonorable means, in a similar heroic spirit.

MARY MAPES DODGE (1838-1905), XIX. 157.

608. HANS BRINKER: OR, THE SILVER SKATES (1865), VII. 259. 1. Youth. 2. Skating. 3. Dutch Life and Customs. Two poor children of an afflicted father, by their fortitude and self sacrifice, win the love and esteem of their comrades, and restore their father to health and sanity. Dutch customs and sport, especially skating, are described.

ALBION W. TOURGEE (1838-1905), XIX. 406.

609. A FOOL'S ERRAND (1880), XVI. 490. 1. History. 2. Politics. The experiences of a "carpet-bagger" and his family in the days of Reconstruction.

ANALYSIS OF THE WORLD'S STORIES 91

JOHN HAY (1838-1905), XIX. 252.

610. THE BREADWINNERS (1883), X. 192. 1. Labor. 2. Crime and its Detection. 3. Love. An employer is compromised by a bold working-girl who is in love with him. His sweetheart thereupon repulses him. A strike arises among his workmen. His sweetheart fears for his safety, and, watching him, is able to save him from a murderous assault, and, by her testimony, exonerates an innocent employee upon whom the guilty man has attempted to fasten the crime.

F. HOPKINSON SMITH (1838-   ), XIX. 378.

611. COLONEL CARTER OF CARTERSVILLE (1891), XV. 299. 1. Character. 2. Humor. 3. Business. A character study of an old Virginian, a visionary railroad promoter who is supported and saved from financial wreck by his aunt, though he imagines that it is he who is the protector and benefactor.

BRET HARTE (1839-1902), XIX. 248.

612. GABRIEL CONROY (1876), X. 88. 1. Western Life. 2. Melodrama. 3. Mining. 4. Gambling. A tale of wild adventures in the mining regions of the West, in which the passions of love, revenge, gambling, etc., have free play.

GEORGE CARY EGGLESTON (1839-   ), XIX. 168.

613. DOROTHY SOUTH (1902), VIII. 162. 1. History. 2. Virginia Life and Character. 3. Love. 4. Music. 5. Medicine. A woman who is a musical genius forsakes her husband and child for the stage. She loses her beauty and becomes very poor. Her daughter at home in Virginia chooses her guardian, a doctor from the North, who teaches her chemistry. Going to Europe to pursue the study, she meets her mother, who reveals herself to her. The Civil War breaks out. Mother and daughter return home, the one to be a nurse, the other to aid her guardian in his medical work. But it is as his wife and not as his ward that she does it.

JAMES M. LUDLOW (1841-   ), XIX. 299.

614. THE CAPTAIN OF THE JANIZARIES (1886), XII. 64. 1. History. 2. Adventure. The romance of Scanderbeg, an Albanian rebel against Turkish rule at the time of the capture of Constantinople by the Turks (1453).

ELLEN OLNEY KIRK (1842-   ), XIX. 285.

615. THE STORY OF MARGARET KENT (1866), XI. 337. 1. Marriage. 2. Love. 3. Ethics. The wife of a worthless man, whom she supports, falls in love with a noble man, but resists the temptation to get a divorce, and remains faithful to him to his death.

JOHN HABBERTON (1842–), XIX. 238.

616. Helen's Babies (1876), IX. 310. 1. Youth. 2. Humor. 3. Love. One of two impish brothers involve their bashful bachelor uncle in an awkward situation with the young lady he adores, and then by his artlessness precipitates a declaration and acceptance of love.

CHRISTINE CHAPLIN BRUSH (1842–1892), XIX. 69.

617. The Colonel's Opera-Cloak (1879), III. 315. 1. Humor. 2. Character. The story of a poor aristocratic Southern family, and the multifarious uses to which the father's opera-cloak was put.

EDWIN LASSETTER BYNNER (1842–1893), XIX. 75.

618. Agnes Surriage (1886), IV. 231. 1. Love. 2. History. An English gentleman, appointed to office in the colony of Massachusetts, falls in love with a beautiful servant girl, and makes her his mistress. He succeeds to a title, and returns to England, taking his wife with him. His family fails to receive her, and he accepts office in Portugal. In the earthquake at Lisbon he is saved from death by her, and a sailor, her first sweetheart. The gentleman marries her.

HENRY JAMES (1843–), XIX. 273.

619. Daisy Miller (1878), XI. 96. 1. Character. 2. Travel. 3. Society. 4. Love. A character study of an American girl travelling in Switzerland and Italy. She is a coquette, and yet so innocent that she breaks all European conventions ruling the relations of the sexes, and compromises herself. She dies, leaving a compatriot who had been her severest censor in doubt whether he had loved her or not.

620. The Portrait of a Lady (1881), XI. 108. 1. Character. 2. Society. 3. Ethics. An American heiress refuses the suit of a compatriot, and marries a shallow dilettante, an Englishman living in Italy. She bravely tries to prevent her step-daughter making a similar mistake; she is unsuccessful in this, but is rewarded by the approval of a dying man, who had reproached her for her loveless marriage.

GEORGE WASHINGTON CABLE (1844–), XIX. 76.

621. The Grandissimes: A Story of Creole Life (1880), IV. 241. 1. Creole Life. 2. Psychology. 3. History. A story of a family in New Orleans at the time of the Louisiana purchase. Creole society is vividly presented, and the character of its individual members clearly portrayed.

ELIZABETH STUART PHELPS [MRS. WARD] (1844–), XIX. 339.

622. Friends: A Duet (1881), XIII. 212. 1. Friendship. 2. Love. 3. Temperance. A widow, striving to be true to the memory of her husband, fights off a friend who would marry her, and devotes herself to the reform of a dipsomaniac, who proves incurable. When the suitor is about to leave her, she realizes that her feeling for him is more tender than friendship, and recalls him.

HENRY FRANCIS KEENAN (1845–   ), XIX. 280.

623. The Money-Makers (1885), XI. 195. 1. Labor. 2. Finance. 3. Politics. A tale of the power for evil of corporate wealth, its manipulation of finance, control of the press, and enmity to labor unions. Cf. "The Breadwinners" **(610)**.

JULIAN HAWTHORNE (1846–   ), XIX. 250.

624. Archibald Malmaison (1878), X. 120. 1. Character. 2. Tragedy. The hero receives psychic shocks at intervals in his life, which throw him back to the person he was at the time of the previous shock. On one relapse his sweetheart mysteriously disappears, and it is not until the following shock (and the last), that he comes to the knowledge that many years before he had locked her in a chamber of whose existence he and she alone knew.

ANNA KATHERINE GREEN [MRS. ROHLFS] (1846–   ), XIX. 233.

625. The Leavenworth Case (1878), IX. 239. 1. Detection of Crime. 2. Love. The discovery of the perpetrator of a murder, chiefly by playing upon the criminal's love for a woman.

MRS. BURTON HARRISON (1846–   ), XIX. 248.

626. The Anglomaniacs (1890), X. 78. 1. Society. 2. Love. 3. Intrigue. A rich American girl is separated from her American lover by intrigue, and driven to marry a titled Englishman.

BLANCHE WILLIS HOWARD (1847–1898), XIX. 262.

627. Guenn (1882), X. 345. 1. Artist Life in Brittany. 2. Tragedy. A Breton peasant girl loves the artist for whom she poses as a model. She heroically saves his masterpiece from destruction, and, when she finds he has a sweetheart, drowns herself.

MARY HARTWELL CATHERWOOD (1847–1902), XIX. 85.

628. Lazarre (1901), IV. 308. 1. History. 2. Love. A romance of the "Lost Dauphin" (Louis XVII.), who is supposed to have escaped from prison, an imbecile, and to have recovered his reason in America, upon which he choses the love of a plebeian sweetheart rather than a throne.

ARTHUR SHERBURNE HARDY (1847–   ), XIX. 244.

629. The Wind of Destiny (1886), IX. 399. 1. Love. 2. Fate. A young girl meets the same unhappiness in love that befell her prototype in the former generation.

630. PASSE ROSE (1889), IX. 409. 1. Imagination. 2. Love. 3. History. A romantic idyl of the time of Charlemagne telling the love of a madcap girl and a gallant youth.

(HERE MAY FOLLOW 695.)

FRANCES COURTENAY BAYLOR (1848–), XIX. 38.

631. ON BOTH SIDES (1886), II. 370. 1. English and American Society. 2. Character. 3. Humor. A story of Americans living in England, and Englishmen travelling in the United States, in which racial customs and characteristics are contrasted with lively humor.

WILLIAM WALDORF ASTOR (1848–), XIX. 18.

632. SFORZA (1889), I. 352. 1. History. 2. Adventure. A romance in which there figure the historical characters of Ludovico Sforza, the great Duke of Milan, Cæsar Borgia, and the Chevalier Bayard. The hero is a nephew of the Duke.

JOEL CHANDLER HARRIS (1848–1908), XIX. 247.

633. GABRIEL TOLLIVER (1902), X. 66. 1. Youth. 2. Politics. 3. Psychology. 4. Love. A story of Reconstruction days in the South, in which youths and children are the main characters. The delineation of the characters of hero and heroine is the marked feature.

FRANCES HODGSON BURNETT (ENGLAND, 1849–), XIX. 72.

634. THAT LASS O' LOWRIE'S (1876), IV. 185. 1. Mining. 2. Heroism. 4. Love. A "pit girl" in a Lancashire mine saves the life of an engineer by her heroism, and gains his love by her devotion and her study to raise herself to his condition.

635. LITTLE LORD FAUNTLEROY (1886), IV. 195. 1. Youth. 2. Family Love. 3. Benevolence. 4. Humor. An American boy becomes heir to an English title and estate, held by his misanthropic grandfather, and, by thinking the old man a loving, benevolent person and treating him as such, transforms his character to this ideal. The love between the little fellow and his self-sacrificing mother is a charming feature in the story, and a comedy touch is given it by the character study of an aristocracy-hating grocer, who comes to own a shop patronized by nobility.

636. A LADY OF QUALITY (1896), IV. 205. 1. Tragedy. 2. Love. 3. Youth. A tomboy, growing up, marries an old lord, for social position, and, on his death, a young one for love. She spurns the advances of a former suitor, and upon his pressing his attentions, strikes him dead with a loaded whip-handle. Her sister, who secretly loves the murdered man, aids her to make way with the body.

SARAH ORNE JEWETT (1849–), XIX. 275.

637. A COUNTRY DOCTOR (1884), XI. 133. 1. Medicine. 2. Ethics. 3. Semi-Autobiography. A country doctor adopts an orphan girl and

ANALYSIS OF THE WORLD'S STORIES

makes her his professional companion. She refuses a suitor whom she could love if she would, to become a physician. The country doctor is a portrait of the author's father, and the scenes depicted are of her youth, in and near Portsmouth, N. H.

JAMES LANE ALLEN (1849-   ), XIX. 13.

638. SUMMER IN ARCADY: A TALE OF NATURE (1896), I. 207. 1. Youth. 2. Love. An idyl of Kentucky, presenting the frank amorousness of a lad and girl, who are disciplined by the church for dancing.

639. THE CHOIR INVISIBLE (1897), I. 216. 1. Love. 2. Pathos. A story of pioneer days in Kentucky. The hero is saved by the influence of a noble married woman from entanglement with her unworthy niece, who is betrothed to another. He comes to love the aunt, who has made a loveless marriage, and who secretly loves him in return. He is beloved by a good girl, and promises to marry her, telling her the state of his heart. Then his old love is freed by the death of her husband, but honor keeps both from breaking the heart of the hero's betrothed.

CHRISTIAN REID [MRS. FRANCES FISHER TIERNAN] (PRESENT DAY), XIX. 350.

640. MORTON HOUSE (1871), XIV. 1. 1. Melodrama. 2. Southern Life. An English governess in a Southern family (in the United States) meets with many misfortunes through her connection with a villain, which are succeeded, however, by a happy marriage, when the secret of her life is disclosed, relieving her of blame.

ARLO BATES (1850-   ), XIX. 38.

641. A WHEEL OF FIRE (1885), II. 348. 1. Insanity. 2. Love. 3. Tragedy. 4. Psychology. The story of a girl who inherits insanity. She refuses to marry on this account, is over-persuaded by her lover, and goes mad on the day set for her wedding. Her state of mind is described in detail.

EDWARD BELLAMY (1850-1898), XIX. 46.

642. LOOKING BACKWARD (1888), III. I. 1. Social Reform. 2. Imagination. A story of the world regenerated by socialism—the nationalization of all means of production.

643. THE DUKE OF STOCKBRIDGE (1900), III. 12. 1. History. A romance dealing with Shay's Rebellion.

LAFCADIO HEARN (1850-1905), XIX. 254.

644. YOUMA (1890), X. 212. 1. History. 2. Character. 3. Superstition. 4. Tragedy. 5. Heroism. A romance of the negro insurrection in Martinique, in which the character of a Creole negress, a nurse, is presented—her superstition, her loyalty to the white family who own her, and finally her heroic death with a child whom she refused to leave in a burning house.

RUTH McENERY STUART (1850–   ), XIX. 395.

645. CARLOTTA'S INTENDED (1894), XVI. 182.   1. Italian Life and Character. 2. Love.   3. Renunciation.   A crippled Irish shoemaker, in the Italian quarter of New Orleans has loved an Italian girl from childhood. When she is being forced into unwelcome marriage with a rich old Italian, she asks the shoemaker to marry her. They become engaged. Then the girl meets a young musician and loves him. But she is faithful to her troth, till released by the shoemaker who divines the situation. He loses his life by attempting to rescue a kitten from the river.

NATHAN HASKELL DOLE (1852–   ), XIX. 158.

646. NOT ANGELS QUITE (1893), VII. 269.   1. Love.   2. Marriage.   A study of love and marriage, showing how two engaged couples rearranged their pairing in accordance with temperamental affinity.

ROBERT GRANT (1852–   ), XIX. 231.

647. UNLEAVENED BREAD (1900), IX. 209.   1. Character.   2. Society. 3. Politics.   4. Marriage.   5. Ethics.   A woman who desires social success, advances by the divorce of one husband, whom she had neglected, the demise of another, whom she had driven to death, and the moral disintegration of a third, which she had caused by her ambition, to the proud position of wife of a Senator.

FRANCIS MARION CRAWFORD (1854–1909), XIX. 105.

648. MR. ISAACS (1882), VI. 20.   1. Character.   2. Philosophy.   3. Anglo-Indian Life.   4. Love.   5. History.   A character study of a Persian in an Anglo-Indian community. He exhibits athletic prowess and bravery in war (with the Afghans). His English sweetheart dies, and he is comforted by a religious adept of Thibet with the thought that they will be reunited in a subsequent incarnation. An exposition of Hindu philosophy is presented.

649. A ROMAN SINGER (1883), VI. 31.   1. Italian Life and Character. 2. Music.   3. Love.   4. Tragedy.   The love romance of an Italian tenor and the daughter of a German count, whom he is teaching incognito. A jealous woman reveals his secret to the count, and then commits suicide. He is accused of the murder, but is exonerated. His beloved has been spirited away, but she steals away from the man chosen for her husband, and rejoins the tenor.

F. J. STIMSON (1855–   ), XIX. 391.

650. KING NOANETT (1896), XVI. 102.   1. History.   2. Adventure.   3. Self-Sacrifice.   An English Royalist, fleeing in disguise with his daughter from the commonwealth, becomes an Indian chief in New England. They are followed by two lovers of the daughter, each ignorant of the other's affection. These become friends. They fight side by side in

King Philip's war, whose ally the outlawed Englishman has become. Discovering that the object of his friend's quest is that of his own, one of the men eliminates himself by throwing away his life.

SARAH PRATT McLEAN GREENE (1856   ), XIX. 234.

651. CAPE COD FOLKS (1881), IX. 258. 1. New England Life and Character. 2. Love. 3. Tragedy. 4. Humor. The experiences of a school ma'am on Cape Cod, the quaint folk of which are described. The schoolma'am is beloved by a pupil, who dies saving the life of the betrayer of a trusting girl.

HAROLD FREDERIC (1856–1898). XIX. 194.

652. THE DAMNATION OF THERON WARE (1896), IX. 37. 1. Religion. 2. Character. A self-seeking ignorant country minister is taken up, for motives of kindness, by cultured people, one of whom is a lady whom he egotistically thinks is in love with him. He proves himself such a cad that they drop him. He moves West with his neglected wife with the intention of going into real estate and politics. The "business" of a revivalist is described.

CHARLES MAJOR (1856–   ). XIX. 304.

653. DOROTHY VERNON OF HADDON HALL (1902), XII. 149. 1. History. 2. Love. A love romance in which Queen Elizabeth and her courtiers and Mary Queen of Scots are important figures.

MARGARETTA DELAND (1857–   ). XIX. 122.

654. THE AWAKENING OF HELENA RITCHIE (1906), VI. 290. 1. Character. 2. Morality. 3. Adoption. A deserted wife has a lover who visits her in a small town, in the guise of a brother. She adopts an orphan boy, whom she comes greatly to love. This makes her a better woman. Her husband dies. She reveals her character to a young man of the neighborhood, who urges her to marry him; refused, he commits suicide. She then demands that her lover marry her. He wishes to continue the same life elsewhere. For the adopted boy's sake she refuses, and decides to go away alone leaving him in an old doctor's hands. But when she goes she finds the doctor has smuggled the boy along with her.

DUFFIELD OSBORNE (1858–   ). XIX. 333.

655. THE LION'S BROOD (1901), XIII. 127. 1. History. 2. Love. A love romance of the days of the Roman struggle against Hannibal.

WILL N. HARBEN (1858–   ). XIX. 243.

656. ABNER DANIEL (1902), IX. 381. 1. Georgian Character. 2. Business. 3. Humor. A North Georgian farmer enters into a land speculation in which he is saved from ruin at the hands of rascals by the help of a shrewd, humorous ne'er-do-well.

IRVING BACHELLER (1859–   ), XIX. 24.

657. EBEN HOLDEN (1900), II. 24. 1. Character. 2. Youth. 3. History. 4. Journalism. A story in autobiographical form of a journalist, who, as boy and man, had as friend a great-hearted countryman. Horace Greeley is introduced as a character, and the battle of Bull Run forms one of the scenes.

MOLLY ELLIOT SEAWELL (1860–   ), XIX. 369.

658. PAPA BOUCHARD (1901), XV. 188. 1. Comedy. 2. Character. A sketch of French life and character in which the chief personage, a paterfamilias, is involved in comical complications.

WOLCOTT BALESTIER (1861–1891), XIX. 25.

659. BENEFITS FORGOT (1892), II. 35. 1. Western American Life. 2. Love. 3. Family Relations. 4. Mining. 5. Rascality. Troubles in business and love of a generous, hot-headed father and a good son, and a bad son. The scene is in the mining district of Colorado.

HENRY HARLAND (1861–1905), XIX. 245.

660. THE CARDINAL'S SNUFF-BOX (1900), X. 43. 1. Love. 2. Authorship. A cardinal makes use of his snuff-box as a means of reuniting lovers, who have had a misunderstanding due to the man's being a novelist and presumably in love with the original of his heroine.

MARY E. WILKINS-FREEMAN (1862–   ), XIX. 424.

661. JANE FIELD (1892), XVII. 248. 1. Character. 2. Ethics. 3. Religion. A poor New England woman, a religious fanatic, is mistaken for another, and, suppressing the truth, receives an inheritance. At last remorse of conscience causes her to reveal the deception, and to the end of life she remains a monomaniac, repeating her confession to every stranger she meets.

EDITH WHARTON (1862–   ), XIX. 423.

662. THE HOUSE OF MIRTH (1905), XVII. 221. 1. New York Society. 2. Character. 3. Pathos. A fortune-hunting woman in the Four Hundred fails in all her schemes owing to her weakness at the critical moment, which is due to her love for a comparatively poor man. So, while she dies in want and social disgrace, she saves her soul.

AMELIE RIVES [PRINCESS TROUBETZKOY] (1863–   ), XIX. 353.

663. THE QUICK OR THE DEAD (1888), XIV. 88. 1. Ethics. 2. Love. 3. Marriage. The spell of a dead love overcomes the passion of a living one.

JOHN JACOB ASTOR (1864–), XIX. 18.

664. A Journey in Other Worlds (1894), I. 340. 1. Science. 2. Imagination. 3. Adventure. Some Americans, utilizing the apergy of the earth, take a trip in a projectile to Jupiter and Saturn, where they observe strange phases of life and nature.

RICHARD HARDING DAVIS (1864–), XIX. 113.

665. Soldiers of Fortune (1899), VI. 215. 1. South American Life. 2. Adventure. 3. Love. 4. Mining. An American party is involved in a South American revolution. A mining engineer and a yachtsman are rivals for the hand of a society belle, but the revolution brings out the finer character of her younger sister, and the engineer transfers his devotion to her.

PAUL LEICESTER FORD (1865–1902), XIX. 190.

666. The Honorable Peter Stirling (1894), VIII. 411. 1. Politics. 2. Labor. 3. Social Reform. 4. Character. A study of the character of a politician, based on Grover Cleveland's. He becomes boss of the "machine" by earnestly furthering betterment of the condition of the poor. As a militia captain, he risks his life in quelling a strike, and wins a wife by his heroism.

ROBERT WILLIAM CHAMBERS (1865–), XIX. 87.

667. Ashes of Empire (1899), IV. 334. 1. History. 2. Journalism. 3. Love. The love story of two American journalists and two Parisiennes during the siege of Paris.

GEORGE BARR McCUTCHEON (1866–), XIX. 301.

668. Graustark (1900), XII. 96. 1. Adventure. 2. Love. 3. Heroism. A young American meets with strange adventures in a mythical Balkan kingdom, winning the hand of a princess, by his giving himself up to death, though innocent of the murder with which he is charged, for the honor of the kingdom.

BOOTH TARKINGTON (1869–), XIX. 399.

669. The Gentleman from Indiana (1899), XVI. 250. 1. Character. 2. Journalism. 3. Politics. 4. Love. A story of Indiana life and character. A young editor has incurred the enmity of "whitecaps," and these assault him, leaving him senseless. During his slow recovery, a girl who loves him edits the paper and works up a congressional nomination for him, of all of which he is ignorant.

MARY JOHNSTON (1870–), XIX. 277.

670. To Have and to Hold (1890), XI. 149. 1. History. 2. Melodrama. A melodramatic tale of the settlement of Virginia, dealing with the hero's deeds of derring-do among Indians and pirates, with a titled villain, etc.

FRANK NORRIS (1870-1902), XIX. 328.

671. THE PIT (1902), XIII. 46. 1. Business. 2. Love. A romance of love, and a close approach to a tragedy of marriage centering about the wheat pit in Chicago. Love comes back when its rival, money-making, disappears.

WINSTON CHURCHILL (1871–   ), XIX. 94.

672. RICHARD CARVEL (1899), IV. 400. 1. History. 2. Adventure. 3. Love. A romance of American and English history preceding and during the Revolution. The hero in his travels meets distinguished men such as John Paul [Jones], Charles Fox, Horace Walpole, etc. He is victorious in love as in war, discomfiting a villainous rival.

ELLEN GLASGOW (1874–   ), XIX. 208.

673. THE DELIVERANCE (1904), IX. 126. 1. Virginian Life. 2. Character. 3. Crime and its Penalty. 4. Ethics. A scion of an old Virginian family plots to ruin the family of the man who robbed him of his estate. He leads the son astray, until he becomes a parricide. But in the meantime he has learned to love the daughter, who desires to make restitution. Therefore, he gives himself up for the murder of the old man, of which he feels himself morally guilty.

JACK LONDON (1876–   ), XIX. 295.

674. THE SEA-WOLF (1903), XII. 29. 1. Sea-Life. 2. Character. 3. Adventure. 4. Love. A ship-captain, fierce and tyrannical, oppresses his crew and plans to make a girl, picked up from a wreck, his own. He is thwarted by a young sailor who escapes with the girl and marries her.

SWITZERLAND

(HERE MAY FOLLOW 9.)

JOHANN WYSS (1781-1830), XIX. 426.

675. THE SWISS FAMILY ROBINSON (1813), XVII. 268. 1. Adventure. 2. Natural History. A Swiss family are wrecked on a Pacific island. By their ingenuity they utilize the plants and animals of the island, developing a model colony.

(HERE MAY FOLLOW 94.)

RUSSIA

ALEXANDER PUSHKIN (1799-1837), XIX. 346.

676. THE CAPTAIN'S DAUGHTER (1836), XIII. 289. 1. History. 2. Army Life. The hero is a Russian soldier who is condemned as a spy of the pretender Poggatchoff, but saved by Catherine II., by the plea of his sweetheart.

NIKOLAI GOGOL (1809-1852), XIX. 225.

677. DEAD SOULS (1842), IX. 170. 1. Russian Character. 2. Satire.

A satire upon Russian politics and society, in which the rank of a person was conditioned by the number of serfs, or "souls" owned by him. These "souls" are counted from the previous census, serfs dead since that time being reckoned as living. The hero in order to get political preferment goes over the country buying title to these "dead souls." He meets with every type of Russian character, and each is minutely described. But the government gets after him, and, after bitter experiences with courts and prisons, he runs away a physical and financial wreck.

IVAN TURGENIEV (1818–1883), XIX. 411.

678. FATHERS AND SONS (1862), XVII. 85. 1. Character. 2. Politics. 3. Nihilism. The beginning of the clash between the conservative elder generation of Russians, and the radical younger generation is depicted, individual types of each class being presented.

679. SMOKE (1867), XVII. 96. 1. Character. 2. Politics. 3. Nihilism. The second stage of the revolutionary ferment in Russia, where theory is concentrating into a program of action. The author attacks the charlatans among the advanced thinkers.

LYOF TOLSTOY (1828–   ), XIX. 405.

680. WAR AND PEACE (1865), XVI. 433. 1. History. 2. Russian Life and Character. 3. Philosophy. A romance of all phases of Russian life and character in the first quarter of the nineteenth century. Napoleon I., Alexander I., and their generals appear in the story, which in purpose is philosophic history rather than fiction.

681. ANNA KARENINA (1878), XVI. 448. 1. Marriage. 2. Ethics. 3. Tragedy. The heroine is a married woman who has a lover. Though discovered by the husband and forgiven by him, she elopes with the lover. Seeing that he is tiring of her, she kills herself.

682. THE KREUTZER SONATA (1890), XVI. 459. 1. Marriage. 2. Music. 3. Tragedy. A man and wife nag each other into mutual hatred. She meets a violinist, and their common love for music draws them together. The husband becomes madly jealous and kills them.

683. MASTER AND MAN (1895), XVI. 470. 1. Religion. A master and his servant are overtaken in a blizzard. Through an impulse of divine love, the master, formerly cruel and selfish, protects the body of the servant from freezing with his own, which is frozen to death.

684. RESURRECTION (1902), XVI. 479. 1. Social Reform. 2. Religion. A juryman recognizes in a prostitute that is before the bar a former servant he had seduced. Convicted of sin, he accompanies her to Siberia, to which she is exiled, to comfort her. Convinced also that the life of his order of society is contrary to the Gospels, he gives up his lands to the peasants, and finds peace of soul. The woman loves him, but for his sake pretends to love another, and is happy in her renunciation.

SERGIUS STEPNIAK [SERGIUS KRAVCHINSKI] (1852–1895), XIX. 386.

685. THE CAREER OF A NIHILIST (1889), XV. 452. 1. History. 2. Politics. 3. Tragedy. A story of Russian revolutionists in Switzerland and Russia, reaching its climax in an unsuccessful attempt to assassinate the Czar.

SWEDEN

FREDRICKA BREMER (1802–1865), XIX. 63.

686. THE NEIGHBORS (1835), III. 203. 1. Family Life. 2. Love. 3. Melodrama. The story of a wayward son, who repents and is reconciled to his mother, and who marries a girl of his rank, whereupon a servant girl, who is in love with him, attempts to murder his wife, and, being prevented from so doing, commits suicide.

DENMARK

HANS CHRISTIAN ANDERSEN (1805–1875), XIX. 14.

687. O. T. (1836), I. 226. 1. Youth. 2. Crime. 3. Love. A boy and a girl, illegitimate children of a rich man's son, are born in a House of Correction. An inmate, a juggler, tattooes on the boy's arm the letters O. T., meaning House of Correction. The boy and girl are separated; he takes high social position, which the juggler threatens to endanger by exposing his low birth. The juggler attempts to foist his own daughter, a thief, on him as his sister. The real sister is discovered—a cultivated girl, the friend of the hero's sweetheart.

688. THE TWO BARONESSES (1840), I. 236. 1. Youth. 2. Love. The love romance of an illegitimate youth and a foundling girl.

HOLLAND.

EDUARD DOUWES DEKKER (1820–1887), XIX. 120.

689. MAX HAVELAAR (1860), VI. 269. 1. Dutch East Indian Life. 2. Politics. 3. Pathos. An honest official in Java tries to prevent abuses of the natives, and is persecuted and finally dismissed and impoverished because of his humane efforts.

MAARTEN MAARTENS [J. M. W. VAN DER POORTEN-SCHWARTZ] (1858–   ), XIX. 300.

690. GOD'S FOOL (1892), XII. 84. 1. Character. 2. Blindness. 3. Crime. 4. Self-Sacrifice. 5. Philanthropy. A rich man, a blind deaf mute, attempting to do good to his fellows, is made a dupe by one of his twin step-brothers, and strikes him. The other step-brother, coming in and discovering his twin's infamy, gets into an altercation with him, and kills him. The mute falsely confesses the crime to save the murderer.

HUNGARY.

MAURUS JÓKAI (1825-1904), XIX. 279.

691. TIMAR'S TWO WORLDS (1888), XI. 171. 1. Hungarian Life and Character. 2. Ethics. A Hungarian boat-captain on the Danube unwittingly comes into possession of a treasure which he knows belongs to a girl, the ward of a dishonest promoter. He converts it to his use, and becomes wealthy by trading. He successfully plots the ruin of the promoter, and saves the ward from poverty and indignity. Though in love with another, in gratitude she marries the captain. But he is leading a double life, having a peasant wife, who knows him only as a poor captain. Discovering his acknowledged wife's love for another, and her loyalty to himself, he retires to his "other world" under circumstances that indicate his death, leaving the supposed widow in possession of his wealth, and free to marry her lover.

NORWAY

BJÖRNSTJERNE BJÖRNSON (1832-   ), XIX. 50.

692. ARNE (1858), III. 66. 1. Peasant Life. 2. Youth. 3. Love. An idyllic tale of a youth, his mother, and his sweetheart, written in a poetic vein, and containing original songs.

693. THE FISHER-MAIDEN (1868), III. 77. 1. The Theatre. 2. Peasant Life. 3. Youth. 4. Love. The story of a girl possessed of an artistic temperament, who lost her lover through coquetry, and who found her vocation on the stage, her lover becoming her friend, and finally the sweetheart of her girl companion. Her patron, a village pastor, who opposed the theatre, is brought to see its usefulness in supplying an outlet for such emotional natures as the girl's.

JONAS LIE (1833-   ), XIX. 294.

694. THE PILOT AND HIS WIFE (1874), XII. 20. 1. Jealousy. 2. Sea Life. A pilot becomes suspicious of his wife's relations with another man previous to his marrage, and becomes morose and cruel. His doubts are cleared at last, he repents and, though fallen in fortune, husband and wife become supremely happy.

HJALMAR HJORTH BOYESEN (1848-1895), XIX. 62.

695. GUNNAR (1874), III. 172. 1. Peasant Life. 2. Love. 3. Youth. 4. Sport. The love story of a poor boy and a well-to-do girl, whose mother opposes the match, but is won over to it by the son of her old lover. Norwegian customs and sports, dances, songs, ski-races, are described.

ALEXANDER KJELLAND (1849–   ), XIX. 286.

696. ELSA (1882), XI, 345.   1. Satire.   2. Psychology.   3. Social Reform. The story of a foundling, whom "organized charity" allows to develop into a prostitute.

CANADA.
(HERE MAY FOLLOW 394.)

JAMES DE MILLE (1833–1880), XIX. 126.

697. CORD AND CREESE (1867), VI. 344.   1. East Indian Life and Character. 2. Melodrama.   3. Crime and its Detection.   4. Maritime Adventure. A wild tale of assassination (by thugs of India), conspiracy, discovery of buried treasure at sea, and detection of villainy.

CHARLES G. D. ROBERTS (1860–   ), XIX. 353.

698. A SISTER TO EVANGELINE (1898), XIV. 98.   1. History.   2. Love. A romance of the expulsion of the French from Acadie, in which the English are justified in the act.

RALPH CONNOR (1860–   ), XIX. 48.

699. THE SKY PILOT (1899), VI. 83.   1. Frontier Life.   2. Religion. A preacher wins a frontier settlement, individually and *en masse* to religion by his fine, healthy character and good fellowship.

GILBERT PARKER (1862–   ), XIX. 335.

700. THE RIGHT OF WAY (1901), XIII. 157.   1. Melodrama.   2. Law. 3. Religion. A lawyer saves a guilty man from death, and wins a wife thereby. In remorse, he attempts suicide; and is saved by the murderer, though with loss of memory. He recovers, but keeps his existence a secret; becoming a tailor. He is an atheist, and his employer, a religious fanatic, steals a holy metal cross from the church, and with it brands him, sleeping. The village postmistress loves him, and saves him from the charge of church desecration. He saves her from the burning church, and dies of his wounds, converted from his atheism.

AUSTRALIA.
(HERE MAY FOLLOW 423 AND 424.)

BRAZIL.

SYLVIO DINARTE [ALFRED D'ESCRAGNOLLE TAUNAY] (1843–   ), XIX. 152.

701. INNOCENCIA (1838), VII. 123.   1. South American Life and Customs. 2. Love.   3. Tragedy.   A doctor loves a girl betrothed to another.

She returns his love, but betrothal in South America is as binding as marriage, and the lovers die, the man assassinated by the fiancé, and the woman of a broken heart.

POLAND.

HENRYK SIENKIEWICZ (1846–   ), XIX. 375.

702. QUO VADIS (1895), XV. 266. 1. History. 2. Religion. A tale of early Christian martyrs in Rome under Nero. Saints Peter and Paul, and Petronius, the Roman "Arbiter Elegantiarum" appear in the story.

MODERN GREECE.

(HERE MAY FOLLOW 162.)

SOUTH AFRICA.

(HERE MAY FOLLOW 421.)

(HERE MAY FOLLOW 488 AND 489.)

OLIVE SCHREINER (1862–   ), XIX. 362.

703. THE STORY OF AN AFRICAN FARM (1883), XIV. 232. 1. Religion. 2. Youth. 3. Character. 4. Pathos. Two English girls and a German boy are reared on a Boer farm. They have strange religious impulses, out of harmony with the life about them, and, as they grow older, tragedy results from this incompatibility.

INDEXES

1. PROPER NAMES

		PAGE
I. Persons	. . . . .	109
II. Places .	. . . . .	114

2. SUBJECTS 116

INDEX OF PROPER NAMES

I. PERSONS

NOTE: Numbers refer to analyses on pages 3 to 105

Achilles: Greek hero, 1
Agamemnon: Greek hero, 1
Æneas: Trojan hero, 1, 2
Alaric, the Goth, 266
Alcott, Louisa M., American author, touch of autobiography, 599. (See also AUTHORS, page iii.)
Aldrich, Thomas Bailey, American author, touch of autobiography, 603. (See also AUTHORS, page iii.)
Alençon, Duke of, 48
Alexander I., Czar of Russia, 680
Alexius Comnenus, Emperor of Constantinople, 253
Allen, Ethan, general in American Revolution, 552
Angelo, Michael, Italian artist, 266
Anjou, Duke of, 49, 50
Anne of Austria, Queen of Louis XIII., 19, 43, 47
Aphrodite, Greek goddess, 1
Ares, Greek god, 1
Arnold, Benedict, general in American Revolution, 552
Arnold, Dr. Thomas, English schoolmaster, 399
Aram, Eugene, an English murderer, 288
Argyle, Duke of, intercedes for childmurderess, 235
Athene, Greek goddess, 1

Bailly, French revolutionist, 60
Balsamo, Joseph, name of Cagliostro, q. v.
Bayard, Chevalier, French knight, 632
Bernadotte, marshal of Napoleon I., 186
Bismarck, German statesman, 320
Blucher, German general, 186
Boabdil, King of Granada, 294
Boccaccio, Italian author, touch of autobiography, 150. (See also AUTHORS, page iii.)
Bolingbroke, English statesman, 200, 286

Borgia, Cæsar, murderous Italian prince, 153, 573, 632
Borrow, English author, touch of autobiography, 309. (See also AUTHORS, page iii.)
Bright, John, English statesman, 316
Brissot, French revolutionist 60,
Brontë, Charlotte, English author, touch of autobiography, 375. (See also AUTHORS, page iii.)
Brougham, Lord, English statesman, 310
Bruce, Robert, King of Scotland, 254, 263
Buckingham, Duke of, 43
Bungay, Friar, a necromancer, 297
Burgundy, Duke of, war with Louis XI., 245; war with Swiss, 252
Burdett-Coutts, Lady, English philanthropist, 310, 320
Burr, Aaron, American politician, 572
Bussy d'Ambois, 49, 50
Bute, Marquis of, English statesman, 319
Byron, Lord, English poet, 315

Cagliostro, French charlatan, 54, 55, 56, 59, 60
Calvin, religious reformer, 35
Canonche, Indian chief, 528
Capel, Monsignore, prelate, 319
Carlyle, Thomas, English author, 367
Caroline, English queen, 235
Catherine II., Empress of Russia, 262, 676
Catherine de' Medicis, French queen, 35, 48, 51
Cenci, The, noble Italian family, 154
Charles I., King of England, 45, 237, 258
Charles II., King of England, restored to throne, 47; satirized, 200; conspiracy against, 244; escape, 250
Charles IX., King of France, 35, 48
Charles Stuart, pretender to English throne, 229, 247

PROPER NAMES—PERSONS

Chesterfield, Lord, English author, 342
Christ, see Jesus
Cid, The, Spanish champion, 142
Cinq-Mars, Marquis of, 19
Claverhouse, Colonel, persecutor of Scotch Covenanters, 233
Cleveland, Grover, President of United States, original of hero in 666
Cobden, Richard, English statesman, 320
Colbert, French statesman, 47
Coligny, French admiral, 48, 51
Colonna, Italian noble family in feud with Orsini family, 291
Columbus, Christopher, discoverer of America, 266
Condé, French general, 47
Condorcet, French statesman, 60
Cooper, James Fenimore, American author, touch of autobiography, 534. (See also AUTHORS, page iii.)
Coppée, François, French author, touches of autobiography, 128. (See also AUTHORS, page iii.)
Craven, Charles, Colonial governor of South Carolina, 560
Cromwell, English Protector, 45, 250

Danton, French statesman, 60, 130
Dantzic, Duchess of, Napoleon I.'s laundress, 131
Darnley, Lord, husband of Mary of Scotland, 398
David, Prince royal of Scotland, in Crusade, 249
David, son of Robert III., of Scotland, 251
Derby, Earl of, English statesman, 320
Desmoulins, French revolutionist, 296
De Witt, execution of the brothers, 57
Dickens, Charles, English author, 320; touch of autobiography, 345. (See also AUTHORS, page iii.)
Diomed, Greek hero, 1
Disraeli, Benjamin, English author and statesman, touches of autobiography, 310, 316, 319, 320. (See also AUTHORS, page iii.)
Douglas, James, Scots earl, 254
Du Barry, Madame, mistress of Louis XV., 54, 55, 56
Dudevant, Madame, see Sand, George
Du Guesclin, French knight, 494
Dumas, René, French revolutionist, 296
Dumouriez, French general, 60

Edward the Confessor, King of England, 299
Edward I., King of England, 254
Edward III., English king, 494
Edward, the Black Prince, English warrior, 494
Edward IV., King of England, 297
Elizabeth, English queen, 242, 653
Epicurus, Græco-Roman philosopher, 264, 443
Erasmus, Dutch theologian, 358
Esterhazy, Prince, European diplomat, 310

Fairfax, Lord, English nobleman, 54
Ferdinand and Isabella, sovereigns of Spain, 294
Fern, Fanny, touch of autobiography, 569 (See also AUTHORS, page iii.)
Fouquet, chief of police, troubles with Louis XIV.
Fox, Charles, English statesman, 672
Francis II., King of France, 35, 51
Frederick the Great, King of Prussia, 181
Fuller, Margaret, American author, 557

Gama, Vasco de, Portuguese explorer, 197
Gambetta, French statesman, original of character in 118
Garibaldi, Italian patriot, 319
Gilbert, Sir Humphrey, English sea-captain, 383
Gladstone, W. E. English statesman, 316
Godwin, Earl, English king-maker, 299
Goethe, German author, touch of autobiography, 168. (See also AUTHORS.)
Goffe, English pirate, 239
Gonzaga, Marie de, in Conspiracy of Cinq-Mars, 19
Gortschakoff, Prince, Russian diplomat, 310
Greeley, Horace, American editor, 657
Grenville, Sir Richard, English sea-captain, 383
Guillotine, Dr., inventor of beheading machine, 59
Guise, Duke of, 48, 50, 51
Gustavus Adolphus, King of Sweden, 237

Hamilcar, Carthagenian general, 82
Hannibal, Carthagenian general, 655

PROPER NAMES—PERSONS

Harcourt, Lord, English statesman, 320
Harold, English King, 299, 386
Hawkins, Sir John, English sea-captain, 383
Hawthorne, Nathaniel, American author, touch of autobiography, 557. (See also AUTHORS, page iii.)
Haydn, German musical composer, 69
Hector, Trojan hero, 1
Henry II., King of France, 51
Henry III., King of France, 48, 49, 50, 480
Henry IV., King of France, 35, 48, 49, 50, 480
Henry VI., King of England, 297
Henry VIII., King of England, 180
Henrietta Maria, Queen of Charles I., 47
Hera, Greek goddess, 1
Hereward, Saxon (English) patriot, 253, 386
Heriot, George, banker of James I., 243
Hertford, Marquis of, English statesman, 310, 316
Honorius, Emperor of Rome, 402
Hook, Theodore, English wit, 310, 316
Hopkins, Dr., New England clergyman, 572
Hortense, Queen of Belgium, 320
Hypatia, Alexandrian philosopher, 382
Humboldt, Baron von, German scientist, 316
Hunt, Leigh, English poet, 346

Ireton, general in English Revolution, 281
Isabella, equal consort of Ferdinand of Spain, 294

James I., King of England, 243
James II., King of England, satirized, 200; war in Ireland, 279
James Stuart, pretender to English throne, 232
Jeffrey, Judge, presides at "Bloody Assizes," 411
Jesus Christ, 73, 266, 591
Joan of Arc, French patriot, 461
Jewett, Sarah Orne, American author, touch of autobiography, 637. (See also AUTHORS, page iii.)
John, English King, 238
Jones, Paul, sea hero of American Revolution, 54, 523, 672
Joseph, Father, French prelate, associate of Richelieu, 19

Josephine, Empress, Queen of Napoleon I., pardons prisoner, 20
Juno: see Hera, 1

Kali, Hindu goddess of murder, 268
Kirke, English general in Ireland, 270

Lafayette, Marquis de, French statesman, 58, 59, 60
Lamartine, French author and statesman; his own love story, 17. (See also AUTHORS, page iii.)
Landor, Walter Savage, English author, 346
Laud, Archbishop, English prelate, 433
Launay, de, governor of the Bastile, 58
Lavater, physiognomist, 54
Leicester, Earl of, murders wife, 242
Leonardo da Vinci, Italian artist, 174
Lespinasse, Julie de, French literary woman, 476
Liszt, musical composer, 32
Loti, Pierre, touch of autobiography, 138. (See also AUTHORS, page iii.)
Louis XII., King of France, 63, 245
Louis XIII., King of France, 19, 43
Louis XIV., King of France, 45, 47, 80
Louis XV., King of France, 54, 55
Louis XVI., King of France, 55, 56, 58, 59, 60, 130, 182
Louis XVII., "Lost Dauphin" of France, 182, 628
Lucas, Vrain, literary forger, original of character in 121
Luther, Martin, religious reformer, 266, 418
Lyly, English dramatist, 240

Macgregor, Rob Roy, Highland chief, 234
Manning, Cardinal, English prelate, 319
Marat, French revolutionist, 55, 59, 60
Margaret of Anjou, Queen of Henry VI. of England, 297
Marguerite of Valois, Queen of Henry IV. of France, 48
Maria Theresa, Queen of Austria, 181
Marie Antoinette, Queen of Louis XVI. of France, 53, 54, 55, 56, 58, 59, 60, 130, 182
Mars: see Ares, 1
Mary, Queen of Scots, 35, 51, 241, 398, 653

PROPER NAMES—PERSONS

Mazarin, Cardinal, French premier, 45, 47.
Mendelssohn-Bartholdy, Felix, musical composer, original of hero, 422
Menelaus, Greek hero, 1
Mesmer, discoverer of hypnotism, 56
Metternich, Austrian diplomat, 186
Michelangelo, Italian artist, 266
Minerva, see Athene, 1
Mirabeau, French revolutionist, 59
Mohammed, founder of Moslem religion, 266
Moncey, marshal of Napoleon I., 147
Monk, English general, 47
Monmouth, Duke of, rebellion of, 233, 411
Montgomery, Count, accidentally kills Henry II. of France in tourney, 51
Montrose, Earl of, Scots general, 237
Moreau, marshal of Napoleon I., 186
Murger, Henri, French author, touch of autobiography, 86. (See also AUTHORS, page iii.)
Musset, Alfred de, French author, his relations with George Sand, 75. (See also AUTHORS, page iii.)

Napoleon I., French emperor, at Waterloo, 16; pardons prisoner, 20; 23; idealized, 25; empire of, 36; rise of, 60; soldier of, 91, 474; his laundress, 131; campaign in Germany, 177, 186, 271; oppressor of Toussaint, 282; Irish soldier and, 323, 324; Waterloo, 331; in Russia, 680
Napoleon III., French emperor, 91
Narbonne, French statesman, 60
Necker, French statesman, 58
Nelson, Horatio, English sea-captain, 539
Nero, Roman emperor, 266
Ney, marshal of Napoleon I., 186
Nicot, Doctor, French revolutionist, 296
Norton, Mrs. Caroline, poetess, original of heroine, 417

Orleans, Duke of, French nobleman, 59
Orsini, Italian noble family in feud with Colonna family, 291
Ouida, Anglo-French author, touch of autobiography, 445. (See also AUTHORS, page iii.)

Palafox, Spanish general, 147
Palmerston, Lord, English statesman, 320

Paris, Trojan hero, 1
Parr, Catherine, last wife of Henry VIII., 180
Parton, Sarah Payson, see Fern, Fanny
Paul, Saint, in Rome, 702
Pausanius, Regent of Sparta, 307
Peter the Great, Czar of Russia, 584
Peter, Saint, Roman martyr, 702
Petrarch, Italian poet, 266
Petronius, "arbiter elegantiarum" of Rome, 702
Philip IV. of Spain, Gil Blas procures mistress for, 6
Philip, King, American Indian chief, 528, 650
Planche, Gustave, French critic, 32
Poggatchoff, Russian pretender, 676
Porpora, musical composer, 69

Rameses II., King of Egypt, 193
Reni, Guido, Italian artist, 174
Reynard, Earl, mediæval noble, 166
Richard I., English king, 238, 249, 503
Richard III., as Duke of Gloucester, 297
Richelieu, French premier, in Conspiracy of Cinq-Mars, 19; character in novel, 43
Rienzi, Roman patriot, 291
Robert III., King of Scotland, 251
Robespierre, French revolutionist, 59, 60, 296
Robin Hood, English outlaw, 238
Rohan, Cardinal de, French prelate, 56
Roland, Madame, French noblewoman, 60
Rothschild, Baron de, European financier, 316, 318, 320
Rouget de l'Isle, author of Marseillaise, 60, 130
Rousseau, French author, 54, 55. (See also AUTHORS, page iii.)

Saladin, Saracen paladin, 249
Sand, George, French author, character in fiction, 32, 75. (See also AUTHORS, page iii.)
Sarsfield, Patrick, general of James II., in Ireland, 279
Savonarola, Italian religious reformer, 390, 573
Scanderbeg, Albanian hero, 614
Schomberg, general of William III., in Ireland, 279
Sforza, Ludovico, duke of Milan, 632
Shelley, Percy Bysshe, English poet, 315.

PROPER NAMES—PERSONS 113

Sheppard, Jack, English criminal, 322
Smith, Goldwin, English publicist, 319
Smollett, English author, touch of autobiography, 212. (See also AUTHORS, page iii.)
Solomon, King, mines in Africa, 488
Staël, De, Madame, French author, 58, 60. (See also AUTHORS, page iii.)
Stern, Daniel, character in novel, 32
Sterne, Laurence, English author, touches of autobiography, 209, 210. (See also AUTHORS, page iii.)
St. Just, French revolutionist, 59
St. Maur, general in English Revolution, 281
Swedenborg, Emanuel, Swedish mystic, 24, 28, 54

Taylor, Bayard, American author, touch of autobiography, 587. (See also AUTHORS, page iii.)
Temple, Charlotte, woman buried in Trinity churchyard, New York, 517
Thackeray, William Makepeace, English author, 320. (See also AUTHORS, page iii.)
Titus, Roman emperor, 266
Torquemada, Spanish inquisitor, 294
Toussaint L'Ouverture, liberator of San Domingo, 282

Venus, see Aphrodite, 1
Vergniaud, French statesman, 60

Viaud, Louis M. J., see Loti, Pierre
Voltaire, French philosopher, 54, 181. (See also AUTHORS, page iii.)

Wallace, William, Scots patriot, 263
Walpole, Horace, English statesman, 672. (See also AUTHORS, page iii.)
Warwick, Earl of, English king-maker, 297
Washington, George, American patriot, 335, 521
Wellington, Lord, English general and statesman, 310
Wilberforce, Bishop, English philanthropist, 315
Wilde, Oscar, English author, satire on, 511. (See also AUTHORS, page iii.)
William the Conqueror, King of England, 299, 386
William III., English king, 200; war in Ireland, 279
William of Nassau, Dutch patriot, 57
Willis, N. P., American author, 569
Wiseman, Cardinal, English prelate, 320
Woffington, Margaret, English actress, 353
Wolfe, English general, 335

Ximenes, Cardinal, 54

Zanoni, name of Cagliostro, q. v.

II. PLACES

NOTE: Numbers refer to analyses on pages 3 to 105

Abyssinia, 208
Algiers, 113, 444, 512
Arabia, 3, 223, 303
Australia, gold discovered, 355; transportation to, 361; bush-ranging, 423

Babylon, philosopher of, 7
Belgium, Waterloo, 331; school in, 375
Bourbon, Isle of, 68
Brazil, life in, 701

Canada, novels of, 697–700
Carthage, ancient, 82
Corsica, island of, 46

Denmark, novels of, 687, 688

East Indies, life in Java, 689; Malaysia, 697
Egypt, ancient, 193, 264, 382
England, see Great Britain
Europe, Americans in, 562, 619, 620. (See also particular countries, e.g., France.)

Florence, 390
France, novels of, 5–141; execution of Louis XVI., 182; Englishman travels through, 210; English soldier in, 212; Scotsman in, 245, 461; French Revolution, 296, 349; siege of Paris, 306, 667; scene of novel, 356, 658; Latin Quarter of Paris, 428, 435; Normandy, 442, 627; soldier of, 480; time of Charlemagne, 630

Germany, novels of, 166–196; English soldier in, 212; Frenchman in, 271; robber, 280; the Reformation in, 418; mythical state of, 467, 506; life in, 475; drinking-bout in, 531
Great Britain, novels of, 198–516; **French soldiers in England, 43, 45, 47; Guernsey, Isle of, 65; vices of English aristocracy, 66; Italian-English romance, 156; court of Henry VIII., 180; society in, 520;** Americans in England, 631, 672; Lancashire, 634; American lad in England, 635; scene of story, 636; court of Elizabeth, 653
Greece, ancient, 1, 307; modern, bandits in, 92
Guernsey, isle of, 65

Holland, novels of, 689–690; tulip mania in, 57; execution of the De Witts, 57; soldier's adventures in, 80; scene of novel, 358; life in, 608
Hungary, life in, 691

Iceland, the Eddas, 4; outlaw, 431
India, worship of Kali, 268; theft of sacred jewel, 406; Sepoy rebellion, 465; Persian in, 648.
Ireland, novels of, 227, 228, 276, 278, 279, 308, 323, 324, 329
Italy, novels of, 149–165; travel in, 12; Scotsman in, 12; priest's adventures in, 16; life in, 17; Englishman in, 210, 312, 315; revolution in, 319; Florence, 390; Venice, 532; Rome, 558, 649; Sorrento, 572; Milan, 632

Japan, life in, 138

Lancashire, 634
Lisbon, earthquake, 618
London, see Great Britain

Man, island of, 477
Mauritius, island of, 10
Milan, 632
Moscow, 584

Normandy, 442, 627
Norway, novels of, 692–696; Norse cosmogony, 4; human monster of, 62

Orient, the, life in, 79, 194. (See also particular countries, e.g., Arabia.)

Pacific Islands, see Sea, the
Palestine 149, 248, 249, 266, 313, 318, 503, 591
Panama, proposed canal, 602
Paris, see France

114

Persia, 267
Poland, patriot of, 262
Portugal, story of, 197; Lisbon earthquake, 618

Rome, ancient, 2, 266, 290, 402, 443, 655, 702; mediæval, 291; modern, 558, 649
Russia, novels of, 676–685; Englishman in, 507; Moscow, 584

Sahara, The, "the garden of Allah," 512
Scotland, novels of, 229–237, 239–241, 244, 247, 251, 254, 263, 354, 398, 408, 456, 457, 469, 470, 472, 473, 474, 491, 498, 499, 500
Sea, The, wreck, 10, 459, 470, sailor salves wreck, 65; Vasco da Gama, 197; attack on Carthagena, 212; sea-dogs, 213; pirate, 239; sea-fight in War of 1812, 272; life at sea, 274; castaways, 361, 430, 546, 600; defeat of the Armada, 383; yachting, 395, 457; treasure island, 466; sea-port life, 508; fishing off Newfoundland, 514; sea-fights, 523, 526, 529, 538, 539, 542, 543; pursuit, 534; race, 549; Antarctic exploration, 563; Pacific islands, 578; whaling, 579; tyranny of captain, 674; Norwegian pilot, 694

Sorrento, 572
Soudan, The, war in, 513
South Africa, novel of, 703; diamond mines, 364; gold mines, 488; immortal princess, 489
South America, siege of Carthagena, 212; proposed Panama canal, 602; mining in, 665; life in Brazil, 701. (See also West Indies.)
Spain, novels of, 142–148; Spanish life, 6, 61; Inquisition in, 268; siege of Granada, 294; English soldiers in, 494; American Indian in, 536
Sweden, life in, 686
Switzerland, Englishman in, 252; life in, 453

Turkey, Constantinople, 253, 614

United States of America, novels of, 577–674; early Louisiana, 8; settlement of New York State, 265; Virginia, 332, 335; Englishman in, 343; Adirondacks, 469; Utah, 493

Venice, 532

West Indies, slave life in, 198; castaway in, 199; Negro insurrection in San Domingo, 282; and in Martinique, 644

INDEX OF SUBJECTS

NOTE: Numbers refer to analyses on pages 3 to 105

Abduction, see Kidnapping.

Adoption, merchant and wife adopt girl, 132; squire adopts foundling, 206; merchant adopts foundling, 339; miser adopts foundling, 389; deserted wife adopts orphan, 654

Adultery, ethics of, 149; woman shields clergyman, the father of her child, 553. (See also Courtesan and Mistress in CHARACTER; Seduction.)

Adventures, picaresque, 6, 143, 145; of soldier-priest, 16; of comrades-in-arms, 43, 45, 47; of band of guards, 49, 50; of convict, 64; sailor's fight with octopus, 65; of wandering Jew, 73, 266; of girl disguised as a cavalier, 76; of strolling player, 77; of soldier, 80; of mad knight, 144, 215; of wife disguised as a man, 149; of Vasco da Gama, 197; of castaway sailor, 199; of poor young man, 204; of foundling, 206; of sentimental philosopher, 210; of ship's surgeon, 212; of political aspirant, 213; of sharper, 214, 329; of servant on tour, 216; of madman, 218; of English officer in Scotland, 229; of mercenary soldier, 237, 245; chivalric, 238, 249, 253; of Englishman in Switzerland, 252; of young Persian, 267; of madman, 268; of British sailor in War of 1812, 272; of youth seeking father, 273; of young naval officer, 274; of boy Crusoe, 275; of Cavalier in English Revolution, 281; of wandering man among gypsies, 309; of mystics in Orient, 313, 318; of Jack Sheppard, 322; of Irish soldier, 323, 324; of runaway scholar, 358; of English sea-captains, 383; of yeoman among outlaws, 411; of Scotch monk in France, 461; expedition after buried treasure, 466, 488; of kidnapped heir and outlaw, 470, 472; of boy in War of Roses, 471; of French nobleman of Henry IV., 480; of English troop in Spain, 494; mediæval romance, 502; of Richard I., 503; of Oxford student in English Revolution, 505; of Englishman in mythical Balkan country, 506; in Antarctic, 563; of sailor among Pacific cannibals, 578; trip to planets, 664; of journalists in siege of Paris, 667; of American, in Balkan state, 668. (See also Adventurer, Aeronauts, Bandit, Explorer, Hero, Indian, Knight, Outlaw, Patriot, Pioneer, Pirate, Rascal, Sailor, Soldier, Spy, in CHARACTER.)

Æronautics, trip to planets, 664

Æstheticism, evils of, 490; satire of 511

Agnosticism, see Religion

Alchemy, the Wandering Jew, 266

Allegory, see Symbolism

Altruism, allegory of, 79, 175. (See also Heroism, Patriotism, Philanthropy, Self-Sacrifice.)

Ambition, of priest, 15, 16; of conspirator, 19; of woman, 23; of place-hunter, 26; of poet, 30; of politician, 41, 118, 136, 310, 311, 316, 317, 319, 320; of soldier, 80; of lion-hunter, 113; of millionaire, 116; social, 121, 409, 476, 626, 647, 662; thwarted, 128, 165; of journalist, 136; of student, 165; of author, 485, 501, 569; renounced, 594; of preacher, 652; of actress, 693

Anarchy, evils of, 112

Anger, at image of saint by girl whose prayer he had not answered, 141; at lover by woman he had saved from rascal, 176

Animals, sailor fights with octopus, 65; rational horses, 200; knight fights with tiger and orang-utan, 253; boy Crusoe tames seal, 275; half-witted boy pets raven, 342; fairy tale of water animals, 385; wolf-boy masters forest beasts, 515; dog saves life, 532; prenatal influence on girl of snake, 566; magic whale, 579

Antiquarianism, see Antiquary in CHARACTER

Archæology, mediæval Paris, 63; ancient Carthage, 82; ancient Egypt, 264; Pompeii, 290
Architecture, Notre Dame Cathedral, 63; "Golden House" of Nero, 592
Aristocracy, see Aristocrat and Nobleman in CHARACTER; Society
Army, see Soldier in CHARACTER; Chivalry, Combat, History
Arson, by insane adventuress, 440
Art, see Artist in CHARACTER; Architecture, Painting, Sculpture
Assassination, see Murder in DEATH
Astrology, Catherine de Medici's devotion to, 35; astrologer casts hero's horoscope, 230; youth dabbles in, 289
Astronomy, voyage among planets, 664
Atheism, see Religion
Athletics and Sports, at school, 399; archery, 400; man brutalized by, 407; skating, 475, 608; horse-racing, 478; prize-fighting, 483; sleigh-riding on ice, 541; boat-racing, 568; chariot-racing 591; polo, 648; ski-racing, 695
Authors, of stories in the *Authors' Digest;* see page iii
Authorship, plagiarism, 485, 496; bookstore clerk becomes poet, 501; career of Jewish authoress, 510; career of writer, 569, 587; love troubles of novelist due to his heroine, 660. (See also Author, Journalist and Poet in CHARACTER; Literature.)
Autobiography, see Alcott, Louisa M.; Aldrich, Thomas Bailey; Boccaccio; Borrow, George; Brontë, Charlotte; Cooper, James Fenimore; Coppée, François; Dickens, Charles; Disraeli, Benjamin; Fern, Fanny; Goethe; Jewett, Sarah Orne; Lamartine; Loti, Pierre; Murger, Henri; Musset, Alfred de; Ouida; Smollett, Tobias; Sterne, Laurence; Taylor, Bayard; in AUTHORS, page iii
Avarice, greed for gold, 26, 389, 437, 452; for land, 109; pretended, 351; (See also Ambition, Miser and Usurer in CHARACTER.)

Banking, bandit as bank depositor, 92; bank robbery, 97; Heriot, goldsmith of James I., 243; bank failure, 333; embezzlement, 359. (See also Usurer in CHARACTER.)

Bankruptcy, see Business
Betting, see Gambling
Bigamy, see Marriage
Biography, see INDEX OF PROPER NAMES: I. PERSONS on page 109; AUTHORS on page iii; and HISTORY
Blackmail, of banker's wife, 97
Blindness, blind heroine, 66; loyal subject blinds prince by accident, 117; blind man recovering sight is repelled by sight of ugly sweetheart, 148; girl attends to blind man wronged by her grandfather, 187; blind heroine of Pompeii, 290; blind witness of murder, 462; blind man throws himself into fight to be killed, 513; blind deaf-mute, 690
Botany, prisoner grows a flower, 20; magic flower ingredient of elixir of life, 559. (See also Botanist in CHARACTER.)
Burlesque, see Satire
Business, rivalry, 30, 450; career, 31, 37, 185, 190, 412; bankruptcy, 114; promotion, 300; ruined merchant, 344; mill-owner ruined by American embargo, 374; congregation of shop-keepers, 419; boy, magically changed to man, plays hob with business, 484; satire of, 533; crook, 586; railroad promotion, 611; evils of trusts, 623; land speculation, 656; wheat speculation, 671. (See also Banking, Clerk, Grocer, Inventor, Manufacturer, Promoter, Usurer, in CHARACTER; Forgery; Invention; Manufacture; Wealth.)

Cannibalism, of savages, 199, 578

CHARACTER

[Listed by professions and moral characteristics, such as Doctor, Adventuress. For proper names of characters in this and other fiction, see Vol. XX. of AUTHORS' DIGEST.]

Actress, courtesan, 107; stage-dancer as governess, 336, 352; wife of Highland laird, 457; friend of artist girl, 601; stage-smitten girl, 693
Actor, 77, 168
Adventurer, 42, 80, 267; rascally, 143, 145; among gipsies, 309; military, 323, 324; Irish, 329; wandering youth, 358; sailor among Pacific islanders, 578; Swiss family

on Pacific island, 675. (See also Explorer.)
Adventuress, 45, 331, 344; redeemed, 404; bigamous, 405, 440, 476, 502
Adulteress, shields lover, 553
Æronauts, 664
Æsthete, 490, 511
Agitator, labor, 381, 623; New York anti-rent rioters, 545. (See also Reformer.)
Antiquary, 40, 231
Aristocracy, poor, 421; English, 520, 631; American, 626, 631; grandfather, 635; "Four Hundred," 662. (See also Nobleman.)
Artist, 36, 183; theatrical, 353, 354, 442; tricked by magic, 487; blind, 513; colony in Rome, 558; prefers true friendship of actress to selfish love of doctor, 601; loved by model, 627
Astrologer, 230
Atheist, 34; persecuted, 492; converted, 700
Athlete, murderous, 407
Author, rising, 345, 346; Transcendentalists as farmers, 557; saves country girl, 587; in love, 660. (See also Journalist, Poet.)
Authoress, rivals, 32, 417; Jewish, 510; marries editor, 569
Avenger, 44, 46, 271

Bachelor, 400, 662
Bandit, professional, 92; heroic, 287
Banker, of King James I., 243
Barber, 486
Barmaid, entraps author, 496
Beggar, 231
Bigamist, 405, 440, 690
Blind girl, in love with disfigured man, 66; man, witnesses murder, 462; artist, 513; deaf mute confesses murder to save step-brother, 690
Boston types, 607
Botanist, 92
Boy, see Youth
Braggart, 113
Broker, wheat, 671
Brother, avenging, 46, 246; loyal, 295; spendthrift and his good brother, 335; wayward, 377, 388; brothers at enmity, 469

Castaway, 430, 459, 546; widows, 600
Charlatan, 54, 55, 56, 59, 60, 439
Child, see Girl, Youth

Clergyman, simple-minded, 217; grafting, 367, 368; curate, 396, 419; murderous, 497; young Scotch, in love with gipsy, 499; father of illegitimate girl, 500; shielded by his fellow in adultery, 555; New England, 571; opinion of, changed by girl, 582; selfish missionary, 600; circuit rider, 605; revivalist, 652; opposes theatre, 693; frontier preacher, 699
Clerk, loyal, 31, 185; disloyal, 222; bookstore, becomes poet, 501
Conspirator, 53
Convict, see Criminal
Coquette, 18, 332, 396; punished, 446
Courtesan, 8, 119; noble-souled, 88, 102; congenital, 89; actress, 107; Algerian, 113; Japanese, 138; self-sacrificing, 684; victim of organized charity, 696. (See also Mistress.)
Coward, 495
Creole types, 621, 644
Criminal, repentant, 64, 190, 322; grateful, 350; converted, 355; innocent convict, 361; merchant, 361; in business and politics, 586; juggler, 687. (See also Bandit, Forger, Murderer, Poisoner, Rascal, Robber, Villain.)

Deaf-mute, blind, confesses murder to save step-brother, 690
Daughter, assassin's, 292; adopted, 350; outlaw's, 411; perjurer's, 472
Detective, 42, 64, 97, 98, 352, 406, 493, 625
Dilettante, marries heiress, 620
Doctor, country, 25, 637, 654; murderous, 95; patriot, 156; swindling, 337, 364; woman, 365; saved from snakes by girl, 566; mulatto, 594; selfish, 601; in Civil War, 613; Brazilian, 701
Doctrinaire, democratic, 274
Drunkard, 105, 565, 622
Dupe, 42, 121, 116, 279; blind, 690
Dutchman, New York, 519

Egotist, 22, 30, 83, 85, 121, 124, 416, 533
Employer, see Manufacturer, Master, Merchant
Employee, see Clerk, Mechanic, Servant, Working Girl, Workingman
English types, county gentry, 256–261; eccentric, 270; aristocracy, 314, 319; village, 327; boarding

house, 334; girl in America, 427; rustics, 448–451
Euphuist, 240
Evangelist, woman, 120, 387
Executioner, noble, 532
Exile, Polish, 262
Explorer, of underworld, 304; Elizabethan, 383; companion of Columbus, 536; in Antarctic, 563; among the planets, 664

Family, poor, 157, 159, 617; Lutheran, 418; French, 658; Swiss, 675
Fanatic, religious, 120, 433, 499, 700
Farmer, Transcendentalists, 557; farm girl, 580; farmer saves fugitive slave, 589; land-speculating, 656
Father, self-sacrificing, 27; unhappy, 122; brutal, 149; incestuous, 154; conscience-stricken, 163; loving, 333; swindling, 337; stern, 344, 347, 415; scapegrace, 379, 426; blackleg, killed by son, 423; wicked, 454; judge sentences son, 473; becomes boy, 484; hotheaded, 659; Russian, 678
Faun, reincarnation of, 558
Forger, woman, 369; literary, 485, 496, 574, 583
Foundling, squire adopts, 206, 273; rescued from thieves, 339; adopted by miser, 389; exploited by juggler, 687; girl, 688; prostitute, 696
French, see Parisian
Friend, false, 445, 501; man resigns wife to, 504; journalist and artist, 513; changes to lover, 622

Gambler, 36; titled, 248; aged, 341; 365; princess, 507, 605; Western, 612
Gipsy, Spanish, 61; French, 63; girl, 125; English types, 309; girl, in love with minister, 499
Girl, self-sacrificing, 148, 196, 347, 488, 505; religious, 34; romantic, 38; noble-born working girl, 78; self-willed, 87, 269; schoolgirl, 101, 585; wronged girl, 126, 202, 246, 345, 517; husband-seeking, 139, 662; heroine of siege, 147; repentant, 187, 189; dependent, 188, 409; untutored, clever, 221; terrorstricken, 224, 225; blind, 290; gambler's granddaughter, 341; fisher girl, 354; orphan, 377; wayward, 378; light-minded, 387; disciple of Savonarola, 390; philanthropic, 395; saves life of bachelor, 400; intellectual, 421, 501; clever, 426; English, in America, 427; victimized, 454; Australian girls, 460; disguised as boy, 471, 505; with prenatal affinity to snakes, 566; flower girl, 574; farm girl, 580; changes views of clergyman, 582; saved by journalist, 587; waif adopted by lamplighter, 588; Knickerbocker, 597; nurse in Civil War, 613; unsophisticated American, abroad, 619; coal-mining lass, 346; tomboy, 636; orphan adopted by doctor, 637; Italian American, 645; Acadian, 698; loves atheist, 700. (See also Woman.)
Goldsmith, philanthropic, 243
Gothic types, 382, 402
Governess, in love with husband of maniac, 373, 396, 640
Greek types, 382
Grocer, aristocrat-hating, 635
Guardian, faithful, 248, 567; eccentric, 351; rival guardians, 357
Gunmaker, 584

Heir, mean, 326; kidnapped, 470, 472
Heiress, suspicious, 84, 357, 370; proud, 374; romantic, 421; in disguise, 516; saved by guardian, 567; American, marries, foreign dilettante, 620
Hero, 1, 2, 3; dissolute, 349; Saxon, 386; Icelandic, 431; heroes of Sepoy rebellion, 465; Albanian, 614; Revolutionary, 672
Heroine of siege, 147
Highland chief, 234; laird, 457
Horticulturists, rival, 57
Humorist, Scotch, 498
Hunchback, 63
Husband, forgiving, 123; mismated, 165, 169, 482; reconciled, 195; jealous, 360, 392; self-righteous, 372; of maniac, 373; reunited with wife, 379; rascal, 390, 573; selfish, 413; attempts suicide, 602
Hypnotist, 408. (See also Charlatan.)
Hypocrite, 343

Idealist, thwarted, 128
Idler, attractive, 174; sleeper, 518; shrewd, 656
Impostor, 94
Indian, American, 13, 14; chiefs, 522, 525, 527, 535, 536, 537, 540, 541,

545, 548, 553, 560, 561; in California, 596; in Virginia, 670
Inventor, ruined, 30; pirate, 93; wizard, 297; mechanic hounded by trade-union, 362; robbed by capitalist, 581
Insane, gentleman crazed by chivalry, 144; bride, 236, 268, 641; half-witted waif, 340; victims of private insane asylum, 359; wife, 373; villain, 409; blank-minded woman recovers memory of murder, 462; Continental soldiers, 524; Indian-slaying Quaker, 553; lunatic wrongly accused of murder, 556; brother goes mad over burying sister alive, 564; imbecile prince, 628; religious monomaniac, 661
Irish, blundering, servant, 278; lass in America, 394
Italian-American types, 645

Journalist, 33; scheming, 136, 337; rising, 345, 463; chum of artist, 513; saves country girl, 587; rascal, 606, 657; in siege of Paris, 667; Indiana, 669
Jew, prince, 313, 318; exposes villain, 355; types, 382; Zionists, 393; quarter in London, 510; hero, 591
Jewess, succoring, 238; converted, 294; authoress, 510
Judge, sentences son, 473; wicked, 556
Juggler, 687

King, bad, 117, 180; 245, 250, 297, 299; sentimental, 467, 503; czar, 584. (See also Prince.)
King-maker, 297
Knight, 142, 238, 249, 253, 254, 494, good and bad combat, 502; German barons, 531; Italian, 632

Lamplighter, adopts waif, 588
Laundress, ennobled, 131
Lawyer, sharping, 326, 346; judge, 473; wicked, 556; convicts capitalist of robbing inventor, 581; becomes tailor, 700
Libertine, 68, 71, 83, 118, 201, 202, 217, 283, 284, 345, 387, 394, 451, 490, 574, 618, 654, 681, 682
Librarian, 420
Lover, mediæval lovers, 5, 630; faithful girl, 5, 330, 604; boy and girl lovers, 10, 471, 500, 505, 593, 633, 638, 687, 688, 692, 693, 695, 703;

neurotic, 75; opposing affinities, 127; forsworn woman, 151, 572; world-weary lovers, 164; hopeless lover, 167; fate-mastered, 170; young ladies, 256–261; lovers separated by religion, 276, 279; eccentric, 305; broken-hearted woman, 305; predestined lovers, 380, 629; jealous, 397; royal lovers, 398; proud lover, 409; runaway lovers, 415; dream lovers, 434; lovers separated by false friend, 445; self-sacrificing, 554, 571, 668; girl saves lover's life, 610; censorious, 619; dying, 620; lover of temperance reformer, 622; lovers change partners, 646; Roman lovers, 655; lover slain by fiancé, 701. (See also LOVE.)
Lunatic, see Insane
Lutheran, family, 418

Magician, 303
Man, selfish (see Egotist); passionate, 70; honorable, 176, 203, 606, 615, 639; strong-willed, 283; under a cloud, 285; rich, 343; good, but unattractive, 370; brave, 408; suspicious, 410; self-made, 412, 432, 607; innocent, accused of murder, 452; forgiving, 458; with double personality, 468; English traveler impersonates a king, 506; marries mistress, 618; subject to lapses of memory, 624
Maniac, see Insane
Manufacturer, indomitable, 31; ruined, 374; self-made man, 412, 432, 607; in strike, 610
Martyrs, early Christian, 702
Master, blundering, 338; repentant, 683
Mechanic, smith, 251; oppressed by trade-union, 347, 363; marries evangelist, 387; gunmaker, 584. (See also Inventor, Workingman.)
Merchant, ambitious for son, 344. (See also Manufacturer.)
Mesmerist, see Hypnotist
Miner, 108; diamond, 364; Western, 612, 659; English coal-miners, 634; engineer, 665
Miser, 147; weaver, 389; robbed by son, 437
Mistress, penitent, 379; marries lover, 618. (See also Courtesan.)
Monster, blood-drinking, 62; created by man, 277
Mountebank, disfigured, 66

Mother, repentant, 106; bad, 115; strong-minded, 132; loving, 330, 635; forges deed for son's sake, 369; wise, 378; crippled, 498; grief at son's death, 571; opposes marriage of son to quadroon, 589
Murderer, poisoner, 153; remorseful, 222, 477; educated, 288; accidental, of mistress, 307; moral, of wife, 308; moral, 558; caught through his love, 625; of twin brother, 690; Malay thugs, 697; fiancé kills rival, 701. (See also Murder in DEATH.)
Murderess, 298, 328; would-be, repents, 559. (See also Murder in DEATH.)
Musician, 40, 146, 422, 475, 479, 564; prima donna, 69, 365; broken-down singer, 613; tenor, 649; paramour, 682
Mystic, 24, 509; Rosicrucian, 296

Negro, hero, 3; lovers, 198; liberator, 282; self-sacrificing girl, 488; African queen of immortal youth, 489; slaves, 570, 571; fugitive quadroon saved by farmer, 589; aids Union men, 590; doctor, 594; Ku-Klux outrages, 609; Creole nurse, 644
New England, types, 571, 573, 575, Boston, 607; Cape Cod folks, 651, 661
New York types, 519, 586, 592
Nurse, in Civil War, 613
Nobleman, infamous, 342; French, marries Quakeress, 595

Official, honest colonial, 689
Outlaw, 238; Highland, 470, 472; Englishman, becomes Indian chief, 650
Opium-eater, 352
Oriental types, 249, Hindus recover stolen amulet, 406

Pacific islanders, 578
Parents, loveless, 135; melancholy, 491. (See also Father, Mother.)
Parisian types, boarding house, 27; bohemians, 86; Latin Quarter, 102, 306, 428, 435; family, 658; grisettes, 667
Patriot, 252, 263, 575. (See also Hero.)
Peasant, man, 109; woman, 179; girl, the model of artist, 627; Russian, 683
Perjurer, 472

Persian theosophist, 648
Philanthropist, goldsmith, 243; blind, 690
Philosopher, Babylonian, 7; pagan woman, 382; Transcendentalists, 557; theosophist, 648. (See also Mystic.)
Photographer, exonerates lunatic of murder, 556
Pioneer, American, 265, 522, 525, 527, 528, 535, 537, 540, 541, 544, 545, 548, 551, 552, 553, 605, 639
Pirate, 93, 239, 466, 526, 529, 542, 546, 670
Poet, selfish, 30; poets, 315; labor agitator, 381; book-store clerk, 501
Policeman, son kills blackleg father, 423
Politician, 41, 118, 623; carpet-bagger, 609; reform, 666, 669. (See also Statesman.)
Priest, wicked, 15, 16, 255, 286, 424; benevolent, 64; in love, 104; tempted, 160; anchorite, 194; ex-monk marries, 512; monks in drinking bout, 531; cardinal, 660
Prig, reformed, 401
Prince, unfortunate, 182; Jewish, 313, 318; "Lost Dauphin," 628
Prisoner, 20; for debt, 348; French, in Scotland, 474
Prizefighter, loved by intellectual woman, 483
Promoter, 300, 421; visionary, 611
Prostitute, see Courtesan

Quakeress, marries French nobleman, 595
Queen, 35, 48, 117, 241, 242; unfortunate, 321; brilliant, 467; African, of immortal youth, 489; Balkan, loved by English traveller, 506, 668; English and Scotch rivals, 653; Russian, 676

Rascal, 6, 94, 143, 145, 149, 227, 300, 325, 343, 370, 390, 464, 573, 615
Recluse, deformed, 232
Reformer, social, 391, 438, 642, 684; temperance, 622
Regicide, of Charles I., 528
Renegade, Englishman becomes Indian chief, 650
Revolutionist, 58; Russian, 678, 679, 685. (See also HISTORY.)
Robber, London thieves, 339; thieves of sacred Oriental jewel, 406. (See also Bandit.)

Roman types, 402; convert to Christianity, 443; rival of Jew, 591
Rosicrucian, 296
Russian types, 676–685

Sailor, indomitable, 65; resourceful, 199; keeps log in War of 1812, 272; officer, 274; lover, 357; mutineers, 459; retired sea-captain, 508; rich boy as common, 514; pilot, 523, 694; sea-captain, 534, 547; admirals, 538; searchers for treasure, 549; among savages, 578; whaler, 579; rescues former sweetheart, 618; tyrannical sea-captain, 674; Hungarian boat captain, 691. (See also Pirate.)
Scholar, absent-minded, 300
Schoolmaster, 161; cruel, 340; despised, by heiress, 374; man and woman, 376; Yankee, 519
Schoolmistress, 376, 384
Scotch types, 580
Servant, chaste girl, 201; loyal, 236; blundering, 278; clever, 338; devout, 408; girl, 478; avenges master, 576; becomes mistress, 618; saved by master, 683; murderous girl, 686
Shoemaker, self-sacrificing, 645
Sister, faithful, 235, 356, 636; sisters in love, 257, 371, 388; Australian, 460; subject of her brother's magic, 509; four sisters, 599; rivals in love, 607, 665
Smith, brave, 251
Social functionary, poor, 429
Soldier, comrades-in-arms, 43, 45, 47; humane, 67; private, 110; English in Scotland, 229; religious, 233; mercenary, 237; self-sacrificing, 444; German officer, 455; Scotch, in mediæval France, 461; heroes of Sepoy rebellion, 465; French gentleman, 480; student, 505; British in American Revolution, 524, 559; Continental, 559, 560, 561, 672; Russian, 676
Son, cruel, 137; avenging, 135; noble, 228, 454; thoughtless, 330; good, 337, 429, 659; policeman, kills blackleg father, 423; rascal, 437, 659; sentenced to death by father, 473; loving boy, 635; Russian, 678; wayward, 686
Southern (U. S.) types, visionary promoter, 611; poor, proud family, 617, 633; Kentucky, 639; Georgia, 656
Spendthrift, 335

Spy, female, 21; in American Revolution, 521
Squire, simple-minded, 144
Statesman, ruined by woman, 162; young, 316, 317; premier, 320. (See also Politician.)
Step-mother, wicked, 441
Subject, loyal, 250
Swiss types, 453; family, 675

Theosophist, Persian, 648
Thief, see Bandit, Robber
Transcendentalists as farmers, 557
Traveller, 312, 562
Tyrant, doge of Venice, 530

Usurer, 340, 341

Ventriloquist, 325
Villain, 218, 293, 302, 355, 365, 576, 640, 697; seducer, 71, 574; revengeful suitor, 379; sacrilegious, 394; villains and victims, 403; hypnotist, 408; insane, 409; monster, 425; Borgia, 572; capitalist robs inventor, 581; libertine pursues fugitive quadroon, 589; titled, 670; repentant, 673; step-brother of mute, 690. (See also Criminal, Rascal.)

Ward, 343; neglected, 344
Wife, tempted, 68; unfaithful, 81, 114, 134, 150, 372, 681, 682; cruel, 133; mismated, 169, 482; reconciled, 195, 379; "child-wife" and "soul-mate," 345; suspected, 356; deceiving, 363; extravagant, 364; disguised as governess of her children, 366; of rascal, 390; noble, 413; jealous, 447; abused, 456; free lover, 481; intellectual, of prize-fighter, 483; unwitting bigamist, 504; of ex-monk, 512; shrew, 518; disguised, follows husband to sea, 547; adopts child of husband's mistress, 573; separated from husband by memory of early love, 598; gives her blood to restore husband to life, 602; of rascally journalist, 606; spurns divorce, 615; ambitious, 647; deserted, 654
Witch, 52, 239, 279
Woman, ambitious, 23; self-sacrificing, 26, 639; perfect, 29; revengeful, 39, 50; strong-minded, 76; selfish, 92, 533; unhappy in love, 129; wicked, 192, 502; loyal peasant, 179; noble, 332; eccentric rich old,

350, 452; good aunt, 377; widow of unknown antecedents, 397; wicked stepmother, 441; vivandière, 444; crippled Scotchwoman, 498; innocent, convicted of murder, 550; inspires murder, 558; repents of contemplated murder, 559; buried alive, 564; college, saves youth from burning, 568; religious, 577; widows as castaways, 600; loves dead man, 663. (See also Actress, Authoress, Coquette, Daughter, Evangelist, Gipsy, Girl, Governess, Heiress, Jewess, Laundress, Lover, Mistress, Mother, Murderess, Nurse, Quakeress, Queen, Servant, Sister, Wife, Witch, Working-girl.)
Woman-hater, 365
Woodsman, rescues persecuted inventor, 581; befriends boy, 657
Working-girl, noble-born, 78; laundress, 131; loves employer, 610. (See also Servant.)
Workingman, honest, 74; strikers, 610. (See also Farmer, Mechanic, Peasant, Servant.)

Yachtsman, 395, 665
Yeoman, 411
Youth, brave, 5; ambitious, 37, 310, 311; proud, 100; boy Crusoe, 257; influenced by women, 289, 332; spirited, 340, 343; half-witted, 340, 342; dying, 344; aristocratic, ruins poor girl, 345; aids convict, 350; wandering, 358; chimney-sweep, 385; schoolboys, 399; college, 414; kidnapped heir, 470, 472; boy suddenly becomes man, 484; beautiful but vicious, 490; rich boy as common sailor, 514; wolf-boy, 515; with antipathy to young women, 568; impish, 603, 616; foundlings, 687; Norwegian, 692, 693, 695; children on Boer farm, 703. (See also Lover, Man.)

Zionists, 393.

Charity, see Philanthropy
Chastity, woman resists outlaw, 70; princess risks virtue to save city, 82; girl chaste in soul though not in body, 102; of tempted wife, 149; of tempted anchorite, 194; of tempted servant girl, 201; of tempted young man, 204; of Irish emigrant lass, 394; equal duty of man and woman to be chaste, 451, 553, 684
Chemistry, drug changes man to villain, 468; girl studies, 613
Child-bearing, advantages of, 111; purpose of marriage, 134, 135; obstetrics, 209
Childhood, see Girl and Youth in CHARACTER
Chivalry, the Cid, 142; satire of, 144, 215; mediæval feuds in Italy, 152; in mediæval Great Britain, 238, 251, 254; Crusades, 238, 248, 249, 253; War of Roses, 471; French nobleman under Henry IV., 480; English troop in Spain, 494; mediæval romance, 502; Richard I., 503. (See also History.)
Christianity, see Religion
Church, The, see Religion
Combat, sailor's fight with octopus, 65; knightly, 152, 153, 155, 238, 248, 249, 251, 253, 254; knight's fight with tiger and orang-utan, 253; mediæval feuds, 291; pugilism, 309, 483; outlaw father kills policeman son, 423; outlaw fights ghost, 431; mayor fights rival in love, 450; seekers for buried treasure fight pirates, 466; naval, 523, 526, 529, 538, 539, 542, 543; Indian, 525, 527, 528, 535, 537, 540, 548, 561, 670; timber-stealer fights surveyor, 544; South American revolution, 655. (See also History.)
Comedy, coquette fixes her escapades on friend, 18; heiress makes love to poet, who sends his secretary to impersonate him, 38; girl disguised as cavalier, 76; escapades of Parisian students, 86; man falls in love with his grandchild, 91; boastful lion-hunter, 113; prayer of girl for husband strangely granted, 141; demented knight-errant, 144; heiress disguised as man enters monastery, 158; young man resists seduction, 204; servant conceals poverty of master, 236; young naval officer attempts to practice "equal rights" on shipboard, 274; boarding house, 334, 453; widower marries stage-dancer, 336; guardian pretends to be avaricious to cure money-worshiping ward (girl), 351; actress poses as portrait to confound art critics, 353; proud woman found to have been cook, 354; woman wins resisting

bachelor, 400; college pranks and vacation love-making, 414; rich woman tests heirs by disguising herself as poor, 452; boy and father magically exchange places, 484; statue of Venus comes to life and makes love to barber, 486; statue of god of mischief plays hob in artist's studio, 487; sea-captain, attempting to get his son "crimped," is crimped himself, 508; man after sleeping twenty years, finds marvellous changes in village, 518; lover scares off rival by pretending to be headless horseman, 519; man too busy to make love at right time, finds woman too busy when he does take time, 533; widows run boarding house on deserted island, 600; old aunt supports railroad promoter who thinks he is the benefactor, 611; *enfant terrible* as Cupid, 616; multifarious uses of opera cloak in poor aristocratic family, 617; aristocrat-hating grocer is patronized by nobility, 635; cardinal uses snuff-box to reconcile lovers, 660

Comradeship, see Friendship

Conjugal Relations, see Husband and Wife, in CHARACTER; Marriage

Conscience, perverted, 95. (See also Repentance.)

Coquetry, see Coquette in Character

Cosmogony, Norse, 4

Crime, satire of exaltation of criminals, 200, 328, 329; career of Jack Sheppard, 322. (See also Arson; Criminal in CHARACTER; Murder in DEATH; Forgery.)

Crime, detection of, 7, 42, 56, 64, 90, 95, 97, 98, 222, 352, 355, 403, 404, 405, 406, 407, 462, 493, 497, 527, 532, 550, 574, 581, 604, 625, 697

Cruelty, toward husband by wife, 23, 481, 602, 647; toward child by mother, 23, 106, 115; toward man by beloved, 25, 32, 84, 189, 350, 374; toward woman by beloved, 26, 33, 148, 475, 490, 601; toward father by daughters, 27, 122; persecution of girls by relatives, 34, 409; toward poor relation, 39, 40; persecution of ex-convict, 64; mountebanks maim foundling, 66; toward convicts, 72, 355, 684; toward hospital patients, 72; toward brother by sister, 87; toward captives by bandit, 92; toward man by mistress, 119, 162; toward man by wife, 133; toward wife by husband, 136, 171, 329, 372, 397, 403, 407, 451, 456; toward mother by son, 137; toward brother by brother, 137; toward daughter by father, 149 (4), 426; torture, 154; of Inquisition, 268; toward child by father, 163, 344, 347; toward dependent girl by woman, 188; toward negroes, 198, 384, 540, 571, 589, 609; persecution of vicar, 217; toward girl by outlaws, 224, 225; toward foundling in workhouse, 339; toward nephew by uncle, 340, 470; toward waif by schoolmaster, 340; toward old man and grandchild by usurer, 341; toward the insane, 359; toward adopted boy, 380; mob tears woman to pieces, 382; toward sister by brother, 388, 569; toward man by cousin, 401; toward son by father, 415, 473; toward ward by guardian, 425, 471; toward poor boy, 432; toward his victim by hypnotist, 435; toward girl by stepmother, 441, 703; toward mother-in-law, by woman, 449; toward castaways by mutineers, 459; toward child by human fiend, 468; toward good brother by bad, 469; toward old man become schoolboy, 484; toward Indians by whites, 540, 541, 553, 596; toward fellow heirs by judge, 556; bereaved mother charges God with, 571; toward inventor by capitalist, 581; toward Southern Unionists, 590; outrages of "white-caps," 669; of sea-captain, 674; abuses of Javanese by Dutch officials, 689; toward wayward girl by organized charity, 696; religious fanatic brands atheist, 700; ancient Christian martyrs, 702. (See also Infidelity, Marital; Jealousy; Revenge.)

Dancing, church opposes, 638; Norwegian, 695

DEATH

Personification of, 172

Accidental, in wreck, 10; in hunting, 11; of Henry II., in tourney, 51; child drowns, 169; Shelley drowns, 315; usurer drowned, 341; maniac wife burned, 373; brother and sister drown, 388; forger burned, 403; bad man entombed alive in tree,

425; heroic husband drowned, 442; wife drowns with paramour, 449; husband and wife drown, 457; man buried alive, 469; repentant murderer dies saving life, 477; negro girl gives up life to save white explorers, 488; princess with gift of youth perishes in magical flame, 489; magical death of murderer, 490; of duellist, 495; electrical adept killed by lightning, 509; of ruffian, 554; woman buried alive, 564; madman buried under falling house, 564; of sailors in whaling, 579; girl entombed alive in secret chamber, 624; child burns to death, 644; shoemaker drowns in rescuing kitten, 645; sailor perishes in saving life, 651; master and servant freeze to death, 683; converted atheist burned to death in rescuing holy relic, 700

Execution of murderous priest, 15; of woman spy, 21, 43; of Charles I., 45; of Marie Antoinette, 54, 60, 130, 182; of De Witt brothers of Holland, 57; of Louis XVI., 60, 130, 182; invention of guillotine, 59; of witch, 63; of humane general for treason, 67; hanged man resuscitated, 91; of murderers of Count Cenci, 154; of thief, 205, 322; of murderer, 222; of William Wallace, 263; of Jesus Christ, 266; of Eugene Aram, 288; of victims of French Revolution, 296, 349; of Lady Jane Grey, 321; murderess, 328, 451; of Savonarola, 390; of Christian martyrs, 443, 702; character of executioner, 532

In Combat, Hector, 1; of knights, 153; in duel, 46, 71, 87, 189, 202, 218, 264, 474; of soldier, 99, 429; of rioter, 317; outlaw done to death by ghost, 431; blind man killed in battle, 513; of lunatic and simpleton in Revolutionary War, 524; of Indian chief, 525; of admiral in sea-fight, 538; of red-coat in Revolution, 559; of lover in Civil War, 575

Murder, victim of priest, 15, 16; husband executes traitorous wife, 43; assassination of Bussy d'Amboise, 49; assassination of Henry III., 50; lover kills gypsy, 61; husband kills wife to save her from becoming prostitute, 89; mysterious, 90, 97, 342, 352, 493, 625; doctor kills usurer, 95; of seducer, 123; 473; mother kills bad son-in-law, 132; father kills daughter's paramour, 150; assassination in feuds, 152; of Count Cenci, 154; fairy wife kills mortal husband, 171; father kills child, 218; mother kills child, 235, 387; bride kills husband, 236; Earl of Leicester murders wife, 242; of villain, 248; assassination of Duke of Burgundy, 252; murderous monk carried away by Devil, 255; son kills those who had maltreated his parents, 271; man-monster kills his creator, 277; of gambler, 284; assassination of Rienzi, 291; villains assassinate lady, 292; maniac kills assassin, 293; Jew kills daughter, a Christian convert, 294; murderess poisons son by mistake, 238; Englishman murders Arabian sorcerer, 303; Pausanias slays mistress by mistake, 307; husband causes secret wife to be slain, 308; thief kills mistress, 339; mob assassinates Hypatia, 382; assassination of Lord Darnley, 398; husband kills wife's double, 403; secret society kills traitor, 403; of villainous husband, 419; outlaw kills policeman, his son, 423; son murders traducer of mother, 434; lover kills rival, 448; wife kills her betrayer, 451; of miser, 452; blind man witnesses a murder, 462; man kills his cousin, 477; man kills painter of his portrait, 490; of Mormon, 493; clergyman kills father of girl he seduced, 497; of emigrant, 527; of betrothed man, 532; Indian kills insulter, 540, 541; timber thief kills surveyor, 544; mad Quaker massacres Indians, 553; Italian and American artist (woman) murder man, 558; drunkard commits murder, 565; servant kills master's enemy, 576; mulatto doctor assassinated, 594; man killed by strikers, 604; wife kills would-be seducer, 636; parricide, 673; husband kills wife and her seducer, 682; fratricide, 690; assassination by East Indian thugs, 697; fiancé kills lover of betrothed, 701

Non-violent, of courtesan, 8, 88, 102; of lover, 10, 13, 66, 128, 148, 156, 159, 170, 219, 305, 380, 430, 446, 481, 505, 536, 554, 620, 663, 701; of self-indulgent man, 22; of melancholy bereaved sister, 87; of consumptive courtesan, 88; of child, 106, 163, 293, 341, 344, 491, 570; of millionaire, 116; of gipsy girl, 125; of mother, 128, 420, 491; of priest, 160; of preacher and wife, 178; of king's mistress, 179; of recluse, 188; of wronged girl, 202, 246, 517; of bride of Wallace, 263; of wife in love with paramour, 283; of Jewish "Prince of the Captivity," 313; of Byron, 315; of false heir in debtor's prison, 326; of father, 333; of child wife, 345; of estranged wife, 366; of penitent mistress, 379; of labor agitator, 381; of unfaithful husband, 390, 573; of jealous husband, 392; of drunken husband, 397, 454; of victim of insolence, 401; of hated husband, 404; of shocked wife, 415; of hypnotist and his victim, 435; of mayor, his wife, and his rival's wife, 450; bad wife, 475; of author, 485; murderous clergyman, dies in pulpit, 497; of shrew, 518; of lost daughter, 528; wicked judge is stricken dead, 556; of girl cured of prenatal evil, 566; of poor young husband, 569; of old man charged with murder, 574; of Indians maltreated by whites, 596; of worthless husband, 615; of American girl abroad, 619; of aged husband of young wife, 636; of unloved husband, 639; of insane bride, 641; of English sweetheart of Persian adept, 648; of husband of deserted wife, 654; of reformed fortune-hunting girl, 662

Suicide, lover, 65, 66, 104, 149, 164, 167, 490, 559, 627, 654; of man who had convicted friend of treason, 67; of wife of slain man, 71; of unfaithful wife, 81, 103; race suicide, 111; of ruined man, 114; of husband of religious fanatic, 120; of Academician, 121; husband of dead wife, 128; of governess and father of drowned child, 169; of madman, 268; of wicked father, 340, 574; of would-be parricide, 343; of seduced girl, 345; of adventuress, 405; of lover of supposed thief, 406; of man with double personality, 468; suicide-pact, 495; husband makes way with himself to leave wife free to marry another, 504; mulatto nurse perishes with child in burning house, 644; husband driven to death by bad wife, 647; of jealous woman, 649; of suitor, to give free field to friend, his rival, 650; of wife neglected by paramour, 681; of murderous, jealous servant-girl, 686

Deception, coquette blames her escapades on friend, 18; secretary impersonates poet, 38; woman disguised as man, 52, 76, 149; low-born Jew pretends to be Hungarian noble, 94; self-deception, 113; man wins wagers by stratagem, 149 (2); exiled lover returns in disguise, 149 (3); heiress becomes companion to blind man, 187; subject impersonates Charles I., 250; false father, 269, 325; wife deceives husband as to paternity of child, 363; runaway wife returns in disguise to be governess of child, 366; woman robbed of inheritance becomes adventuress and marries heir, 404; middle-aged adventuress becomes young in looks by arts of "beauty doctor," 405; mother poses as maiden, 420; heiress poses as poor girl, 421, 516; adventuress commits arson to conceal bigamy, 440; rich woman tests heirs by disguising herself as poor, 452; wife disguises herself as twin brother, 481; criminal clergyman by disguise throws crime on friend, 497; lovers tricked at tryst, 500; girl escapes in disguise as boy, 504; double of king saves him by impersonation, 506; lover scares rival by assuming rôle of headless horseman, 519; mistaken identity, 520; wife follows husband to sea in disguise, 547; mad Quaker murders Indians in guise of spirit, 553; lover takes service with seducer to unmask him, 574; woman impersonates another to receive inheritance, 661; thief foists daughter on boy as his sister, 687; "double life." 691. (See also Dupe in CHARACTER; Infidelity, Marital.)

Deformity, man-monster, 62; hunchback bell-ringer, 63; disfigured mountebank, 66; desiccated man with broken ear, 91; dwarf (girl) loves blind man, 148; dwarf recluse, 232; dwarf lover, 265; crippled mother, 498

Destiny, see Fate

Detection of Crime, see Crime, Detection of
Disaster, Financial, see Ruin
Disaster, Moral, see Ruin
Disaster, physical, maritime, see Sea, the; volcanic explosion, 170, 290; burning building, 67, 373, 440, 644, 700; flood, 388; fall of house, 564; earthquake at Lisbon, 618
Disgrace, see Ruin
Disguise, see Deception
Divination, by witch, 52, 239, 279; Cagliostro foretells fate of Marie Antoinette, 54; by dreams, 150
Divorce, see Marriage
Dreams, divination by, 150; of travel, 312; living in, 434
Drunkenness, see Temperance
Duel, 8, 46, 71, 87, 133, 189, 202, 207, 218, 236, 246, 285, 415, 474, 527. (Cf. Combat.)

Earthquake, Pompeii, 290; Lisbon, 618
Economics, study of, defeated by love, 165; communism, 557. (See also Business, Social Reform, Wealth.)
Education, advantage of, to laborer, 74; sentimental, 83; Italian schoolmaster, 161; of boy on philosophical principles, 209; treatise on, 220; traveler teaches assassin's daughter, 292; abuses of private schools, 340; runaway wife returns in disguise to be governess of child, 366; English teacher's experiences in Belgian school, 375, 376; home, 377, 378; childish lessons in natural history and morals, 385; at Rugby, 399; moral education of young man, 408, 415; student life in Paris, 428; of the poor, 438; of women, 481; man becomes schoolboy, 484; spoiled rich boy made man of on fishing boat, 514; guardian watches over moral development of ward, 567; pit girl raises herself by study, 634. (See also Scholar, Schoolmaster, and Schoolmistress in CHARACTER.)
Egotism, see Selfishness
Electricity, represented as divine power, 509
Embezzlement, see Theft
Emigration, Irish, 394
Engineering, Panama Canal proposed, 602
Escape, see Rescue

Ethics, priest shields criminal, 64; general commits treason to save life, 67; princess risks virtue to save city, 82; sister exposes immoral brother, causing his death, 87; ethics of bandit, 92; doctor murders man who proposes murder to him, 95; girl chaste in soul though not in body, 102; ethics of marriage, 134, 135, 169, 481; virtuous man tortures his mother and her bastard son, 137; ethics of adultery, 149 (3), 476; woman absolved of vow of virginity, 151; ethics of murder, 163, 308; ethics of suicide, 164, 167; worship of criminals, 205, 328, 329; employee denounces kind master as murderer, 222; avenger kills relative of his beloved, 271; man creates human monster who destroys him, 277; woman lies to save sister, 356; wife deceives husband to circumvent villain, 363; governess refuses to marry husband of maniac wife, 373; daughter conceals mother's theft, 384; prig's intolerance of cousin's frailties causes his death, 401; woman marries man to secure property rightfully hers, 404; Hindu priests recover their property by crime, 406; woman tricks her betrayer into marriage, 407; policeman fights criminal father, 423; son takes on himself crime of which he believes father is guilty, 429; son kills mother's traducer, 434; equal duty of man and woman to be chaste, 451, 553, 684; allegory of good and evil natures in one man, 468, 490; judge condemns son to death, 473; ethics of marriage, 481, 482; ethics of plagiarism, 485; man fails to fulfill suicide pact, 495; sinning preacher denounces sin, 497; ex-monk breaks vow of celibacy, 512; ethics of property in land, 544, 545, 684; ethics of property in man, 570, 571, 589, 590; ethics of wealth, 592; man refuses to allow beloved to sacrifice herself for her sister, 607; preaching as a business, 652; woman suppresses truth to gain inheritance rightfully but not legally hers, 661; lawyer defends man he believes guilty, 700. (See also Chastity, Deception, Forgiveness, Heroism, Revenge, Self-Sacrifice.)

Family Relations; see Brother, Daughter, Father, Husband, Mother, Sister, Son, Wife, in CHARACTER.
Famine, in siege, 147
Farming, English rustic life, 448–451; colony of philosophers, 557; farm-girl, 580; in South Africa, 703. (See also Farmer and Peasant in CHARACTER.)
Fate, measures life of man, 22; decrees man's love, 170; decrees man's madness, 268; inherited affinity of boy and girl, 380; fulfilment of prophecy, 556, 576; house falls at death of inmates, 564; girl meets fate of prototype, 629
Feuds, mediæval, 152, 155, 291
Fidelity, see Loyalty
Filial Relations, see Daughter and Son in CHARACTER
Floriculture, prisoner grows flower, 20; tulip mania, 57; gardening, 361; flower-girl, 574; magic flower, 559. (See also Botany.)
Forgery, business, 119, 361, 403, 574, 581; of manuscripts, 121; of deed, 369; by adventuress, 405; by brother, 444; plagiarism, 485; of will, 583. (See also Deception.)
Forgiveness, husband forgives wife's love for tutor, 9; wronged women forgive betrayer, 15; jilted girl aids lover, 26; wife forgives jealous husband, 149, 356; friend forgives sharper, 214; old man forgives heir, 343; daughter forgives cruel father, 344; wife forgives erring husband, 353, 360, 379, 415; fisher lass forgives proud mother of her lover, 354; husband forgives wife, 364, 366, 481, 482; girl forgives repentant, sacrilegious lover, 394; man spares enemy who is at his mercy, 450, 458; man forgives deceiving beloved, 516
Fortune-hunting, lover, 26, 132, 133, 329, 421; woman, 662
Fraternal Relations, see Brother and Sister in CHARACTER
Friendship, of husband for wife's lover, 9, 356; of antiquary and musician, 40; of four soldiers, 43, 45, 47; of Frederick the Great and Voltaire, 181; of old recluse (woman) and girl, 188; man rescues friend who had misused him, 214; gold-miners, 355; of former lovers, 358; of old and young Jew, 393; of young girl and boyish lord, 410; of artists in Paris, 435; falsity in, 445; of boy and outlaw, 470, 472; of boy and girl disguised as boy, 451; of tenor and married woman disguised as twin brother, 481; of author and woman, 496; of rivals in love, 504; of boys and girls, 599; of widow and lover, 622; of actress and former lover, 693

Gambling, man bets he will seduce friend's wife, 149; wife of losing gambler wins fortune, 365; on horse races, 478; Russian government interferes with marriage of gambling princess, 507; in mining camp, 612. (See also Gambler in CHARACTER.)
Gardening, see Floriculture
Geography, see Index on page 114 of PROPER NAMES: II. PLACES.
Ghost, see Magic
Giants, see Magic
Gipsies, see Gipsy in CHARACTER
Goldsmith, see Banking
Government, see Politics
Gratitude, convict aided to escape by boy, makes him his heir, 350; of Indian, 540; of prostitute to noble defender, 684
Grief, for dead love, 8, 10, 11, 14, 15, 16, 88, 128, 156, 167, 170, 219, 434, 624; for dead brother, 87; for estranged daughters, 122; of estranged lover, 125, 445; of deserted woman, 129, 171; runaway wife returns to be governess of child, 366; anguish of unloved husband, 481; of parents for dead child, 491. (See also Suicide in DEATH; Repentance; Self-Sacrifice.)

Happiness, reward of labor and child-bearing, 111; of philanthropy, 173; secret of, 208
Heroism, in Trojan war, 1; in Latin war, 2; of Arabian chief, 3; of young lover, 5; of woman spy, 21; of comrades-in-arms, 44, 45, 47; of bravo, 49; at storming of the Bastile, 58; of hunchback, 63; of convict, 64; of sailor, 65; of mountebank, 66; of opposing generals, 67; of outlaw, 70; of Carthaginian princess, 82; mock-heroism, 113; the Cid, 142; heroine of siege of Saragossa, 147; of negro prince and

princess, 198; of sister of child-murderess, 235; of Scotch soldier in France, 245; of armorer, 251; of Crusaders, 253; William Wallace, 263; Toussaint, 282; of robber, 287; blind girl of Pompeii, 290; Rienzi, 291; son repudiates bad father, 337; fisher lass saves artist from drowning, 354; son refuses farm procured by mother's forgery, and stands by her, 369; husband burned in vain attempt to rescue maniac wife, 373; of Elizabethan sea-captains, 383; Hereward the Wake, 386; moral and physical courage at school, 399; girl saves life of sailor, 430; Icelandic outlaw, 431; life-savers, 442; of Englishman in French army, and vivandière, 444; Joan of Arc, 461; girl repudiates perjured father, 472; man saves girl from her folly, 476; outcast saves community, 477; spy in American Revolution, 521; John Paul Jones, 523; of admiral, 538; Lord Nelson, 539; surveyor killed by timber-thief, 544; girl saves doctor from snakes, 566; girl saves young man from burning building, 568; heroine of fire at sea, 588; mistress saves lover in Lisbon earthquake, 618; pit girl saves life of engineer, 634; negro nurse dies rescuing child, 644; shoemaker drowns rescuing kitten, 645; in Afghan war, 648; schoolboy lifesaver, 651; militia captain in strike, 666; atheist dies in rescuing cross from burning church, 700. (See also Self-Sacrifice.)

HISTORY

(See also INDEX OF PROPER NAMES—PERSONS, page 109.)

Ancient: Trojan war, 1; founding of Latin kingdom, 2; Carthage, 82, 655; Egypt, 173, 264, 382; destruction of Pompeii, 290; Sparta, 307; Honorius of Roman Empire, 402; Roman persecution of Christians, 443, 702; Roman rule in Palestine, 591; Hannibal, 655.

Australian: discovery of gold, 355

British: Revolution, 45, 237, 281, 508, 628; Charles II., 47, 200, 244, 250; Anne, 66; Henry VIII., 180, 321; James II., 200, 279; William III., 200; attack on Carthagena, 212; Pretender Charles Edward, 229, 247, 470; Pretender James, 232, 332; Monmouth's rebellion, 233, 411; Revolution of 1715, 234; Porteous Riot in Edinburgh, 235; Richard I., 238, 503; Elizabeth, 240, 241, 242, 383, 653; James I., 243; Robert III. of Scotland, 251; Edward I. and Robert Bruce, 254; Wallace, 263; war of 1812 with U. S., 272; Bolingbroke, 286; War of Roses, 297, 471; William the Conqueror, 299, 386; William IV., 310; Victoria, 316, 317, 319, 320, 381, 391, 417, 438; war with Napoleon I., 323, 324, 331, 474, 539; American Revolution, 335, 672; Gordon riot, 342; Mary of Scotland, 398 (see also Elizabeth); Sepoy rebellion, 465; the Black Prince, 494; war in Soudan, 513; George II., 538

Canadian: expulsion of French from Acadie, 698

Crusades: 248, 249, 253

Dutch: William of Nassau, 57; Erasmus, 358; colonial government of Java, 689

French: Napoleon I., 16, 20, 23, 25, 36, 60, 91, 131, 147, 177, 186, 271, 282, 323, 324, 331, 474, 680; conspiracy of Cinq-Mars, 19; Vendean insurrection, 21, 67; Catherine de' Medici, 35; French Revolution, 36, 53, 58, 130, 182, 296, 349; Louis XIII., 43; Louis XIV., 45, 80, 595; Massacre of St. Bartholomew, 48; Henry III., 49, 50, 51, 480; Henry II., 51, 52; Louis XV., 54, 55; Louis XVI., 55, 56, 58, 59, 60; Louis XI., 63, 245; Revolution of 1832, 64; Prussian war, 110, 306, 667; Gambetta, 118; battle of Dettingen, 212; war in Algiers, 444; Joan of Arc, 461; "Lost Dauphin," 628; Charlemagne, 630

German: Earl Reynard, 166; war with Napoleon I., 177, 271; Frederick the Great, 181; Luther, 418

Icelandic: Grettir, 431

Italian: plague at Milan, 151; mediæval feuds, 152, 155; Borgia, 153, 572, 632; Cenci, 154; Sicilian revolution, 156, 319; present day politics, 160-162; Rienzi, 291; Savonarola, 390; insurrection of Molinos, 433; tyranny of Venetian doges, 530

Polish: war with Catherine of Russia, 262

Portuguese: Vasco da Gama, 197; Lisbon earthquake, 618

Russian: Catherine II., 262, 676; Peter the Great, 584; Nihilism, 678, 679, 684, 685; Napoleonic war, 680

Spanish: in 17th century, 6; the Cid, 142; war with Napoleon I., 147, 323; Inquisition, 268; Ferdinand and Isabella, 294, 536

Swiss: war with Burgundy, 252

United States: War of 1812, 272, 543, 548, 551, 552; Revolution, 335, 518, 521, 523, 540, 541, 559, 561, 672; French war of 1756, 525, 535; King Philip's War, 528, 650; French war after Revolution, 542; New York anti-rent agitation, 545; slavery agitation, 570, 589; Civil War, 575, 590, 594, 613, 657; treatment of California Indians, 596; Colonial New York, 597; Hayes and Tilden campaign, 606; Reconstruction, 609, 633; Louisiana Purchase, 621; Shay's Rebellion, 643; President Cleveland, 666; settlement of Virginia, 670

West Indian: insurrection in San Domingo, 282; in Martinique, 644

Honesty, advantage of, to laborer, 74
Horror, magical, 211, 223, 224, 225, 277, 283, 303, 468, 489, 509, 564; insane, 218, 236, 255, 268, 373, 553, 641. (See also Death, Insanity, Magic.)
Humanity, see Philanthropy
Humor, escapades of bombastic lion-hunter, 113; demented master and simple-minded servant, 144; child reared on philosophic principles, 209; stupid servant, 216; untutored girl in society, 221; eccentric character 270, 300, 301, 327, 341, 343; stupid Irish servant, 278; practical jokes of ventriloquist, 325; master gets into awkward situations from which he is rescued by servant, 338; a Scotch "humorist," 498; burlesque of Oscar Wilde, 511; boyish pranks, 603; backwoods philosopher, 656, 657; French pater-familias, 658. (See also Comedy.)
Hypocrisy, of heirs, 343; of criminal clergyman, 497. (See also Religion.)
Hypnotism, see Psychic Phenomena

Imagination, see Magic; Poetry
Imposture, see Deception
Incest, girl loves brother, 14; Count Cenci, 154
Indian, American, abuse of, 596. (See also Indian, American, in CHARACTER.)
Industry, future of, 304. (See also Business, Labor, Manufacture.)
Infidelity, see Religion
Ingratitude, convict steals from benevolent bishop, 64; secretary betrays employer, 222
Insanity, demented gentleman plays knight-errant, 144, 215; insane husband drives wife mad, 218; mad bride kills husband, 236; adventures of madman, 268; girl goes insane over conviction of lover, 276; assassin goes mad, 292, 293; murderess of son goes mad, 298; murderous mad gipsy woman, 309; half-witted lad, 340, 342; old man demented by gambling, 341; abuses of private insane asylums, 359; maniac wife, 373; villain incarcerates wife's double in madhouse, 403; villain uses insane woman as accomplice, 407; villain becomes insane for love, 409; prisoner goes mad upon death of his beloved, 434; insane adventuress, 440; insane stepmother separates wife from husband, 441; past a blank, 462; maniacal rage, 490; mild lunacy, 491; mad Quaker murders Indians, 553; judge persecutes lunatic, 556; brother of sister buried alive goes mad, 564; capitalist sends inventor to poorhouse as lunatic, 581; imbecile Dauphin recovers reason, 628; woman inheriting insanity goes mad on wedding day, 641; religious monomania, 661; loss of memory, 200
Insurance, ship, 361

Intellect, inductive reasoning, 7; student succumbs to love, 165; girl's head develops in advance of heart, 421. (See also Crime, Detection of; Education; Invention; Philosophy.)

Intemperance, see Temperance

Invention, paper-making, 30; the guillotine, 59; submarine boat, 93; devices of castaway sailor, 199; satire of, 200; printing, 266; mechanical, 362; electrical, 482. (See also Inventor in CHARACTER.)

Jealousy, of daughters against stepmother, 122; of artist's wife against model, 183; of rival lovers, 206; of courtesan, 207; of husband, 356, 360; dying husband forbids widow to remarry, 392; of lover of widow against her brother, 397; of stepmother, 441; of young wife of older husband, 447; of princess against lover's Indian captive, 536; of woman against tenor's sweetheart, 649; of husband against musician, 682; of pilot, 694. (See also Love.)

Journalism, control of press by trusts, 623; Horace Greeley, 657. (See also Journalist in CHARACTER.)

Kidnapping, of tourists, 92; of violinist by rival in love, 146; of girl, 192, 217, 224, 649; of lad, 339; Highland laird kidnaps actress, 457; of heir, 470; sea-captain, endeavoring to have his son "crimped," is kidnapped himself, 508; prevented, 547; of ladies by Indians, 561

Knighthood, see Chivalry

Labor, sailor salves wreck, 65; career of a mason, 74; heiress becomes work girl, 78; drunken workingman, 105; riots and strikes, 108, 317, 604, 610, 666; peasant's greed for land, 109; advantages of industry and child-bearing, 111; labor reform, 112; laundress becomes duchess, 131; lumbermen, charcoal-burners, glassmakers, 175; evils of war on peasants, 177; Irish tenants, 228; English tenants, 316; the unemployed, 317; mechanic oppressed by trade-unions, 347, 361; proud mother found to have been cook and grocer's wife, 354; difficulties of ruined mill-owner, 374; Chartist agitation, 381; leader in riot, 391; bond labor in American colonies, 470; servant girl in racing family, 478; Anti-rent agitation in New York, 545; lamplighter adopts waif, 588; murder results from labor troubles, 604; labor unions, 623. (See also Barber, Clerk, Farmer, Inventor, Sailor, Working-girl, Workingman, in CHARACTER; Social Reform.)

Land, property in, ethics of, 544, 545. (See also Labor.)

Law, trial for witchcraft, 64, 238; satire of, 200; imprisonment of witness, 207; disputed inheritance, 326; breach of promise, 338; delays of Chancery court, 346; imprisonment for debt, 348; sane man sent to private insane asylum, 359; innocent man convicted of forgery, 361; injustice of law leaves heiress penniless, 404; marriage under Scotch law, 407; father as judge sentences son to death, 473; innocent woman convicted on circumstantial evidence, 550; photography reveals forgery, 581; disputed will, 583; lawyer falsely declares his own belief in innocence of client, 700

Legend, of Wandering Jew, 73, 266; of Reynard the Fox, 166; Grettir the Outlaw, 431; Childe Christopher, 436; Rip Van Winkle, 518; Headless Horseman, 519

Literature, Madame de Staël, 58, 60; George Sand and Daniel Stern, 32; relations of Musset and George Sand, 75; forger victimizes French Academician, 121; Euphuism, 240; Petrarch, 266; Byron and Shelley, 315; Dickens's start as writer, 345; Landor and Leigh Hunt, 346; Mrs. Caroline Norton, 417; literary salon of Julie de Lespinasse, 476; Margaret Fuller and Nathaniel Hawthorne at Brook Farm, 557; N. P. Willis, 569. (See also Autobiography; Author in CHARACTER; Poetry; AUTHORS on page iii.)

Love, heroic, 3; mediæval, 5, 630; infatuation for courtesan, 8; of wife for tutor, 9; of boy and girl, 10, 633, 639, 687, 688, 692, 693, 695, 703; ethics of love, 11; renunciation in love, 12, 126, 349, 506, 554, 571, 594, 602, 615, 627; love of American Indian, 13, 596; incestuous love, 14,

154; forgiving love, 15, 645, 650, 668, 691; love of a coquette, 18; in a prison, 20; strife between love and loyalty, 21; sweetheart nurses cataleptic lover, 24; faithful sweetheart of fortune-seeker, 26; too critical a wooer, 29; young man's first love, 32; girl's pure love, 34; heiress's infatuation for poet, 38; slighted old maid, 39; girl disguised as page loves duke, 52; jealous lover kills gipsy girl, 61; sailor resigns sweetheart to another, 65; love of disfigured mountebank and blind girl, 66; Creole wife saved from villain by friend, who loves her, 68; love of outlaw for captive, 70; of neurotic youth, 75; woman loves woman in disguise, 76; heiress becomes workgirl to save lover from dissipation, 78; low-born soldier wins high-born lady, 80; love of chief for priestess of the enemy, 82; selfish man returns to first love, to find her married, 83; poor man wins heiress, 84, 100, 344; love of a consumptive courtesan, 88; grandfather in love with grandchild, 91; captive in love with fellow captive, 92; poor doctor in love with school teacher, 95; heiress restores ill-gotten wealth to its owner, whom she loves, 96; young girl beloved by her brother, who is ignorant of their kinship, 99; school-girl's love confessions, 101; student truly loved by harlot, 102; lawless love, 103; priest's love, 104, 158, 160, 194, 512; doctor loves married patient, 106; subject loves his queen, 117; courtesan loves student, 119; love of a divorced man for a divorcée, 122; of Hungarian noble for gipsy, 125; loves of persons of complementary qualities, 127, 169; unsatisfied love, 128; wife has two lovers, 129; jilted sister, 132; lover weds girl in love with a villain, 133; wife has a faithless paramour, 134; girl loves her mother's paramour, 136; love of French officer for Japanese girl, 138; passionate love, 139, 612; love triumphs over obstacles, 140; lovesick girl, 141; love and music, 146, 422, 475, 479, 649, 682; officer loves heroine, 147; unreturned love, 148; lovers separated by monk, 149; father kills daughter's lover, 149; emotions of unfaithful wife, 150; English girl loves Italian revolutionist, 156; tragedies of love and poverty, 159; statesman ruined by love, 162; suicide for love, 164, 167, 681; intellectual man succumbs to commonplace woman, 165; affinity, 169, 314, 646; controlled by destiny, 170; love of man for watersprite, 171; idler's love for supposed countess, 174; hate changed to love, 176; woman disappointed in love, becomes actress, 178; soldier loves artist's model, 183; man resigns heiress to wed poor girl, 185; girl loves man wronged by her father, 187; man foregoes fortune to wed girl he loves, 188; girl learns to love man she has injured, 189; love affairs of artists, 191; adopted son loves daughter of the house, 192; girl loves her guardian, 196; love of negro slaves, 198; master infatuated with servant, 201; passion of libertine, 202; engaged man resists a new passion, 203; man in love with a girl wrongly reputed his sister, 204; rivalry in love of a foundling and an heir, 206; man in love rescues the girl from a villain, 217; poor man in love dies of sorrow because of inability to marry, 219; romance of an untutored but clever girl, 221; girl in love with her rescuer, 224, 225; lovers united, 226; complications of English officer with two Scotswomen, 229; historical love romances, 231, 233, 234, 237, 653, 655, 672, 698; girl saved from loveless marriage to wed true lover, 232; girl forced to give up her lover and marry another, becomes insane and murders husband, 236; Jewess loves knight, 238; love of a pirate, 239, 243; king unites lovers, 244; soldier wins princess, 246; unlawful love resisted, 248; blacksmith wins his sweetheart from seductions of prince, 251; Englishman loves Swiss noblewoman, 252; single combat over lady love, 254; love problems among English country gentry, 256–261; love of Polish refugee, 262; love story of Wallace, 263; love troubles of headstrong girl, 269; avenger kills grandfather of his beloved, 271; love of Catholic and Protestant, 276, 279; love adventures of a Cavalier, 281; a man loves the sister of a suspected assassin, 284; rivalry in love of brothers, 285, 295; 286; 289; a blind girl's love, 290; assassin's daughter loves a captive, and saves him, 292; man mistakenly suspects sweetheart is his daughter, 293; tragic love of Moorish general for Jewess, 294; 297; 299; love of poet and outcast, 301; woman thwarts her lover's villainies, to keep him in her power, 302; girl, resigned by her lover to her benefactor, dies of grief, 305; king kills his beloved by mistake, 307; gentleman secretly married to peasant girl, loves a lady, whence tragedy results, 308; adventurer beats a bully and wins his woman, 309; love romances of budding statesman, 310, 311, 316, 317; love saves girl from nunnery, 312; unfortunate love, 313; love romances of Byron and Shelley, 315; Oriental love, 318; love of soldier and maid-of-honor, 324; a girl's patient love, 330; love of man and his stepmother, 332; widower's love for governess, 336; lovers tested, 343; child-wife and soul-mate, 345; love compensates for misfortune, 348; man loves woman who in their youth had tortured him, 350; a lesson in love, 351; love and crime, 352, 369, 558, 625, 636, 673; actress resigns her lover to his wife, 353; artist loves fisher-girl, 354; villain separates lovers, 355; tragedies of love due to misunderstanding, 356; love at sea, 357, 674; lovers, separated, enter the Church, 358; good son circumvents his wicked father who would prevent his marriage, 359; jealous love, 360, 447, 694; innocent convict wins the betrothed of the real criminal, 361; mechanic overcomes villainous rival in love, 362; a wife saves a maiden from her villainous husband, and falls in love with the maiden's brother, 365; rival suitors, 370, 397; 371; governess loves a man with maniac wife, 373; return to first love, 374; love in school, 375, 376; mother's guidance in love, 378; girl loves man who wrongly suspects her of robbery, 384; mechanic loves seduced girl, 387; children of enemies love each other, 388; foundling refuses to give up her lover, a laborer, to go to rich father, 389; woman resigns wealth to marry poor reformer, 391; a widow of a jealous man resigns his wealth to marry her choice, 392; love of two "Zionists," 393; repentant love, 394; transference of lover's rights, 395; supplanting in love, 396; bachelor ensnared, 400; lover saves wife of villain from madhouse, 403; adventuress saved by good man's love, 404; lover saves girl from evil designs of hypnotist, 408; a poor and proud lover, 409; guardian loves ward, 410; yeoman loves outlaw's daughter, 411; love in vacation, 414; gentleman forbids his son to marry farmer's daughter, 415; selfishness alienates love, 416; heiress poses as poor and wins lover, 421; love troubles of a scamp's daughter, 426; love affairs of English girl in America, 427; love in the Latin Quarter, 428, 435; girl ships as sailor to be with her lover, 430; poor boy loves his employer's daughter, 432; a prisoner visits his beloved in dreams, 434; love and social reform, 438; 439; artist and model, 442; woman of the regiment dies to save a soldier, 444; Ouida's own love story, 445; coquette drives away lover, 446; English rustic love tragedies, 448–451; Swiss love affairs, 453; merchant contrives the marriage of a poor girl, loved by his son, to a villain, 454; German officer and English girl, 455; love in the Hebrides, 456; Highlander and London actress, 457; love in Australia, 460; love and journalism, 463, 513, 587, 606, 667, 669; man loves daughter of a rascal, 472; former lover of girl kills her seducer, 473; French peasant and Scotswoman, 474; love in a salon, 476; love and religion, 477, 605, 700, 703; love and athletics, 483; love and literature, 485, 501, 510, 587, 660; love and magic, 486–489, 559; love and suicide, 490, 495, 686; calf-love, 496; preacher and gipsy, 499; tricked at the tryst, 500; love and chivalry, 502; loves of Richard I., 503; love and friendship, 504; love and war, 505; love and gambling, 507; love in a seaport, 508; love in disguise, 516, 520; Revolutionary and pioneer love stories, 521-525, 535, 537, 541, 544, 551; Indian and Christian rivals in love, 536; preacher and adulteress, 555; love among the Transcendentalists, 557; love and travel, 562; love and medical science, 566; guided love, 567; man in love, yet with antipathy to woman, 568; editor and authoress, 569; love breaks vow of virginity, 572; flower-girl weds heir, 544; love and patriotism, 575; love and religion, 577, 584, 593; orphan girl and adopted brother, 580; love and melodrama, 584, 588; school-girl love, 585, 599; negro and white, 589, 594; French nobleman and New England Quakeress, 595; Englishman and colonial New York girl, 597; early love estranges wife from husband, 598; love on an island, 600; physician and artist, 601; sweetheart loyal to man accused of murder, 604; choice between sisters, 607, 665; love and labor, 610; love and medicine, 613; lovers brought together by *enfant terrible*, 616; gentleman and servant girl, 618; unconventional American girl in Europe and her censor, 619; ambitious wife and reproachful lover, 620; love and friendship, 622; cataleptic lover unwittingly kills sweetheart, 624; love and society, 626, 662; "Lost Dauphin" and American girl, 628; love and atavism, 629; engineer and "pit girl," 634; love and insanity, 641; love and reincarnation, 648; schoolma'am and pupil, 651; woman forsakes paramour to adopt orphan, 654; a dead love blocks a living one, 663; love and business, 671; sacredness of betrothal, 701

Loyalty, of old soldier for Napoleon I., 25; of clerk, 31; of subject, 117, 179, 250; of servant, 199, 216, 236, 308, 576; of family to Pretender, 247; queen loyal to deposed king, 467; of admirals, 538. (See also Patriotism.)

Magic, talisman measures life of man, 22; unites man and maiden, 170; water-sprite marries man, 171; knight contends with Devil, 172; man sells shadow to Devil, 173; fairies of Black Forest, 175; marvellous voyages, 200; horrors, 211, 224, 225; Oriental, 223; tutelary spirit, 240; monk sells soul to devil, 255; devil prophesies man will go mad, 268; man creates human monster, 277; man meets ghost of his beloved at assignation, 283; Rosicrucian barters supernatural power for love, 296; wizard inventor, 297; necromancer, 297, 299; elixir of youth, 303, 559; woman's ghost haunts house of lover, 380; fairy-tale of child among water animals, 385; outlaw fights ghost, 431; drug changes man to monster, 467; amulet causes boy and father to change places, 484; statue comes to life, 486; image of god makes mischief, 487; African princess discovers secret of immortal youth, 489; portrait reveals vices of subject, 490; of electricity, 509; man sleeps for twenty years, 518; lover frightens rival by assuming guise of legendary spirit, 519; judge falls dead according to ancient curse, 556; bond between house and inmates, 564; fulfilment of prophecy, 576; magic white whale, 579; girl meets fate of prototype, 629. (See also Mysticism, Psychic Phenomena.)

Manufacture, printing and paper making, 30; perfumery, 31; flour, 132; ironmaster, 133; nails, 265; leather, 412; paint, 607. (See also Business, Invention.)

Marriage, girl goes disguised as cavalier among men and, disgusted with them, forswears matrimony, 76; divorce, 122, 136, 647; woman monk marries head of monastery, 158; couples re-pair according to affinity, 169; Henry VIII., 180; alienation of husband and wife, 195, 441; treatise on, 220; ethics of, 258; secret tragedy of, 308; breach of promise, 338; bigamy, 356, 360, 390, 405, 440; wife deceives husband as to paternity of child, 363; runaway wife returns in disguise to be governess of child, 366; husband alienates wife by his self-will, 372; husband estranged from wife by his evil past, 379; "Scotch marriage," 407; drunkard sells wife and children, 450; husband and wife mutually confess lapses from chastity, 451; matrimonial scheming, 453;

runaway Scotch wife of cruel Londoner, 456; loyal queen of deposed king, 467; ethics of, 481; incompatibility in, 482; union of opposites in learned woman and prize-fighter, 483; a sacrament, 572; study of temperaments in, 646; for ambition, 647; ethics of, 681, 682. (See also Husband and Wife in CHARACTER.)

Medicine, catalepsy, 24, 564; country doctor, 25, 81, 637; skeptical physician, 34; hospital abuses in Paris, 72; Wandering Jew spreads cholera, 73; love of a neurotic youth, 75; unfaithful wife of country doctor, 81; death of consumptive, 88; physiologist suspends animation by desiccation, 91; doctor hypnotizes wife to learn her secrets, 95; doctor seduces patient, 106; physiological basis of character, 124; plague, 149, 151; Italian doctor as revolutionist, 156; transfusion of blood, 195, 360, 602; satire of, 200, 209; ship's surgeon, 212; doctor frustrates hypnotist, 303; doctor ruined by extravagant wife, 364; woman doctor, 365, 637; "beauty doctor," 405; villain stricken with paralysis, 407; doctor with second evil personality, 468; resuscitation of man buried alive, 469; temperamental melancholy, 491; prenatal influence on girl of snakes, 566; antipathy of youth against young womanhood, 568; Jesus cures leprosy, 591; mulatto doctor gives up position among whites to work for blacks, 594; surgeon and nurse in Civil War, 613. (See also Blindness, Chemistry, Doctor and Nurse in CHARACTER, Psychic Phenomena.)

Melodrama, see Death, Love

Mining, tragedies of, 108; discovery of gold in Australia, 355; discovery of diamonds in South Africa, 364, 488; coal, 634; gold in Colorado, 659. (See also Miner in CHARACTER.)

Misery, see Cruelty, Deformity, Death, Prison, Punishment

Misfortune, see Ruin

Mob, see Riot

Modesty, heroic blacksmith refuses wealth and title, 251

Motherhood, solace of, 134; agony of, 135. (See also Mother in CHARACTER.)

Murder, see Death

Music, Liszt, 32; the Marseillaise, 130; fanatic destroys musical scores, 188; draws lovers together, 365, 682; Felix Mendelssohn-Bartholdy, 422; conductor hypnotizes tone-deaf girl into prima donna, 435; recalls scene of murder to girl whose mind has been a blank, 462; German conservatory, 475; musical temperament, 479; singer loses voice, 613; career of tenor 649; Norwegian folk-songs, 692. (See also Musician in CHARACTER.)

Mutiny, of sailors, 199, 459

Mystery, mysteries of Paris, 72; of girl's birth, 221, 325; mistaken identity disclosed, 301; unknown benefactor, 350; of widow's antecedents, 397; of governess's life, 640; of foundling's parentage, 687. (See also Murder in DEATH; Crime, Detection of.)

Mysticism, Swedenborgianism, 24, 28, 54; Jewish, 313; Oriental, 318; Catholic, 433; electricity as divine power, 509; strange savages who fear color white, 563. (See also Magic; Psychic Phenomena.)

Mythology, classic, 1, 2; Norse, 4; faun, 558. (See also names of gods in index on page 109, PROPER NAMES: I. PERSONS.)

Nature, love of, 99, 504

Natural History, of Pacific island, 675. (See also Animals.)

Navy, see Sea, The

Negro, Arabian mulatto chief, 3; tragedy of negro prince and princess, 198; Toussaint, 282; Englishman aids slave girl to escape, 384; evils of slavery, 570, 571; fugitive slave, 589, 590; negro philanthropist, 594; Ku-Klux outrages, 609; negro heroine of Martinique, 644.

Nihilism, see Politics

Numismatics, 189

Opium-eating, 352, 406

Paganism, see Religion

Painting, artist life in Paris, 86, 435; Leonardo and Reni, 174; artist life in Munich, 191; Michael Angelo, 266; actress poses as picture to confound art critics, 353; magical portrait, 490; revengeful model destroys artist's masterpiece, 513;

artist colony in Rome, 558. (See also Artist in CHARACTER.)
Parable, see Symbolism
Pardon, Queen Josephine pardons prisoner, 20; of convict who saved warden's life, 190; Queen Caroline pardons child murderess, 225; Cromwell pardons impersonator of Charles II., 250; seducer secures reprieve for child murderess, 387; Catherine II. pardons spy, 676. (See also Forgiveness.)
Parental Relations, see Father and Mother in CHARACTER
Pathos, see Cruelty, Death, Grief, Negro, Poverty
Patience, allegory of, 175; in love, 330, 345
Patriotism, bond of love, 125; of Polish exile, 262; of spy in American Revolution, 521; in Civil War, 575, 613, 657; of American in England during Revolution, 672. (See also Heroism, History, Loyalty.)
Penology, prisoner converted by flower, 20; abuses of French penal system, 72; of English, 338, 348, 355; abuses of private insane asylums, 359. (See also Prison, Social Reform.)
Persecution, see Cruelty, Religion
Philanthropy, of ex-convict, 64; man repents of bargain with devil, and devotes himself to good deeds, 173; allegory of, 175; banker founds hospital, 243; abuser of benefaction, 367; helping people to help themselves, 395; of Dutch official in Java, 689; of blind deaf-mute, 690; (See Social Reform, Wealth.)
Philosophy of life, 7, 208, 210, 443; of Swedenborg, 24; Epicureanism, 191, 264; satire of, 200; democratic, 274, 297; materialistic, 347; Neo-Platonism, 382; Trancendentalists form farm colony, 557; reincarnation, 558; sentience of inorganic world, 564; Hindu, 648; philosophic history of Russia, 680. (See also Mysticism, Religion.)
Photography, reveals forgery, 581
Physiognomy, satire of, 209
Physiology, see Medicine
Pigmies, see Magic
Pioneer Life, see Pioneer in CHARACTER

Piracy, hotel porters taken for pirates, 113. (See also Pirate in CHARACTER.)
Plagiarism, 485
Poetry, the Iliad, 1; the Æneid, 2; Antar, 3; Eddas, 4; Aucassin and Nicolette, 5; the Cid, 142; the Lusiad, 197; Icelandic saga, 431; Norse idyl, 692.
Politics, intrigue for French deputy's seat, 41; millionaire in, 116; political idol, 118; rascality in, 136; mediæval Italian, 155; priest denounces politicians, 160; schoolmaster's fight with politicians, 161; Italian politician ruined by intrigue, 162; ban against misalliance of clergy, 184; satire of, 200, 533; adventurer in, 213; rascals in, 219; youth dabbles in, 289; democratic principles, 274, 297; studies in, 301; French in Prussian War, 306; British Victorian, 310-320; bribery in, 370; Chartist agitation, 381; political secret society kills traitor, 403; woman meddles in, 417, 476, 647; crook, 586; Presidential campaign, 606; Reconstruction of South, 609, 633; minister goes into, 652; President Cleveland, 666; journalist in, 669; Russian, satire of, 677; Russian Nihilism, 678, 679, 685; abuses of Dutch Government in Java, 689. (See also History.)
Poverty, abuses of poor of Paris, 72; romance of poor young man, 84, 100; poor students of Paris, 86, 102; poor Italian family, 157, 159; makeshifts of servant of poor gentleman, 236; old maid, 327; son repudiates bad father and suffers poverty, 337; prevents marriage of workingman, 347; People's Palace for the poor, 438; London ghetto, 510; waif adopted by lamplighter, 588; makeshifts of poor aristocratic family, 617
Prejudice, of Scotch against Americans, 580
Pride, of birth, 257, 354; of wealth, 374
Prison, imprisonment for debt, 34, 348; escape from, 44; conspiracy to rescue Marie Antoinette from, 53; bandit holds tourist for ransom, 92; Italian revolutionist, 156; escape of the Dauphin, 182, 628; witness of assault, 207; sharper, 214; child-murderess, 235; escape of soldier

and Highland chief, 237; Jewess succors English knight in, 238; Mary, Queen of Scots, 241; man imprisoned for religion, 276; spendthrift heir dies in, 326; man goes to prison rather than pay damages in breach of promise suit, 338; innocent man imprisoned for theft, 355; sane men escape from private insane asylum, 359; Chartist agitator in, 381; prisoner lives in dreams, 434; Christian martyr, 443; French prisoners of war, in Scotland, 474; Danish house of correction, 687. (See also Penology.)
Prophecy, see Divination
Prostitution, 8, 88, 89, 102, 103, 107, 119, 684. (See also Courtesan in CHARACTER.)
Psychic Phenomena, hypnotism, 34, 55, 56, 95, 303, 406, 408, 435; telepathy, 46; presentiment, 178; vril, 304; inherited affinity of boy and girl, 380; spiritualism, 434, 439; music recalls scene of murder to girl whose mind had been a blank, 462; double personality, 468; lapses of memory, 624; girl meets fate of ancestor, 629. (See also Magic, Mysticism.)
Psychology, "child is father to the man," 586; woman's moods, 598. (See also Character, Intellect, Love, Psychic Phenomena, Will.)
Pugilism, 309
Punishment, for self-indulgence, 22, 83, 85; for infidelity, 23; soldier executes wicked wife, 43; of crime, 211; of seducer, 246; of headstrong girl, 269; of abusers of husband and wife, 271; of assassin, 293; murderess of son goes mad, 298; of sharping lawyer and false heir, 326; of heartless father, 340; of contemptuous girl toward lover, 351; of forger, 361; of bribing politician, 370; villain entombed alive in tree, 425; of wicked uncle, 470; for adultery, 555; wicked judge falls dead, 556; conscience-stricken murderess, 558. (See also Criminal, Rascal and Villain in CHARACTER, Penology, Prison.)

Race-suicide, see Child-bearing
Railroads, see Business
Rascality, see Rascal and Villain in CHARACTER; Crime

Real-estate, Jew finances wateringplace, 134; minister goes into, 652; land speculation, 656
Religion, converts among American Indians, 13, 14, 536; prisoner converted by flower, 20; Swedenborgianism, 24; converted physician, 34; persecution of Huguenots, 35, 51; the Wandering Jew, 73, 266; idolatry, 82; fanaticism, 120, 188, 309; parable of religious tolerance, 149; Woman absolved of vow of virginity, 151; priest denounces abuses of Church, 160; strife of Christianity with paganism, 172, 264, 382, 402, 443, 702; man sells shadow to devil, 173; English Reformation, 180; ban against misalliance of clergy, 184; conversion of pagan, 194; Catholic girl resigns betrothed to Protestant, 203; reflection on, 210; vicar, 217; persecution of Scotch Covenanters, 233; Reformation in Scotland, 240, 241; plot to restore Catholicism in England, 244; monk sells soul to devil, 255; woman missionary teaches young castaway, 275; strife between Catholics and Protestants, 276, 279, 424; converted Jewess, 294; Jewish "Prince of the Captivity," 313; Judaism and Christianity harmonized, 318; Anglican movement toward Rome, 319; satire of foreign missions, 346; preferment in Anglican church, 367, 368; Savonarola, 390, 572; sacrilege, 394; devout Scotch steward, 408; Martin Luther, 418; Dissenters, 419; Catholic becomes Quietist, 433; conversion of dying outcast, 477; religious music, 479; converted atheist, 492; Mormonism, 493; preacher convicted of sin falls dead in pulpit, 497; minister's love for gipsy girl creates scandal in church, 499; emancipated Trappist monk marries, 512; clergyman confesses adultery, 555; New England Puritanism, 571, 573; diary of religious woman, 577; Calvinist softened by little girl, 582; Jesus Christ, 591; obligations of, 593; circuit rider, 605; ban of church on dancing, 638; the business of a revivalist, 652; religious monomania, 661; divine love, 683, 684; pastor opposes theatre, 693; preacher converts frontier settle-

ment, 699; conversion of atheist, 700; of children on Boer farm, 703. (See also Clergyman and Priest in CHARACTER; Ethics; Philosophy.)

Remorse, see Repentance

Renunciation, see Self-Sacrifice

Repentance, of murderer, 15, 16, 222, 292, 308; of agnostic, 20; of woman lover, 21; of convict, 64; of wicked priest, 106; of bad mother, 106; of runaway wife, 123, 482; of murderous father, 163; of man who bargained with devil, 173; of King's mistress, 179; of libertine, 202; of denouncer of his employer as murderer, 222; of robber, 287; of rascal, 300; of adventuress, 344; of contemptuous girl to her lover, 350, 374; of man-hating old woman, 350; of money-worshiping girl, 351; of erring husband, 353; of woman forger, 369; of sacrilegious young Irishman, 394; of prig whose intolerance had caused cousin's death, 401; stepmother repents of separating husband and wife, 441; of jealous wife, 447; of deserting husband, 451; of cruel husband, 457; of murderer and outcast, 477; of wayward wife, 481; of plagiarist, 485; of married ex-monk, 512; clergyman confesses adultery, 555; would-be murderess slays herself, 559; of gambler, 605; of woman who received inheritance by deception, 661; of fortune-hunting girl, 662; of moral murderer, 673; of wayward son, 686; of jealous husband, 694. (See also Grief.)

Rescue and Escape, abortive attempt to save Charles I., 45, and Marie Antoinette, 53; of children from burning castle, 67; of bandits' prisoners, 92; of abducted girl, 217, 224, 225; dwarf recluse rescues girl from loveless marriage, 232; sister saves child-murderess, 235; of lad from thieves, 339; of simple-minded waif from cruel school-master, 340; of girl from scoundrels, 340; of runaway grandfather and grandchild, 341; youth rescues old woman from burning house, 350; vain attempt to rescue maniac wife from burning house, 373; adventuress redeemed by love, 404; young man rescues girl from hypnotist, 408; lover rescues girl from insane villain, 409; brother rescues sister charged with murder, 419; of castaways, 430, 459; of wrecked crew, 442; of English men and women, in Sepoy Rebellion, 465; jail delivery, 473; escape of French prisoner of war in Scotland, 473; escape of Englishman imprisoned in mine, 488; of student soldier, 505; Englishman runs away with Russian Princess, 507; lunatic saves life of British soldier, 524; in Indian wars, 525, 527, 528, 535, 537, 540, 548, 560, 561; in naval battles, 526, 538; escape of sleigh riders on breaking ice, 541; Indian saves friends, 540, 548; Gov. Craven saves South Carolina, 560; girl saves man from burning building, 568; of girl from Borgias, 572; woodsman rescues persecuted inventor from poorhouse, 581; journalist saves country girl, 587; railroad promoter saved from ruin by aunt, 611; in Lisbon earthquake, 618; escape of sailor and girl from tyrannical ship captain, 674; of attempted self-slayer, 700

Restitution, heiress restores property to true heir, 96, 187; son restores property to true heiress, 188; heirs righted, 226, 369; stolen money restored by thief's daughter, 384; "board money" restored to landlord, 600

Revenge, repented of too late, 21; of slighted poor relation, 39; of innocent prisoner who escapes, 44; of son of executed woman, 45; man kills murderer of twin brother, 46; injured man turns pirate, 93; mediæval feuds, 152; son on father, 155; son on parent's abusers, 271; man forgives enemy at his mercy, 450, 458; model destroys artist's masterpiece, 513; Indian revenges insult, 540, 541; wife of dead lover plans to kill slayer, 559; of servant of injured man, 576; among miners, 612; man leads astray son of his enemy, 673

Riot, the Porteous, 235; mob tears pagan teacher (woman) to pieces, 382; Ku-Klux, 609, 633; "white caps," 669. (See also Labor.)

Romance, see Adventure, Love, Heroism

Royalty, kings in exile, 117; corruption of court, 179; court of Henry VIII., 180; court of Frederick the Great, 181; court of Elizabeth, 242, 653; court of James I., 243; sentimental king deposed, 467; court of Louis XIV., 595. (See also King and Queen in CHARACTER; History.)

Ruin, moral, 8, 14, 22, 85, 95, 119, 120, 255; financial, 30, 31, 114, 333, 344, 361, 388, 444, 607, 611; social, 85, 119; political, 160, 161, 162

Satire, of English women and modern business methods, 92; of abuses of the time, 143; of chivalry, 144, 215; of human race, 200, 533; of "Pamela," 204; of exaltation of criminals, 205, 328; rearing a child on philosophic principles, 209; of naval mismanagement, 212; satirical youth, 214; of foreign missions, 346; of æstheticism, 511; of Russian politics and society, 677, 678, 679, 684, 685; of organized charity, 696

Science, satire of; 200; future of, 304. (See also Aeronautics, Chemistry, Electricity, Engineering, Invention, Medicine, Psychic Phenomena.)

Sculpture, statue of faun, 558

Sea, The, girl lost in wreck, 10; sailor salves wreck, 65; submarine pirate, 93; stoker, 115; naval officer in Japan, 138; exploits of Vasco da Gama, 197; castaway sailor, 199, 546; surgeon, 212; British sailor in War of 1812, 272; young naval officer, 274, boy Crusoe, 275; fisher lass saves artist from drowning, 354; castaways, man and girl, 361, 430; Elizabethan sea-captains, 383; yachting, 395, 457; castaway enemies, 458; mutiny and wreck, 459; search for buried treasure; 466, 549, 697; shanghaied heir, 470; life in a sea-port, 508; fisherman off Newfoundland, 514; naval battles, 523, 526, 529, 538, 539, 542, 543; voyage across Atlantic, 534; island appears and disappears, 546; pursuit of law-breaking vessel, 547; sailor among Pacific cannibals, 578; whaling, 579; French nobleman wrecked on New England coast, 595; castaway widows, 600; Cape Cod folks, 651; tyrannical ship-captain, 674; Swiss family cast away on Pacific Island, 675. (See also Pirate and Sailor in CHARACTER.)

Secret Society, political, kills traitor, 403

Seduction, 15, 71; doctor seduces patient, 106; roué elopes with married woman, 123; man's sweetheart ruined by his friend, 128; of Jew's wife, 134; false, 149; mediæval lust, 155; resisted by servant girl, 201; of girl by libertine, 202; resisted by young man, 204; of girl at watering-place, 246; of married woman by strong-willed man, 283; gambler betrays girl, 284; of hero's mother, 285; of fisher girl by aristocrat, 345; of mechanic's sweetheart by aristocrat, 387; athlete seduces woman, 407; of young husband by siren, 415; aristocrat betrays servant, 451; man kills betrayer of his sweetheart, 473; eloping wife, 482; clergyman seduces girl, 497; of Charlotte Temple, 517; forger seduces woman, 574; prevented, 589; of servant by Russian nobleman, 684. (See also Adultery; Courtesan; Mistress and Libertine in CHARACTER, Sensuality.)

Selfishness, youth gratifies his wishes with talisman, 22; fortune-seeker, 26; heartless daughters, 27; scheming poet, 30; allegory of, 79; of student in Paris, 83; inherited, 85; of mother, 115; of king, 116; of courtesan, 119; of religious fanatic, 120; of political idol, 118; scheming mother and son, 121; selfish elder brother, 124; egoist, 416; of political schemer, 476; of rich, 592; of missionary, 600; of lover, 601; of ambitious woman, 647; of preacher, 652

Self-Sacrifice, mistress resigns lover to pure girl, 12; of country doctor, 25; married woman gives up lover to her daughter, 29; sailor gives up sweetheart to another, 65; general does humane but treasonable act, 67; neurotic youth resigns sweetheart to better man, 75; heiress becomes work-girl to save dissipated lover, 78; chief respects chastity of priestess, 82; true heir allows woman he loves to retain inheritance, 84; courtesan resigns lover, 88; son sacrifices himself for mother, 116;

husband shoulders crime of wife, 123; of brother, 124, 335; girl resigns beloved to friend, 126; girl devotes herself to wronged man, 187; wife heals husband by transfusion of blood, 195, 602; betrothed resigns lover, 203; girl agrees to loveless marriage to save father, 232; man suffers charge of cowardice rather than fight duel, 285; elder brother resigns beloved to younger, 295; husband takes wife's place on guillotine, 296; man resigns beloved to her benefactor, 305; father sacrifices himself for son, 333; man takes place of his rival in love on guillotine, 349; maiden claims child to shield married sister, 356; husband heals wife by transfusion of blood, 360; poor girl resigns ruined lover to heiress, 374; of sister for wayward brother, 377; wife cares for former mistress of husband, 379, 390; adopted daughter of weaver refuses to go with aristocratic father, 389; heiress marries poor labor leader, 391; widow loses fortune to marry man under social ban, 392; Jew adopted by rich Christian goes with his own people, 393; man resigns beloved to his step-brother, 395; poor lover resigns heiress, 409; son takes father's crime on himself, 429; poor laborer refuses to woo owner of farm, 448; of deposed king and faithful queen, 467; husband bears charge of wife's theft, 475; author suffers plagiarist to go unpunished for sake of the man's wife, 485; negro girl dies to save life of Englishman, 488; husband kills himself to make way for wife's lover, 504; girl dies to aid beloved to escape, 505; king's double and queen renounce love for duty, 506; his wife resigns ex-monk to church, 512; of spy in American Revolution, 521; sick lover resigns beloved, 554; bride adopts husband's child by mistress, 573; mulatto doctor renounces position among whites to work among blacks, 594; French nobleman gives up rank for American Quakeress, 595; wife of worthless man puts by temptation of divorce, 615; of sister, 636; girl refuses marriage to become doctor, 637; lovers refuse to have man break engagement to another, 639; lover dies to make way for rival in love, 650; woman resigns lover to care for orphan, 654; American gives himself up to death for honor of princess, 668; master saves servant from freezing, 683; nobleman goes to Siberia with servant he had seduced, 684; Dutch official in Java removed for humanity, 689; blind deaf-mute confesses murder to save brother, 690; husband effaces himself to leave wife rich, 691. (See also Heroism.)

Sensuality, of outlaw, 70; strives with heroism within a man, 113; of political idol, 118; of monk, 149, 255; libertine 201, 202, 217, 283, 284, 345, 387, 394, 451, 490, 574, 618, 654, 681, 682; of women, 204; doctor develops a second and sensual personality, 418; of sea-captain, 674. (See Courtesan and Libertine in CHARACTER.)

Slavery, Russian serfs, 677. (See also Negro.)

Smuggling, 190, 230

Social Reform, profit-sharing, 190; of abuses of tenantry, 228, 316; future of, 304; relief of workingmen, 317, 666; prison reform, 355; abuses of private insane asylums, 359; woman's rights, 365; People's Palace, 438; socialism, 642; Russian nobleman gives up land to peasants, 684; satire of organized charity, 696. (See also Poverty, Temperance.)

Society, intrigue, 30; rivalry, 32; Parisian, 33, 306; untutored girl in, 221; untutored wife in, 227; at watering-place, 246, 261; English country gentry, 256, 261, 270; English aristocracy, 273, 284, 285, 310, 311, 314, 316, 319, 320, 331, 426, 476, 520; murderess in, 298; American, 427, 586, 592, 647, 662; American girl disregards European conventions, 619; Creole, 621; Anglomania, 626; English and American society, 626, 631; Russian, satire of, 677

Sociology, see Labor, Penology, Poverty, Social Reform

Sorcery, see Divination

Sports, see Athletics

Stenography, hero practises, 345

Strikes, see Labor

Suicide, see Death

Supernatural, The, see Magic, Mysticism, Psychic Phenomena

Superstition, negro, 644

Symbolism, of talisman, 22; of man-woman, 26; of complementary women, 29; Oriental allegory of altruism, 79; parable of tolerance in religion, 149; animals symbolize men, 166; Death and Devil personified, 172; man sells shadow to devil, 173; allegory teaching humanity, 175; allegory of life, 208; man creates human monster who destroys him, 277; of debasing effect of self-indulgence, 468

Telepathy, see Psychic Phenomena

Temperance, girl saves drunken lover, 78; tragedy wrought by liquor in home of workingman, 105; drunkard sells wife and children, 450; drinking bout between barons and monks, 531; drink and crime, 565; incurable dipsomaniac, 622. (See also Drunkard in CHARACTER.)

Terror, see Horror

Theatre, The, adventures of strolling player, 77, 168; harlot of the stage, 107; death in, 116; amateur actor, 289; stage-dancer becomes governess, 336; Margaret Woffington, actress, 353; Highland laird kidnaps actress, 457; plagiarism in playwriting, 496; peasant girl goes on stage, 693. (See also Actor and Actress in CHARACTER.)

Theft, robbery of heiress, 34; bandit banks his ransoms, 92; bank robbery, 97; conversion of heiress's estate, 188, execution of thief, 205; stolen fortunes, 226; plot to steal estate, 227; 228; German bandit, 280; heroic robber, 287; uncle robs nephews of inheritance, 295; manager absconds, 344; abused son becomes thief, 347; innocent man convicted of, 355; embezzlement, 344, 359; wrecked man robbed by mother of girl who rescued him, 384; by adventuress, 405; stolen Hindu jewel recovered, 406; of diamonds, 429; husband bears charge of wife's theft, 415; girl to test lover pretends to be thief, 516; timber-stealing, 544; plot to rob heiress frustrated, 567; capitalist robs inventor, 581

Thrift, allegory of, 175

Torture, of Beatrice Cenci, 154

Tragedy, see Death, Love

Transportation, innocent man sent to Australia, 355, 361

Travel, Mediterranean countries and Palestine, 312; Englishman in America, 343; tour of England in phaeton, 455; American tours Europe, 462. (See also Index on page 114 of PROPER NAMES: II. PLACES.)

Treason, conspiracy of Cinq-Mars, 19; criminal spy, 43; conspiracy of Holy League, 50; plot to rescue Marie Antoinette, 53

Trusts, see Business

Vanity, of lion-hunter, 113; of statesman, 118

Vengeance, see Punishment, Revenge

Ventriloquism, 325

Vice, among English aristocracy, 66, 412, 490; among English criminal classes, 328; opium-eating, 352, 406. (See also Gambling, Temperance.)

War, see Soldier in CHARACTER; History

Wealth, unlimited, through talisman, 22; used for vengeance, 44; spendthrift and false heir, 326; mysterious benefactor, 350; worship of, punished, 351; gold discovered in Australia, 355; thrift and extravagance, 432; buried treasure, 466, 469, 488, 549, 556, 697; worship of Mammon, 592; evils of monopoly, 62.3 (See also Business, Philanthropy.)

Will, girl of strong, 87, 269; husband kills wife to save her from harlotry, 89; seducer of compelling will meets ghost of his victim at assignation, 283; physical manifestation of, 304; husband alienates wife by his self-will, 372; self-willed father ruins son's life, 415

Wisdom, see Intellect

Witchcraft, see Divination, Magic, and Witch in CHARACTER

Youth, secret of immortal, 489, 490. (See also Youth in CHARACTER.)

DISCARDED